143 Mallard Street, Suite E
Saint Rose, Louisiana 70087
www.kaplanfinancial.com

KAPLAN REVIEW FOR THE CFP® CERTIFICATION EXAMINATION, VOLUME I: FUNDAMENTALS, 11TH EDITION ©2007 DF Institute, Inc. All rights reserved.

Published by DF Institute, Inc.

Printed in the United States of America.

ISBN: 1-4195-9946-1

PPN: 4302-4202

07	08	10	9	8	7	6	5	4	3	2	1
J	F	**M**	A	M	J	J	A	S	O	N	D

Requests for permission to make copies of any part of the work should be mailed to: Permissions Department, Kaplan Financial, 143 Mallard Street, Suite E, St. Rose, LA 70087.

If found, please notify the following:

Name of CFP® Candidate:_____

Address:_____

City, State, ZIP:_____

Phone:_____

Email: _____

Additional information on review materials and live
instructional review courses near you is available at:

www.kaplanfinancial.com

Please visit our Website regularly
for updates to this and other products.

For answers to your technical questions on the contents of this text, please contact us at:

fpstudent@kaplan.com

PRODUCTS AND SERVICES FOR THE CFP® CERTIFICATION EXAMINATION

KAPLAN FINANCIAL REVIEW COURSES FOR THE CFP® CERTIFICATION EXAMINATION

Kaplan Financial offers several options to meet the diverse needs of candidates—the Live Review Course, which offers both traditional and virtual classrooms, and the Online Review Course.

THE LIVE REVIEW COURSE

Traditional Classroom Program

Kaplan Financial offers the Traditional Classroom Program in over 30 classes in more than 19 states across the country. The Five-Day Review is an intensive program consisting of 38 hours of instruction conducted Wednesdays through Sundays. The Six-Day Review consists of 48 hours of instruction conducted over two (nonconsecutive) weekends, Friday through Sunday. Instruction consists mainly of teaching substantive material and mastering both knowledge and application. The course includes working problems to ensure that the substantive materials taught can be applied to the examlike questions, as well as actual exam-management techniques.

The Virtual Classroom Program

Kaplan Financial's Virtual Review is an instructor-led, Web-based program that provides all the benefits of a classroom review from the convenience of the learner's home or office. This program format is a great option for those who have access to the Web and prefer not to incur the expense of travel. This course is an intensive program consisting of 48 hours of instruction conducted over 17 three-hour sessions held on Mondays, Wednesdays, and Thursdays. Learners receive real-time interaction with the instructor and students and access to a recorded playback option. Playbacks remain active until the first day of the CFP® Certification Examination.

THE ONLINE REVIEW COURSE

For students who have completed the Kaplan University Certificate in Financial Planning, this course provides an extensive review of the concepts covered in our six-course program. The Online Review proceeds through the topics listed by CFP Board, beginning with a detailed outline of each topic to highlight key aspects of the material and concluding with review questions that will help you assess your mastery of each topic. The course also includes a 300-item simulation that can be used by prospective CFP® certificants to prepare for the exam.

VOLUMES I–VI

Volumes I–VI contain complete reference outlines that give detailed coverage of the six tested areas of the CFP® Certification Examination. Each volume contains examples, illustrations, and an index. Combined, the six volumes offer over 1,500 multiple-choice problems to prepare you for the exam. The answers and explanations for each multiple-choice problem are also provided. The answers to the multiple-choice problems are identified by topical categories to assist you in focusing your study efforts. The introduction to each volume presents helpful tips on what to expect when taking the exam, tips for studying, sample study plans, and tips for solving both straight and combination-type multiple-choice problems. The introduction also forecasts the number of questions expected in each area of the exam. Each volume has been updated to reflect law and inflation adjustments through January 2007.

VOLUME VII—CASE BOOK

Volume VII—Case Book provides the exam candidate with 16 comprehensive cases, 40 item sets (minicases), and Cognitive Connection questions. The answers and explanations for each multiple-choice question are provided, and the text has been updated to reflect law and inflation adjustments through January 2007. This text prepares you for the three comprehensive cases given on the exam. Your preparation in this area is extremely important because case questions are weighted more heavily than the general multiple-choice questions. Our students who have used the *Case Book* have said that this book is a must if you want to be prepared for the exam.

VOLUME VIII—MOCK EXAM AND SOLUTIONS

Volume VIII—Mock Exam and Solutions simulates the 10-hour comprehensive CFP® exam. The text is broken up into three mock exams, each containing multiple-choice questions, item sets, and a comprehensive case. This text can serve as a diagnostic tool useful in identifying the areas of strength and weakness in a study plan and can be used to create a unique study program to meet your individual needs. This text is also updated to reflect law and inflation adjustments through January 2007.

UNDERSTANDING YOUR FINANCIAL CALCULATOR

Understanding Your Financial Calculator is designed to assist you in gaining proficiency in using and understanding your financial calculator. In addition to helping master the keystrokes for the financial calculator, it is also designed to assist students with the underlying financial theory problems given on the exam. Being familiar with the financial calculations is critical, because mastering these problems is an important step to passing the exam.

All calculations are worked out step by step, showing keystrokes and displays for five of the most popular financial calculators. These include the HP-17bII, HP-12c, HP-10bII, TI-BAII PLUS, and Sharp EL-733A.

Understanding Your Financial Calculator covers the basic operations of the calculators, basic time value of money calculations, fundamental problems (such as mortgages, education needs analysis, and retirement needs analysis), investment planning concepts, calculations (such as IRR, YTM, YTC, Sharpe, Treynor, Jensen, and standard deviation), and more. This text also includes a student workbook with over 200 basic, intermediate, and advanced practice problems and calculations. This text is a great reference for the exam and for practitioners.

FINANCIAL PLANNING FLASHCARDS

Kaplan Financial's Financial Planning Flashcards were created as a study supplement to *Volumes I–VI* study materials. The Flashcards include over 1,000 cards covering topics in each of the areas on the exam and can help you learn basic concepts and definitions. Flashcards provide an excellent way to learn the material by prompting you to recall facts and information quickly. Their portability makes them a valuable study tool for those on the go.

DRILL & PRACTICE SOFTWARE

Our computerized test bank is an interactive software product including over 1,700 questions taken from *Volumes I-VI, Released Cases and Questions,* and additional practice questions written by our authors. The software will allow you to keep score, track your time and progress, and break down your score by sections.

FROM THE PUBLISHER

This text is intended as the basis for preparation for the CFP® Certification Examination (the exam), either as self-study or as part of a review course. The material is organized according to the six functional areas tested on the exam and is presented in an outline format that includes examples with questions and illustrations to help candidates quickly comprehend the material.

We have structured the material into six manageable study units:

- Volume I—*Fundamentals*
- Volume II—*Insurance Planning*
- Volume III—*Investments*
- Volume IV—*Income Tax Planning*
- Volume V—*Retirement Planning*
- Volume VI—*Estate Planning*

The multiple-choice problems and item sets within each volume have been grouped into primary categories that correspond to the major topic headings in the outlines. In addition, the answers also identify more specific topical categories within each study unit.

We are indebted to Certified Financial Planner Board of Standards, Inc. for permission to reproduce and adapt their publications and other materials.

We welcome any comments concerning materials contained in or omitted from this text. Please send your written comments to Kaplan Financial, 143 Mallard Street, Suite E, St. Rose, Louisiana 70087, or fax your comments to us at (504) 461-9860.

Wishing you success on the exam,

Kaplan Financial

ACKNOWLEDGMENTS AND SPECIAL THANKS

We are most appreciative of the tremendous support and encouragement we have received from everyone throughout this project. We are extremely grateful to the users of out texts who were gracious enough to provide us with valuable comments.

We very much appreciate the continued support of the many registered programs who have adopted our Review Materials. We understand that our success is a direct result of that support.

We greatly appreciate the assistance of the following individuals, who reviewed the outlines and problems and solutions for technical accuracy:

- Kathy L. Berlin
- Cindy R. Hart, CLU, ChFC, CFP®
- Lisa Treece Keleher, MS, CFA
- Bobby M. Kosh, AAMS, CFP®
- James J. Pasztor, MS, CFP®
- Joyce Osche Schnur, MBA, CFP®
- Scott A. Wasserman, CPA/PFS, ChFC, RFC, CFP®

We have received so much help from so many people, it is possible that we inadvertently overlooked thanking someone. If so, it is our shortcoming, and we apologize in advance. Please let us know if you are that someone, and we will correct it in our next printing.

We deeply appreciate the cooperation of CFP Board for granting us permission to reproduce and adapt their publications and other materials. CFP Board's Standards of Professional Conduct, copyrighted by CFP Board, is reprinted (or adapted) with permission.

Thanks to John J. Dardis for granting us permission to use material from "Estate & Benefit Planning Symposium" in *Volume VI—Estate Planning.*

INTRODUCTION

Introduction

PURPOSE OF VOLUMES I–VI

Volumes I–VI serve as the basis for preparation for the CFP® Certification Examination (the exam) either as self-study materials or as part of a review course. These volumes are organized by the six topic areas tested on the exam. Each volume presents its core content in outline format using examples, questions, and exhibits to help candidates quickly comprehend the material. The core content is followed by multiple-choice questions with answers and rationales provided to test candidates' mastery of the material.

Volumes I–VI cover the following topics:

- Volume I—Fundamentals

- Volume II—Insurance Planning

- Volume III—Investments

- Volume VI—Income Tax Planning

- Volume V—Retirement Planning

- Volume VI—Estate Planning

ABOUT THE CFP® CERTIFICATION EXAMINATION (THE EXAM)

EXAMINATION PROCEDURES

Read carefully the procedures outlined in the *Guide to CFP® Certification*. The section entitled "CFP® Certification Examination" covers:

- dates of examinations;
- alternate test dates and test facilities;
- fees for the examination;
- scheduling confirmations;
- withdrawal from the exam;
- medical emergencies;
- items to bring to the examination;
- examination misconduct;
- examination scoring;
- score reports;
- pass score;
- reexamination procedures; and
- review and appeals.

A copy of the *Guide to CFP® Certification* may be obtained from CFP Board, at the following address:

Certified Financial Planner Board of Standards, Inc.
1670 Broadway, Suite 600
Denver, CO 80202-4809
Telephone: 1-800-487-1497
　　　　　　 1-303-830-7500
Fax:　　　　 1-303-860-7388
Website:　　 www.cfp.net
Email:　　　 mail@CFPBoard.org

DATE GIVEN

The exam is generally given on the third Friday and Saturday of March, July, and November each year.

Friday (1 session—afternoon)	4 hours
Saturday (2 sessions)	6 hours
Total	**10 hours**

It is the student's responsibility to verify the exam and registration dates, as well as register for the exam.

For updates and information regarding the CFP® Certification Examination, your exam registration, exam application deadlines, and so forth, please refer to CFP Board's Website at **www.cfp.net**.

For updates to Kaplan Financial study materials (e.g., errata, legislative changes, and inflation-adjusted tax rate summaries), please refer to our updates page at **www.bisyseducation.com/products/fp/exam_review/ material_updates.aspx**.

QUESTION TYPES

The examination consists of approximately 285 multiple-choice questions. The majority of these are stand-alone questions that contain all relevant information within the body of a problem. Also included are item set questions where one fact pattern will be used to answer several questions. A portion of the exam is in the form of case analysis. Each session of the exam contains one case with 15–20 questions. The information needed to answer these questions is generally found within the body of the case. These cases can be several pages long, making it difficult to efficiently organize the information to answer the questions.

The stand-alone questions, item sets, and case questions may test only one particular area of financial planning, such as investments. Many of the questions, however, are integrated questions, meaning that more than one topic is covered in the question. For example, a question might integrate investments and taxation. These integrated questions are designed to test your ability to analyze fact situations involving many planning considerations.

DISTRIBUTION OF TOPICS

The topics on the exam are targeted as follows:

Topic Covered	Percentage of the Exam
Fundamentals	11%
Insurance	14%
Investments	19%
Income tax	14%
Employee benefits*	8%
Retirement	19%
Estates	15%
Total	100%

* The majority of topics within the employee benefits section are discussed in the retirement section. The remaining topics in employee benefits are discussed in the tax and insurance sections. For an in-depth breakdown of all topics, please refer to the updated topic lists found later in this introduction.

Cognitive Levels Tested (Target)	Percentage of the Exam
Knowledge level	5%
Comprehension/application	35%
Analysis/synthesis/evaluation	60%
Total	100%

Scoring Method	Point Value per Question	Approximate Number	Points	Percentage
Stand-alone questions and item sets	2 points	235	470	76%
Case questions	3 points	50	150	24%
Total		285	620	100%

The examination division of CFP Board assigns the value weights to questions according to type, cognitive level, and level of difficulty.

TIME AND TIME ANALYSIS

There are 10 hours of examination time:

- Friday (4 hours)—1 case, item sets, and multiple choice

- Saturday (morning session, 3 hours)—1 case, item sets, and multiple choice

- Saturday (afternoon session, 3 hours)—1 case, item sets, and multiple choice

- Approximately 285 questions overall

- Case questions, 15–20 per case

	Time (minutes)	Approximate Number of Multiple-Choice Questions	Average Time
Average indicated time per stand-alone and item set question	400	235	1.5–1.7 minutes each (Friday and Saturday)
Average indicated time per case question	200	50	4.0 minutes each (Friday and Saturday)
Average indicated time per question	600	285	2.1 minutes each (overall)

You should strive to average 1.5 minutes per question throughout your study of *Volumes I–VI*. The cases and case analyses presented in *Volume VII: Case Book* should provide you with a realistic approximation of exam conditions regarding cases. The case multiple-choice questions should take about 75–90 minutes per set, including reading the case.

PASS RATES

The pass rates have ranged from 42% to 66% on recent exams. This exam is a pass/fail professional exam with no partial credit. Therefore, it is vitally important that you be thoroughly prepared for all the topics covered on this examination.

KAPLAN FINANCIAL'S PASS RATES

The Kaplan Financial Live Instructional Reviews have consistently averaged a 70% to 80% first-time pass rate, which is 20% higher than the national average.

TOPIC LISTS FOR THE CFP® CERTIFICATION EXAMINATION

TOPIC LIST FOR CFP® CERTIFICATION EXAMINATION

The following topics, based on the 2004 Job Analysis Study, are the basis for the CFP® Certification Examinations. Each exam question will be linked to one of the following topics, in the approximate percentages indicated following the general headings. Questions will pertain to all levels in Bloom's taxonomy with an emphasis on the higher cognitive levels. Questions often will be asked in the context of the financial planning process and presented in an integrative format.

In addition to being used for the CFP® Certification Examination, this list indicates topic coverage requirements to fulfill the pre-certification educational requirement. Continuing education (CE) programs and materials that address these topics will be eligible for CFP Board CE credit.

(References to sections (§) in this list refer to sections of the Internal Revenue Code)

First Test Date: November 2006

GENERAL PRINCIPLES OF FINANCIAL PLANNING (11%)

1. Financial planning process
   A. Purpose, benefits, and components
   B. Steps
      1) Establishing client-planner relationships
      2) Gathering client data and determining goals and expectations
      3) Determining the client's financial status by analyzing and evaluating general financial status, special needs, insurance and risk management, investments, taxation, employee benefits, retirement, and/or estate planning
      4) Developing and presenting the financial plan
      5) Implementing the financial plan
      6) Monitoring the financial plan
   C. Responsibilities
      1) Financial planner
      2) Client
      3) Other advisors

2. CFP Board's *Code of Ethics and Professional Responsibility* and *Disciplinary Rules and Procedures*
   A. Code of *Ethics and Professional Responsibility*
      1) Preamble and applicability
      2) Composition and scope
      3) Compliance
      4) Terminology
      5) Principles
         a) Principle 1 – Integrity
         b) Principle 2 – Objectivity

      c) Principle 3 – Competence
      d) Principle 4 – Fairness
      e) Principle 5 – Confidentiality
      f) Principle 6 – Professionalism
      g) Principle 7 – Diligence
      6) Rules
   B) *Disciplinary Rules and Procedures*

3. CFP Board's *Financial Planning Practice Standards*
   A) Purpose and applicability
   B) Content of each series (use most current *Practice Standards*, as posted on CFP Board's Web site at www.CFP.net)
   C. Enforcement through *Disciplinary Rules and Procedures*

4. Financial statements
   A. Personal
      1) Statement of financial position
      2) Statement of cash flow
   B. Business
      1) Balance sheet
      2) Income statement
      3) Statement of cash flows
      4) *Pro forma* statements

5. Cash flow management
   A. Budgeting
   B. Emergency fund planning
   C. Debt management ratios
      1) Consumer debt
      2) Housing costs
      3) Total debt
   D. Savings strategies

6. Financing strategies
   A. Long-term vs. short-term debt

   B. Secured vs. unsecured debt
   C. Buy vs. lease/rent
   D. Mortgage financing
      1) Conventional vs. adjustable-rate mortgage (ARM)
      2) Home equity loan and line of credit
      3) Refinancing cost-benefit analysis
      4) Reverse mortgage

7. Function, purpose, and regulation of financial institutions
   A. Banks
   B. Credit unions
   C. Brokerage companies
   D. Insurance companies
   E. Mutual fund companies
   F. Trust companies

8. Education planning
   A. Funding
      1) Needs analysis
      2) Tax credits/adjustments/deductions
      3) Funding strategies
      4) Ownership of assets
      5) Vehicles
         a) Qualified tuition programs (§529 plans)
         b) Coverdell Education Savings Accounts
         c) Uniform Transfers to Minors Act (UTMA) and Uniform Gifts to Minors Act (UGMA) accounts
         d) Savings bonds
   B. Financial aid

9. Financial planning for special circumstances
   A. Divorce
   B. Disability
   C. Terminal illness
   D. Non-traditional families
   E. Job change and job loss
   F. Dependents with special needs
   G. Monetary windfalls

10. Economic concepts
    A. Supply and demand
    B. Fiscal policy
    C. Monetary policy
    D. Economic indicators
    E. Business cycles
    F. Inflation, deflation, and stagflation
    G. Yield curve

11. Time value of money concepts and calculations
    A. Present value
    B. Future value
    C. Ordinary annuity and annuity due
    D. Net present value (NPV)
    E. Internal rate of return (IRR)
    F. Uneven cash flows
    G. Serial payments

12. Financial services regulations and requirements
    A. Registration and licensing
    B. Reporting
    C. Compliance
    D. State securities and insurance laws

13. Business law
    A. Contracts
    B. Agency
    C. Fiduciary liability

14. Consumer protection laws
    A. Bankruptcy
    B. Fair credit reporting laws
    C. Privacy policies
    D. Identity theft protection

INSURANCE PLANNING AND RISK MANAGEMENT (14%)

15. Principles of risk and insurance
    A. Definitions
    B. Concepts
       1) Peril
       2) Hazard
       3) Law of large numbers
       4) Adverse selection
       5) Insurable risks
       6) Self-insurance
    C. Risk management process

D. Response to risk
   1) Risk control
      a) Risk avoidance
      b) Risk diversification
      c) Risk reduction
   2) Risk financing
      a) Risk retention
      b) Risk transfer
E. Legal aspects of insurance
   1) Principle of indemnity
   2) Insurable interest
   3) Contract requirements
   4) Contract characteristics
   5) Policy ownership
   6) Designation of beneficiary

16. Analysis and evaluation of risk exposures
    A. Personal
       1) Death
       2) Disability
       3) Poor health
       4) Unemployment
       5) Superannuation
    B. Property
       1) Real
       2) Personal
       3) Auto
    C. Liability
       1) Negligence
       2) Intentional torts
       3) Strict liability
    D. Business-related

17. Property, casualty and liability insurance
    A. Individual
       1) Homeowners insurance
       2) Auto insurance
       3) Umbrella liability insurance
    B. Business
       1) Commercial property insurance
       2) Commercial liability insurance
          a) Auto liability
          b) Umbrella liability
          c) Professional liability
          d) Directors and officers liability
          e) Workers' compensation and employers liability

18. Health insurance and health care cost management (individual)
    A. Hospital, surgical, and physicians' expense insurance
    B. Major medical insurance and calculation of benefits
    C. Continuance and portability
    D. Medicare
    E. Taxation of premiums and benefits

19. Disability income insurance (individual)
    A. Definitions of disability
    B. Benefit period

C. Elimination period
D. Benefit amount
E. Provisions
F. Taxation of premiums and benefits

20. Long-term care insurance (individual)
    A. Eligibility
    B. Services covered
    C. Medicare limitations
    D. Benefit period
    E. Elimination period
    F. Benefit amount
    G. Provisions
    H. Taxation of premiums and benefits

21. Life insurance (individual)
    A. Concepts and personal uses
    B. Policy types
    C. Contractual provisions
    D. Dividend options
    E. Nonforfeiture options
    F. Settlement options
    G. Illustrations
    H. Policy replacement
    I. Viatical and life settlements

22. Income taxation of life insurance
    A. Dividends
    B. Withdrawals and loans
    C. Death benefits
    D. Modified endowment contracts (MECs)
    E. Transfer-for-value
    F. §1035 exchanges

23. Business uses of insurance
    A. Buy-sell agreements
    B. Key employee life insurance
    C. Split-dollar life insurance
    D. Business overhead expense insurance

24. Insurance needs analysis
    A. Life insurance
    B. Disability income insurance
    C. Long-term care insurance
    D. Health insurance
    E. Property insurance
    F. Liability insurance

25. Insurance policy and company selection
    A. Purpose of coverage
    B. Duration of coverage
    C. Participating or non-participating
    D. Cost-benefit analysis
    E. Company selection
       1) Industry ratings
       2) Underwriting

2

26. Annuities
    A. Types
    B. Uses
    C. Taxation

EMPLOYEE BENEFITS PLANNING (8%)

27. Group life insurance
    A. Types and basic provisions
       1) Group term
       2) Group permanent
       3) Dependent coverage
    B. Income tax implications
    C. Employee benefit analysis and application
    D. Conversion analysis
    E. Carve-out plans

28. Group disability insurance
    A. Types and basic provisions
       1) Short-term coverage
       2) Long-term coverage
    B. Definitions of disability
    C. Income tax implications
    D. Employee benefit analysis and application
    E. Integration with other income

29. Group medical insurance
    A. Types and basic provisions
       1) Traditional indemnity
       2) Managed care plans
          a) Preferred provider organization (PPO)
          b) Health maintenance organization (HMO)
          c) Point-of-service (POS)
    B. Income tax implications
    C. Employee benefit analysis and application
    D. COBRA/HIPAA provisions
    E. Continuation
    F. Savings accounts
       1) Health savings account (HSA)
       2) Archer medical savings account (MSA)
       3) Health reimbursement arrangement (HRA)

30. Other employee benefits
    A. §125 cafeteria plans and flexible spending accounts (FSAs)
    B. Fringe benefits
    C. Voluntary employees' beneficiary association (VEBA)
    D. Prepaid legal services
    E. Group long-term care insurance
    F. Dental insurance
    G. Vision insurance

31) Employee stock options
    A. Basic provisions
       1) Company restrictions
       2) Transferability
       3) Exercise price
       4) Vesting
       5) Expiration
       6) Cashless exercise
    B. Incentive stock options (ISOs)
       1) Income tax implications (regular, AMT, basis)
          a) Upon grant
          b) Upon exercise
          c) Upon sale
       2) Holding period requirements
       3) Disqualifying dispositions
       4) Planning opportunities and strategies
    C. Non-qualified stock options (NSOs)
       1) Income tax implications (regular, AMT, basis)
          a) Upon grant
          b) Upon exercise
          c) Upon sale
       2) Gifting opportunities
          a) Unvested/vested
          b) Exercised/unexercised
          c) Gift tax valuation
          d) Payment of gift tax
       3) Planning opportunities and strategies
       4) Employee benefits analysis and application
    D. Planning strategies for employees with both incentive stock options and non-qualified stock options
    E. Election to include in gross income in the year of transfer (§83(b) election)

32. Stock plans
    A. Types and basic provisions
       1) Restricted stock
       2) Phantom stock
       3) Stock appreciation rights (SARs)
       4) Employee stock purchase plan (ESPP)
    B. Income tax implications
    C. Employee benefit analysis and application
    D. Election to include in gross income in the year of transfer (§83(b) election)

33. Non-qualified deferred compensation
    A. Basic provisions and differences from qualified plans
    B. Types of plans and applications
       1) Salary reduction plans
       2) Salary continuation plans
       3) Rabbi trusts
       4) Secular trusts
    C. Income tax implications
       1) Constructive receipt
       2) Substantial risk of forfeiture
       3) Economic benefit doctrine
    D. Funding methods
    E. Strategies

INVESTMENT PLANNING (19%)

34. Characteristics, uses and taxation of investment vehicles
    A. Cash and equivalents
       1) Certificates of deposit
       2) Money market funds
       3) Treasury bills
       4) Commercial paper
       5) Banker's acceptances
       6) Eurodollars
    B. Individual bonds
       1) U.S. Government bonds and agency securities
          a) Treasury notes and bonds
          b) Treasury STRIPS
          c) Treasury inflation-protection securities (TIPS)
          d) Series EE, HH, and I bonds
          e) Mortgage-backed securities
       2) Zero-coupon bonds
       3) Municipal bonds
          a) General obligation
          b) Revenue
       4) Corporate bonds
          a) Mortgage bond
          b) Debenture
          c) Investment grade
          d) High-yield
          e) Convertible
          f) Callable
       5) Foreign bonds
    C. Promissory notes
    D. Individual stocks
       1) Common
       2) Preferred
       3) American depositary receipts (ADRs)
    E. Pooled and managed investments
       1) Exchange-traded funds (ETFs)
       2) Unit investment trusts
       3) Mutual funds
       4) Closed-end investment companies

3

5) Index securities
6) Hedge funds
7) Limited partnerships
8) Privately managed accounts
9) Separately managed accounts
F. Guaranteed investment contracts (GICs)
G. Real Estate
   1) Investor-managed
   2) Real estate investment trusts (REITs)
   3) Real estate limited partnerships (RELPs)
   4) Real estate mortgage investment conduits (REMICs)
H. Alternative investments
   1) Derivatives
      a) Puts
      b) Calls
      c) Long-term Equity AnticiPation Securities (LEAPS®)
      d) Futures
      e) Warrants and rights
   2) Tangible assets
      a) Collectibles
      b) Natural resources
      c) Precious metals

35. Types of investment risk
A. Systematic/market/ nondiversifiable
B. Purchasing power
C. Interest rate
D. Unsystematic/nonmarket/ diversifiable
E. Business
F. Financial
G. Liquidity and marketability
H. Reinvestment
I. Political (sovereign)
J. Exchange rate
K. Tax
L. Investment manager

36. Quantitative investment concepts
A. Distribution of returns
   1) Normal distribution
   2) Lognormal distribution
   3) Skewness
   4) Kurtosis
B. Correlation coefficient
C. Coefficient of determination (R^2)
D. Coefficient of variation
E. Standard deviation
F. Beta
G. Covariance
H. Semivariance

37. Measures of investment returns
A. Simple vs. compound return

B. Geometric average vs. arithmetic average return
C. Time-weighted vs. dollar-weighted return
D. Real (inflation-adjusted) vs. nominal return
E. Total return
F. Risk-adjusted return
G. Holding period return
H. Internal rate of return (IRR)
I. Yield-to-maturity
J. Yield-to-call
K. Current yield
L. Taxable equivalent yield (TEY)

38. Bond and stock valuation concepts
A. Bond duration and convexity
B. Capitalized earnings
C. Dividend growth models
D. Ratio analysis
   1) Price/earnings
   2) Price/free cash flow
   3) Price/sales
   4) Price/earnings ÷ growth (PEG)
E. Book value

39. Investment theory
A. Modern portfolio theory (MPT)
   1) Capital market line (CML)
      a) Mean-variance optimization
      b) Efficient frontier
   2) Security market line (SML)
B. Efficient market hypothesis (EMH)
   1) Strong form
   2) Semi-strong form
   3) Weak form
   4) Anomalies
C. Behavioral finance

40. Portfolio development and analysis
A. Fundamental analysis
   1) Top-down analysis
   2) Bottom-up analysis
   3) Ratio analysis
      a) Liquidity ratios
      b) Activity ratios
      c) Profitability ratios
      d) Debt ratios
B. Technical analysis
   1) Charting
   2) Sentiment indicators
   3) Flow of funds indicators
   4) Market structure indicators
C. Investment policy statements
D. Appropriate benchmarks
E. Probability analysis, including Monte Carlo
F. Tax efficiency
   1) Turnover
   2) Timing of capital gains and losses

3) Wash sale rule
4) Qualified dividends
5) Tax-free income
G. Performance measures
   1) Sharpe ratio
   2) Treynor ratio
   3) Jensen ratio
   4) Information ratio

41. Investment strategies
A. Market timing
B. Passive investing (indexing)
C. Buy and hold
D. Portfolio immunization
E. Swaps and collars
F. Formula investing
   1) Dollar cost averaging
   2) Dividend reinvestment plans (DRIPs)
   3) Bond ladders, bullets, and barbells
G. Use of leverage (margin)
H. Short selling
I. Hedging and option strategies

42. Asset allocation and portfolio diversification
A. Strategic asset allocation
   1) Application of client lifecycle analysis
   2) Client risk tolerance measurement and application
   3) Asset class definition and correlation
B. Rebalancing
C. Tactical asset allocation
D. Control of volatility
E. Strategies for dealing with concentrated portfolios

43. Asset pricing models
A. Capital asset pricing model (CAPM)
B. Arbitrage pricing theory (APT)
C. Black-Scholes option valuation model
D. Binomial option pricing

INCOME TAX PLANNING (14%)

44. Income tax law fundamentals
A. Types of authority
   1) Primary
   2) Secondary
B. Research sources

4

CERTIFIED FINANCIAL PLANNER™ | CFP®

45. Tax compliance
   A. Filing requirements
   B. Audits
   C. Penalties

46. Income tax fundamentals and calculations
   A. Filing status
   B. Gross income
      1) Inclusions
      2) Exclusions
      3) Imputed income
   C. Adjustments
   D. Standard/Itemized deductions
      1) Types
      2) Limitations
   E. Personal and dependency exemptions
   F. Taxable income
   G. Tax liability
      1) Rate schedule
      2) Kiddie tax
      3) Self-employment tax
   H. Tax credits
   I. Payment of tax
      1) Withholding
      2) Estimated payments

47. Tax accounting
   A. Accounting periods
   B. Accounting methods
      1) Cash receipts and disbursements
      2) Accrual method
      3) Hybrid method
      4) Change in accounting method
   C. Long-term contracts
   D. Installment sales
   E. Inventory valuation and flow methods
   F. Net operating losses

48. Characteristics and income taxation of business entities
   A. Entity types
      1) Sole proprietorship
      2) Partnerships
      3) Limited liability company (LLC)
      4) Corporations
      5) Trust
      6) Association
   B. Taxation at entity and owner level
      1) Formation
      2) Flow through of income and losses
      3) Special taxes
      4) Distributions
      5) Dissolution
      6) Disposition

49. Income taxation of trusts and estates
   A. General issues
      1) Filing requirements
      2) Deadlines
      3) Choice of taxable year
      4) Tax treatment of distributions to beneficiaries
      5) Rate structure
   B. Grantor/Nongrantor trusts
   C. Simple/Complex trusts
   D. Revocable/Irrevocable trusts
   E. Trust income
      1) Trust accounting income
      2) Trust taxable income
      3) Distributable net income (DNI)
   F. Estate income tax

50. Basis
   A. Original basis
   B. Adjusted basis
   C. Amortization and accretion
   D. Basis of property received by gift and in nontaxable transactions
   E. Basis of inherited property (community and non-community property)

51. Depreciation/cost-recovery concepts
   A. Modified Accelerated Cost Recovery System (MACRS)
   B. Expensing policy
   C. §179 deduction
   D. Amortization
   E. Depletion

52. Tax consequences of like-kind exchanges
   A. Reporting requirements
   B. Qualifying transactions
   C. Liabilities
   D. Boot
   E. Related party transactions

53. Tax consequences of the disposition of property
   A. Capital assets (§1221)
   B. Holding period
   C. Sale of residence
   D. Depreciation recapture
   E. Related parties
   F. Wash sales
   G. Bargain sales
   H. Section 1244 stock (small business stock election)
   I. Installment sales
   J. Involuntary conversions

54. Alternative minimum tax (AMT)
   A. Mechanics
   B. Preferences and adjustments
   C. Exclusion items vs. deferral items

   D. Credit: creation, usage, and limitations
   E. Application to businesses and trusts
   F. Planning strategies

55. Tax reduction/management techniques
   A. Tax credits
   B. Accelerated deductions
   C. Deferral of income
   D. Intra-family transfers

56. Passive activity and at-risk rules
   A. Definitions
   B. Computations
   C. Treatment of disallowed losses
   D. Disposition of passive activities
   E. Real estate exceptions

57. Tax implications of special circumstances
   A. Married/widowed
      1) Filing status
      2) Children
      3) Community and non-community property
   B. Divorce
      1) Alimony
      2) Child support
      3) Property division

58. Charitable contributions and deductions
   A. Qualified entities
      1) Public charities
      2) Private charities
   B. Deduction limitations
   C. Carryover periods
   D. Appreciated property
   E. Non-deductible contributions
   F. Appraisals
   G. Substantiation requirements
   H. Charitable contributions by business entities

RETIREMENT PLANNING
(19%)

59. Retirement needs analysis
   A. Assumptions for retirement planning
      1) Inflation
      2) Retirement period and life expectancy
      3) Lifestyle
      4) Total return
   B. Income sources
   C. Financial needs
      1) Living costs

5

 CERTIFIED FINANCIAL PLANNER™ | CFP®

2) Charitable and beneficiary gifting objectives
3) Medical costs, including long-term care needs analysis
4) Other (trust and foundation funding, education funding, etc.)
D. Straight-line returns vs. probability analysis
E. Pure annuity vs. capital preservation
F. Alternatives to compensate for projected cash-flow shortfalls

60. Social Security (Old Age, Survivor, and Disability Insurance, OASDI)
A. Paying into the system
B. Eligibility and benefit
1) Retirement
2) Disability
3) Survivor
4) Family limitations
C. How benefits are calculated
D. Working after retirement
E. Taxation of benefits

61. Types of retirement plans
A. Characteristics
1) Qualified plans
2) Non-qualified plans
B. Types and basic provisions of qualified plans
1) Defined contribution
a) Money purchase
b) Target benefit
c) Profit sharing
1) 401(k) plan
2) Safe harbor 401(k) plan
3) Age-based plan
4) Stock bonus plan
5) Employee stock ownership plan (ESOP)
6) New comparability plan
7) Thrift plan
2) Defined benefit
a) Traditional
b) Cash balance
c) 412(i) plan

62. Qualified plan rules and options
A. Nondiscrimination and eligibility requirements
1) Age and service requirements
2) Coverage requirements
3) Minimum participation
4) Highly compensated employee (HCE)
5) Permitted vesting schedules
6) ADP/ACP testing
7) Controlled group

B. Integration with Social Security/disparity limits
1) Defined benefit plans
2) Defined contribution plans
C. Factors affecting contributions or benefits
1) Deduction limit (§404(c))
2) Defined contribution limits
3) Defined benefit limit
4) Annual compensation limit
5) Definition of compensation
6) Multiple plans
7) Special rules for self-employed (non-corporations)
D. Top-heavy plans
1) Definition
2) Key employee
3) Vesting
4) Effects on contributions or benefits
E. Loans from qualified plans

63. Other tax-advantaged retirement plans
A. Types and basic provisions
1) Traditional IRA
2) Roth IRA, including conversion analysis
3) SEP
4) SIMPLE
5) §403(b) plans
6) §457 plans
7) Keogh (HR-10) plans

64. Regulatory considerations
A. Employee Retirement Income Security Act (ERISA)
B. Department of Labor (DOL) regulations
C. Fiduciary liability issues
D. Prohibited transactions
E. Reporting requirements

65. Key factors affecting plan selection for businesses
A. Owner's personal objectives
1) Tax considerations
2) Capital needs at retirement
3) Capital needs at death
B. Business' objectives
1) Tax considerations
2) Administrative cost
3) Cash flow situation and outlook
4) Employee demographics
5) Comparison of defined contribution and defined benefit plan alternatives

66. Investment considerations for retirement plans
A. Suitability

B. Time horizon
C. Diversification
D. Fiduciary considerations
E. Unrelated business taxable income (UBTI)
F. Life insurance
G. Appropriate assets for tax-advantaged vs. taxable accounts

67. Distribution rules, alternatives, and taxation
A. Premature distributions
1) Penalties
2) Exceptions to penalties
3) Substantially equal payments (§72(t))
B. Election of distribution options
1) Lump sum distributions
2) Annuity options
3) Rollover
4) Direct transfer
C. Required minimum distributions
1) Rules
2) Calculations
3) Penalties
D. Beneficiary considerations/ Stretch IRAs
E. Qualified domestic relations order (QDRO)
F. Taxation of distributions
1) Tax management techniques
2) Net unrealized appreciation (NUA)

ESTATE PLANNING (15%)

68. Characteristics and consequences of property titling
A. Community property vs. non-community property
B. Sole ownership
C. Joint tenancy with right of survivorship (JTWROS)
D. Tenancy by the entirety
E. Tenancy in common
F. Trust ownership

69. Methods of property transfer at death
A. Transfers through the probate process
1) Testamentary distribution
2) Intestate succession
3) Advantages and disadvantages of probate
4) Assets subject to probate estate
5) Probate avoidance strategies

6

CERTIFIED FINANCIAL PLANNER™   CFP®

6) Ancillary probate administration
B. Transfers by operation of law
C. Transfers through trusts
D. Transfers by contract

70. Estate planning documents
    A. Wills
        1) Legal requirements
        2) Types of wills
        3) Modifying or revoking a will
        4) Avoiding will contests
    B. Powers of Attorney
    C. Trusts
    D. Marital property agreements
    E. Buy-sell agreements

71. Gifting strategies
    A. Inter-vivos gifting

    B. Gift-giving techniques and strategies
    C. Appropriate gift property
    D. Strategies for closely-held business owners
    E. Gifts of present and future interests
    F. Gifts to non-citizen spouses
    G. Tax implications
        1) Income
        2) Gift
        3) Estate
        4) Generation-skipping transfer tax (GSTT)

72. Gift tax compliance and tax calculation
    A. Gift tax filing requirements
    B. Calculation
        1) Annual exclusion
        2) Applicable credit amount
        3) Gift splitting
        4) Prior taxable gifts
        5) Education and medical exclusions
        6) Marital and charitable deductions
        7) Tax liability

73. Incapacity planning
    A. Definition of incapacity
    B. Powers of attorney
        1) For health care decisions
        2) For asset management
        3) Durable feature
        4) Springing power
        5) General or limited powers
    C. Advance medical directives (e.g. living wills)
    D. Guardianship and conservatorship
    E. Revocable living trust
    F. Medicaid planning

G. Special needs trust

74. Estate tax compliance and tax calculation
    A. Estate tax filing requirements
    B. The gross estate
        1) Inclusions
        2) Exclusions
    C. Deductions
    D. Adjusted gross estate
    E. Deductions from the adjusted gross estate
    F. Taxable estate
    G. Adjusted taxable gifts
    H. Tentative tax base
    I. Tentative tax calculation
    J. Credits
        1) Gift tax payable
        2) Applicable credit amount
        3) Prior transfer credit

75. Sources for estate liquidity
    A. Sale of assets
    B. Life insurance
    C. Loan

76. Powers of appointment
    A. Use and purpose
    B. General and special (limited) powers
        1) 5-and-5 power
        2) Crummey powers
        3) Distributions for an ascertainable standard
        4) Lapse of power
    C. Tax implications

77. Types, features, and taxation of trusts
    A. Classification
        1) Simple and complex
        2) Revocable and irrevocable
        3) Inter-vivos and testamentary
    B. Types and basic provisions
        1) Totten trust
        2) Spendthrift trust
        3) Bypass trust
        4) Marital trust
        5) Qualified terminable interest property (QTIP) trust
        6) Pour-over trust
        7) §2503(b) trust
        8) §2503(c) trust
        9) Sprinkling provision
    C. Trust beneficiaries: Income and remainder
    D. Rule against perpetuities
    E. Estate and gift taxation

78. Qualified interest trusts
    A. Grantor retained annuity trusts (GRATs)

B. Grantor retained unitrusts (GRUTs)
C. Qualified personal residence trusts (QPRTs or House-GRITs)
D. Valuation of qualified interests

79. Charitable transfers
    A. Outright gifts
    B. Charitable remainder trusts
        1) Unitrusts (CRUTs)
        2) Annuity trusts (CRATs)
    C. Charitable lead trusts
        1) Unitrusts (CLUTs)
        2) Annuity trusts (CLATs)
    D. Charitable gift annuities
    E. Pooled income funds
    F. Private foundations
    G. Donor advised funds
    H. Estate and gift taxation

80. Use of life insurance in estate planning
    A. Incidents of ownership
    B. Ownership and beneficiary considerations
    C. Irrevocable life insurance trust (ILIT)
    D. Estate and gift taxation

81. Valuation issues
    A. Estate freezes
        1) Corporate and partnership recapitalizations (§2701)
        2) Transfers in trust
    B. Valuation discounts for business interests
        1) Minority discounts
        2) Marketability discounts
        3) Blockage discounts
        4) Key person discounts
    C. Valuation techniques and the federal gross estate

82. Marital deduction
    A. Requirements
    B. Qualifying transfers
    C. Terminable interest rule and exceptions
    D. Qualified domestic trust (QDOT)

83. Deferral and minimization of estate taxes
    A. Exclusion of property from the gross estate
    B. Lifetime gifting strategies
    C. Marital deduction and bypass trust planning
    D. Inter-vivos and testamentary charitable gifts

7

84. Intra-family and other business transfer techniques
   A. Characteristics
   B. Techniques
      1) Buy-sell agreement
      2) Installment note
      3) Self-canceling installment note (SCIN)
      4) Private annuity
      5) Transfers in trust
      6) Intra-family loan
      7) Bargain sale
      8) Gift or sale leaseback
      9) Intentionally defective grantor trust
      10) Family limited partnership (FLP) or limited liability company (LLC)
   C. Federal income, gift, estate, and generation-skipping transfer tax implications

85) Generation-skipping transfer tax (GSTT)
   A. Identify transfers subject to the GSTT
      1) Direct skips
      2) Taxable distributions
      3) Taxable terminations
   B. Exemptions and exclusions from the GSTT
      1) The GSTT exemption
      2) Qualifying annual exclusion gifts and direct transfers

86. Fiduciaries
   A. Types of fiduciaries
      1) Executor/Personal representative
      2) Trustee
      3) Guardian
   B. Duties of fiduciaries
   C. Breach of fiduciary duties

87. Income in respect of a decedent (IRD)
   A. Assets qualifying as IRD
   B. Calculation for IRD deduction
   C. Income tax treatment

88. Postmortem estate planning techniques
   A. Alternate valuation date
   B. Qualified disclaimer
   C. Deferral of estate tax (§6166)
   D. Corporate stock redemption (§303)
   E. Special use valuation (§2032A)

89. Estate planning for non-traditional relationships
   A. Children of another relationship
   B. Cohabitation
   C. Adoption
   D. Same-sex relationships

ADDENDUM

The following topics are an addendum to the *Topic List for CFP® Certification Examination*. Although individuals taking the CFP® Certification Examination will not be tested directly over these topics, CFP Board registered programs are strongly encouraged to teach them in their curricula) Continuing education (CE) programs and materials that address these topics will be eligible for CFP Board CE credit.

1. Client and planner attitudes, values, biases and behavioral characteristics and the impact on financial planning
   A. Cultural
   B. Family (e.g. biological; non-traditional)
   C. Emotional
   D. Life cycle and age
   E. Client's level of knowledge, experience, and expertise
   F. Risk tolerance
   G. Values-driven planning

2. Principles of communication and counseling
   A. Types of structured communication
      1) Interviewing
      2) Counseling
      3) Advising
   B. Essentials in financial counseling
      1) Establishing structure
      2) Creating rapport
      3) Recognizing resistance
   C. Characteristics of effective counselors
      1) Unconditional positive regard
      2) Accurate empathy
      3) Genuineness and self-awareness
   D. Nonverbal behaviors
      1) Body positions, movements, and gestures
      2) Facial expressions and eye contact
      3) Voice tone and pitch
      4) Interpreting the meaning of nonverbal behaviors
   E. Attending and listening skills
      1) Physical attending
      2) Active listening
      3) Responding during active listening; leading responses
   F. Effective use of questions
      1) Appropriate types of questions
      2) Ineffective and counterproductive questioning techniques

8

 CERTIFIED FINANCIAL PLANNER™

PLAN YOUR STUDY TIME

TIME MANAGEMENT

- After you determine your areas of strength and weakness, you should be able to estimate the number of hours you will need to study to pass the exam. At this point, you should take out your calendar and count the number of weeks you have remaining to study before the exam. Divide the number of hours you need to study by the number of weeks until the exam. This will allow you to determine the number of hours you must study per week. This figure can then be further refined into hours to study per weekday and per weekend, and so forth.

- For example, Paul is taking the exam in November. It is now the middle of July, and he has just received his Kaplan Financial materials. He purchased *Volumes I–VIII, Understanding Your Financial Calculator,* the *Financial Planning Flashcards,* and the *Test Bank.* He has registered for and plans to attend a Kaplan Financial Live Instructional Review. He has 17 weeks until the exam and has decided that he needs to study a full 350 hours to pass. On the basis of this information, he will need to study 20 hours per week. To accomplish this goal, Paul decided to study 2 hours each weekday and 10 hours on the weekend (except for the weeks he attends the Live Review). He will always carry at least one section of the flashcards with him so that he can make the best use of any downtime he encounters. Using this information (along with Paul's knowledge of his own areas of strength and weakness), Paul decided the following schedule would be appropriate.

Week	Topics to Cover	Hours
1	*Understanding Your Financial Calculator*	20
2	*Vol. I—Fundamentals of Financial Planning*—text (all) and questions (half)	20
3	*Vol. I—Fundamentals of Financial Planning*—questions (half) and *Vol. II—Insurance Planning* text (all)	20
4	*Vol. II—Insurance Planning* questions (all) and *Vol. III—Investments Planning* text (half)	20
5	*Vol. III—Investment Planning* text (half) and questions (all)	20
6	*Vol. VI—Estate Planning* text (all) and questions (half)	20
7	*Vol. VI—Estate Planning* questions (half) and *Vol. V—Retirement Planning* text (all)	20
8	*Vol. V—Retirement Planning* questions (all) and *Vol. IV—Income Tax Planning* text (half)	20
9	*Vol. IV—Income Tax Planning* text (half) and questions (all)	20
10	*Volume VII—Case Book*—Item Sets, Cognitive Connections, and catch-up	20
11	*Test Bank* and attend Live Review	34
12	*Test Bank* and attend Live Review	34
13	*Vol. VII—Case Book* (half)	20
14	*Vol. VII—Case Book* (half)	20
15	*Vol. VIII—Mock Exam and Solutions* and review	12
16	Review weak topics and catch-up	20
17	Review weak topics	10

MONTHLY CALENDAR

- You might find it beneficial to invest in a large monthly calendar and hang it where you will see it every day. Be sure to mark all of your upcoming commitments with regard to work, family, outside activities, and so forth, on your calendar. This will help you plan and anticipate any time constraints that may lead to obstacles in your study program. For example, during Week 3 of Paul's schedule, he knows that he must attend an out-of-town wedding and will only have time to study the two hours he is on the airplane. Even though he will make good use of his flashcards during that time, he still must adjust his schedule to spend more time studying during Weekend 2 and on the weekdays during Weeks 2 and 3 in order to compensate for the fluctuation in his study program. You may find that you will need to cancel commitments or turn down new commitments you would otherwise accept in order to maintain your focus. Remember, your study time for the CFP® Certification Examination is limited and must be one of your top priorities.

- You will also want to indicate on your calendar the subject areas on which you plan to focus your study time each week. This will help you plan which commitments you will and will not be able to accept as weeks go by. For example, in Week 8 Paul's brother calls and wants to schedule dinner for Week 9. Paul knows that he will be studying Income Tax Planning (his hardest subject) and that this area might require more study time than other areas. Thus, Paul decides that he should not schedule any additional events for Week 9, and declines.

- Make the most of your travel time to and from the Live Review. For example, because Paul will be traveling to and from the Live Review by train, he can study the remaining sections of his flashcards.

WEEKLY CALENDAR

- Before you begin your first week of study, list all of the activities in which you participate. Determine how long each activity takes to complete and whether this activity is performed at a specific time each day, week, or month.

- Make sure to include your work hours, drive time, family time, meals, sleep, and any other miscellaneous activities you might do that take up your time. You may want to use the sample schedule at the end of this section to track your activities.

- Once you have logged your activities in your weekly and monthly calendars, review your schedule, and decide which time slots are full and which are open. Using this information, you should be able to develop a realistic study plan for each day. If you find that your current activities do not leave you enough free time to study, you will need to eliminate enough activities so that you will have adequate study time to prepare for the exam. If you discover that you do not have the appropriate amount of time for exam preparation, it would be to your benefit to postpone taking the exam until it is a higher priority or until you have fewer commitments. Before each week begins, review your weekly schedule and update it for any new commitments. Although you will need to be flexible with your scheduled study time, it is important to stick with your scheduled study time as much as possible. Try to anticipate missed study time and be sure to reschedule the missed time for another day.

MAKE A DAILY TO-DO LIST

- Before you begin each study session, make a tentative list of what you want to accomplish during your study time. You may also want to keep a spiral notebook or binder so you will be able to continuously evaluate and reevaluate your progress. Write down the number of pages that you plan to read or the number of problems that you plan to work during your study session or both. Be realistic when you write this list and work very hard to stick to your study plan.

PREPARE TO STUDY

There are many ways you can maximize the benefits of your study time. The following are some of our suggestions to most efficiently and effectively study.

CREATE A SUITABLE STUDY ENVIRONMENT

The most important thing you can do to help facilitate your studying is to create a suitable study environment.

- Your study area should be quiet. You want to find a place that is free from all extraneous noise (including the television and disruptive people).

- Your study area should be away from distractions. Stay away from areas where there are a lot of distractions. For example, try not to study close to a telephone, since you might be tempted to answer it and talk. You might also want to try to avoid studying at work or at home if coworkers or family members will interrupt you.

- Study in a well lit location. You will want to study in an area where you will be able to see the information as well as stay awake and alert.

- Be comfortable, but not too comfortable. You want to be relaxed so that you see studying as a beneficial activity and not a punishment. You should not, however, let yourself get so comfortable that you will be tempted to fall asleep.

- Have all of your materials readily available. Gather everything you will need during your study session beforehand. This includes pencils, pens, books, highlighters, a calculator, and paper. Try to sit at a desk or table so that you have a firm writing surface and room for all of your materials.

USE THE MULTIPLE-CHOICE QUESTIONS TO DIRECT YOUR STUDY

- Keep in mind that you should not spend the majority of your study time on material you've already learned. There is a natural tendency to do so, because it is a lot more fun and certainly more comforting but, unfortunately, counter-productive. The subject in which you scored the lowest should be studied the most. The multiple-choice questions can be used as a monitoring tool if you keep thorough records. We recommend that you study the multiple-choice questions and the outlines as needed.

BECOME THOROUGHLY KNOWLEDGEABLE ABOUT THE MATERIAL

- The exam is professionally rigorous and tests across Bloom's taxonomy of cognitive learning. You can expect a small percentage of problems to test at the knowledge level and a much larger percentage to test at the application, synthesis, and evaluation levels.

- The difference in passing and failing is the difference between being thoroughly prepared and proactive, versus being casually acquainted and reactive. For example, when you think of IRAs, your mind should create a picture of the following topics that relate to IRAs:

  - Eligibility
  - Deductible/nondeductible
  - Allocation between spouses
  - Transferability
  - Rollover
  - Assignment/pledging
  - Investments

- Penalties
- Distribution before age 70½
- Minimum distributions
- Roth IRAs and Coverdell Education Savings Accounts
- Death
- Inclusion in gross estate
- QDRO
- Active participation in a pension plan
- Joint life distribution

- You should be immediately prepared and ready to answer any question about any subtopic in IRAs. If the mentioning of IRAs does not bring anything to mind, or if only a few of the listed topics come to mind, you are not thoroughly knowledgeable.

- The problem with being only casually acquainted with the material is twofold: (1) you take too much time thinking of an answer, and (2) you let the exam lead you to incorrect answers. You must discipline yourself to aggressively answer the questions and you must monitor the time it takes you to answer the average multiple-choice question. Remember, when you are thoroughly knowledgeable, the questions are fairly easy. When you are only casually acquainted, the questions are much harder and take longer to answer.

TEXTBOOK PREVIEWING

As you are reviewing all of the texts, there are two things you should do.

- Be sure to study the title of each section. Not only will this preview what you are about to read, it will also help you to narrow your scope of study.

- Look for relationships. This is extremely important. By looking for relationships between current information and subjects you have read about previously, you can learn to group concepts together and increase memory retention. Most of the questions on the CFP Exam tie many topics and subjects together into one question, so it is important to look for relationships.

THINGS TO MARK

- **Definitions.** Often knowing a word's definition can help you to distinguish terms that might otherwise prove confusing. On the exam, knowing the definition of key words and concepts can often help you eliminate possible answers on multiple-choice questions.

- **Signal words.** Such words as *and, or, except, not,* and *also* indicate the relationships between concepts.

- **Key words and phrases.** Key words are words or phrases that should instantly bring to mind a number of questions, issues, or ideas relating to the topics identified by the key words or phrases. For example, the phrase *substantial and reoccurring* is a key phrase that relates to the funding of profit-sharing plans. Keywords and phrases are the foundation on which you should build your basis of knowledge.

NOTE-TAKING METHODS

- **Flashcards or note cards.** Notes taken on note cards can also be used as valuable tools for review. You can use them as flashcards, which are much more portable than textbooks or notebooks, and force memory recall, which is a requirement of the exam. You can create your own flashcards or use Kaplan Financial's more than 1,000 Financial Planning Flashcards to enhance your studying when you're on the go.

- **Study notes.** Traditional study notes allow you to trigger key concepts that you have read about. This is crucial for review purposes. Study notes should be rewritten within 48 hours of taking them to clarify any areas that seem ambiguous.

STUDY METHODS

SQ3R Study System

- **Survey.** Glance through material and get a general idea about the key information within the text.

- **Question.** Think about questions that could be asked about the material. If the section title is "Key Concepts of Estate Planning," a possible question might be, "*What are the key concepts of estate planning?*"

- **Read.** Read through the material carefully, marking the text and taking notes as you go.

- **Recite.** After each section, pretend that you are lecturing to a friend or colleague on the material. Are you able to retain the information?

- **Review.** Be sure to go over each section and review information about which you might be confused.

SOAR Study Formula

- **Survey the book.** Skim over the outline topics. Review the table of contents to see the major categories of information. Review the index for important topics and keywords. Also look at each individual section and review the topics, major points, and information contained within each section.

- **Organize.** Organize the information that you have read and taken notes on. Some ways to facilitate this are to:

    - underline books; and

    - make notes for books (e.g., charts and note cards).

- **Anticipate.** Anticipate the information that you think will be tested. Formulate possible test questions, and evaluate your ability to answer these questions correctly in a testing environment.

- **Recite and review.** Just as with the SQ3R method, the SOAR method places final emphasis on being able to recite information as if lecturing on its key points and reviewing any areas where you have deficiencies.

MNEMONICS

- *Mnemonics* literally translates as, "to help the memory." These are techniques that can be incorporated into your study plan to increase your retention of information. The most common use of mnemonics is to create an acronym or a sentence with the first letter of each keyword. For instance, PRIME is an acronym used to help students remember systematic risks. The letters *P, R, I, M,* and *E* stand for purchasing power risk, reinvestment rate risk, interest rate risk, market risk, and exchange rate risk.

KAPLAN'S FINAL TIPS

- **Avoid whining.** Avoid whining about your having to know or learn some area of financial planning that is technical and that most planners have to look up. One purpose of the exam is to serve as gatekeeper to the profession; another is to help you develop a healthy sense of professional humility about what you know. Also, clients will expect you to know everything.

- **Study what you don't know.** Your lowest-scoring subject should be the subject you study the most.

- **Think positively.** It will help you pass.

- **Find a way to make it fun.** Don't fight the problem.

STUDY PLAN

Date	No. Attempted	No. Correct	Correct, %	Average Time per Question	Study Outline	Total Time	Notes

WEEKLY ACTIVITIES/COMMITMENTS

Time	Monday	Tuesday	Wednesday	Thursday	Friday	Saturday	Sunday
12 am							
1							
2							
3							
4							
5							
6							
7							
8							
9							
10							
11							
12 pm							
1							
2							
3							
4							
5							
6							
7							
8							
9							
10							
11							

SOLVING MULTIPLE-CHOICE QUESTIONS

- **Read the last line (the requirement) first.** The last line will generally be the question part of the problem and will identify the types of important information that will be needed to answer the question. See Example 1 on the following page (How many personal and dependency exemptions can Mike and Pam claim on their 2007 income tax return?). This last sentence identifies the type of information needed from the body of the problem. You can now look for key information while reading through the body of the problem.

- **Read the question carefully.** Underline the concepts, words, and data, and make important notes of data or relevant rules to help formulate your answer.

- **Formulate your answer.** Do not look at the answer choices presented on the exam until you have formulated your answer. Looking at the answer choices may have a tendency to distract you or change your thinking.

- **Select your answer if it is presented.** Write your answer or circle it directly on the examination. Watch the clock and enter answers on the answer sheet as you go, or all at once at the end. If at the end, be sure you have enough time. Be consistent.

- **Review other answer choices.** Was your answer sufficiently precise? Was your answer complete?

- **If your answer is not presented**, you know you are incorrect. For alternative answers, reread question and requirements, evaluate answers presented, guess, or skip the question and come back to it later. Note: You are not penalized for guessing, so if time is running out, be sure to fill in all of the open questions.

SOLVING A-TYPE QUESTIONS

STRAIGHT MULTIPLE-CHOICE QUESTIONS

Example 1

Mike and Pam, ages 67 and 65, respectively, filed a joint tax return for 2007. They provided all of the support for their 19-year-old son, who had $2,200 of gross income. Their 23-year-old daughter, a full-time student until her graduation on June 25, 2007, earned $2,700, which was 40% of her total support during the year. Her parents provided the remaining support. Mike and Pam also provided total support for Pam's father, who is a citizen and lifelong resident of Colombia. How many personal and dependency exemptions can Mike and Pam claim on their 2007 income tax return?

Example 1 Analysis

Step 1	Read last line and identify the topic: personal and dependency exemptions.
Step 2	Read question and make notes:

- Mike and Pam ⇒ 2 personal exemptions

- 19-year-old son ⇒ 1 dependency exemption (because gross income test is met)

- 23-year-old daughter ⇒ 1 dependency exemption (because full-time student for 5 months)

- Pam's father ⇒ None because he is not a citizen (note: he could qualify if he were a citizen of Mexico or Canada)

Step 3	Count exemptions (4) and select Choice c.

    a. 2

    b. 3

    c. 4

    d. 5

    e. None of the above

Answer: c

Exemptions are allowed for Mike, Pam, their son, and their daughter. They are not entitled to an exemption for Pam's father because he was not a citizen or resident of the United States or other qualifying country. Their son qualifies as a dependent because his gross income was less than the exemption amount ($3,400 in 2007). The gross income test is waived for their daughter, who was a full-time student for at least 5 months during the year.

Example 2

George, whose wife died in November 2006, filed a joint tax return for 2006. He did not remarry and has continued to maintain his home for his two dependent children. In the preparation of his tax return for 2007, what is George's filing status?

Example 2 Analysis

Step 1	Read last line and identify the topic: filing status for George for 2007.
Step 2	Read question and make notes: • Wife died November 2006 • Joint return filed for 2006 • Unmarried with 2 dependents
Step 3	With these facts and notes, you should immediately recall that the surviving spouse's filing status can be used for the 2 years following the year of death of the first spouse if there is a dependent child.
Step 4	Delete the clearly wrong answers by striking through them (e.g., delete answer d because he is not married). This will help you to focus on the viable alternatives.
Step 5	Select Choice b.

    a. Single

    b. Qualified widow/widower

    c. Head of household

    d. Married filing separately

    e. None of the above

Answer: b

George correctly filed a joint return in 2006. He will file as a qualified widower for 2007.

Example 3

Brenda, an employee of Duff Corporation, died December 25, 2007. During December, Duff Corporation made employee death payments of $10,000 to her widower and $10,000 to her 17-year-old son. What amounts can be excluded from gross income by the widower and son in their respective tax returns for 2007?

Example 3 Analysis

Step 1	Read last line and identify the topic: amounts excluded from gross income for 2007.
Step 2	Read question and make notes:
	• Brenda died during 2007
	• Employee death payments of $10,000 to widow and $10,000 to son
Step 3	With these facts and notes, you should recall that the law allowing an exclusion for death benefits was repealed.
Step 4	Analysis:
	• Total amount excludable = $0
	• Total death benefits = $20,000
Step 5	Select Choice a.

	Widower	Son
a.	$0	$0
b.	$2,500	$2,500
c.	$5,000	$5,000
d.	$7,500	$7,500
e.	$10,000	$10,000

Answer: a

No death proceeds are excludable.

Example 4

Clark wants to retire in 9 years. He needs an additional $300,000 (today's dollars) in 9 years to have sufficient funds to finance this objective. He assumes inflation will average 5% over the long run, and he can earn a 4% compound annual after-tax return on investments. What will be Clark's payment at the end of the second year?

Example 4 Analysis

Step 1	Read last line and identify the topic: TVM serial payment second year-end.
Step 2	Read question and make notes:

- Needs $300,000 in today's dollars in 9 years

- Inflation rate = 5%; earnings rate = 4%

Step 3	Analysis:			
	FV	=	$300,000	
	i	=	-0.95238, or $[(1.04 \div 1.05) - 1] \times 100$	
	n	=	9	
	PV	=	0	
	PMT	=	$34,623.42	Payment at the beginning of the year 1
			$\times 1.05 = \$36,354.60$	Payment at the end of year 1
			$\times 1.05 = \$38,172.33$	Payment at the end of year 2

Step 4	Select Choice b.

---

    a. $38,244.62

    b. $38,172.33

    c. $36,354.60

    d. $34,623.42

    e. None of the above

Answer: b

$36,354.60 × 1.05 = $38,172.33. This is an example of a serial payment. A serial payment is not an annuity due or ordinary annuity level payment. A serial payment increases annually at the rate of inflation.

Example 5

A taxpayer gives her son property with a basis to donor of $35,000 and a fair market value of $30,000. No gift tax is paid. The son subsequently sells the property for $33,000. What is his recognized gain (or loss)?

Example 5 Analysis

Step 1	Read last line and identify the topic: gain or loss on sale of donated property. Note: This topic should bring to mind the important points for this area, such as basis and sales price.
Step 2	Read question and make notes: • FMV < basis • FMV < sales price < basis • If an asset is sold between the gain basis and the loss basis, there will be no gain or loss.
Step 3	Select Choice a.

    a.   No gain or loss

    b.   Loss

    c.   Gain

    d.   None of the above

Answer: a

The son's basis is $35,000 for gains. His loss basis is $30,000. Because his selling price of $33,000 is between the gain and the loss basis, there is no recognized gain or loss.

CALCULATION QUESTIONS

Example 6

Helen, a single taxpayer, purchases an airplane for $130,000. To obtain financing for the purchase, Helen issues a lien on her personal residence in the amount of $130,000. At the time, the residence had a fair market value of $400,000 and a first mortgage of $320,000. For the plane loan, Helen may claim as qualified residence interest the interest on what amount?

Example 6 Analysis

Step 1	Read last line and identify the topic: qualified residence interest/home equity limit.
Step 2	Read question and make notes:
	• QRI limit to $1,000,000 debt or fair market value, whichever is less
	• Home equity line limited to the lesser of equity or $100,000
Step 3	Analysis:

FMV	$400,000	
First Mortgage	– 320,000	
	$80,000	Equity limit

Step 4	Answer $80,000. Select Choice b.

a. $30,000

b. $80,000

c. $100,000

d. $130,000

e. None of the above

Answer: b

Home equity loans are limited to the lesser of:

- the fair market value of the residence, reduced by acquisition indebtedness; or
- $100,000.

Thus, $400,000 (fair market value) minus $320,000 (first mortgage) provides a limit of $80,000. Interest on the remaining $50,000 of the loan will be treated under the consumer interest rules (i.e., not deductible).

Example 7

Connie wants to withdraw $1,200 at the beginning of each month for the next 5 years. She expects to earn 10% compounded monthly on her investments. What lump sum should Connie deposit today?

Example 7 Analysis

Step 1	Read last line and identify the topic: analysis of PMT (AD).
Step 2	Read question and make notes: PV problem.
Step 3	Analysis:

- PV
- n
- i
- PMT
- FV

Step 3	Fill out information and identify objective.

PV	=	?
n	=	60
i	=	10% ÷ 12
PMT	=	$1,200 (annuity due)
FV	=	Not applicable (put 0 in cell to eliminate any numbers)

Step 4	Calculate PV_{AD} = $56,949.10. Answer: b.

If your result was $56,478.44, you calculated an ordinary annuity (payments at the end of the period) instead of an annuity due.

Make sure that your calculator is in "begin" mode.

a. $56,478.44

b. $56,949.10

c. $58,630.51

d. $59,119.10

e. None of the above

Answer: b

PMT_B	=	$1,200
i	=	0.8333 (10 ÷ 12)
n	=	60 (5 × 12)
PVAD	=	$56,949.10

Example 8

Gary has received an inheritance of $200,000. He wants to withdraw equal periodic payments at the beginning of each month for the next 5 years. He expects to earn 12% compounded monthly on his investments. How much can he receive each month?

Example 8 Analysis

Step 1	Read last line and identify the topic: analysis of PMT (AD).
Step 2	Analysis:

- PV
- n
- i
- PMT
- FV

Step 3	Fill out information and identify objective.

PV	=	$200,000
n	=	60
i	=	12 ÷ 12
Objective ⇒ PMT_{AD}	=	$4,404.84 (therefore Choice a)
FV	=	Not applicable

Note closeness of Choice b; make sure you have the annuity due, ordinary annuity issue correct. Does Choice c or Choice d make any sense? No, 60 payments at those levels would be $2–3 million.

Step 4	Select Choice a.

a. $4,404.84

b. $4,448.89

c. $49,537.45

d. $55,481.95

e. None of the above

Answer: a

PV	=	$200,000
i	=	1.00 (12 ÷ 12)
n	=	60 (5 × 12)
PMT_{AD}	=	$4,404.84

EVALUATE ANSWERS

Example 9

On January 1, Mike loaned his daughter Allison $90,000 to purchase a new personal residence. There were no other loans outstanding between Mike and Allison. Allison's only income was $30,000 salary and $4,000 interest income. Mike had investment income of $200,000. Mike did not charge Allison interest. The relevant federal rate was 9%. Which of the following statements regarding the transaction is CORRECT?

    a. Allison must recognize $8,100 (0.09 × $90,000) imputed interest income on the loan.

    b. Mike must recognize imputed interest income of $4,000.

    c. Mike must recognize imputed interest income of $8,100.

    d. Allison is allowed a deduction for imputed interest of $8,100.

    e. None of the above.

Example 9 Analysis

To answer this type of question, you must evaluate each presented option.

Step 1	Read each option and identify the topic(s): lender's imputed interest.
Step 2	Read question and make notes:
	• No interest on loans < $10,000
	• No interest on loans < $100,000 if no income
Step 3	Analysis of answer choices:
	a. No, it is not Allison who would impute interest information.
	b. Looks correct; Mike's imputed interest is equal to lesser of Allison's interest income or federal rate.
	c. Is federal rate; therefore, wrong.
	d. Allison is wrong person.
	e. Choices b and c are both possible.
Step 4	Select Choice b.

Answer: b

The $100,000 exemption applies, and thus Mike's imputed interest income is limited to Allison's net investment income.

Example 10

Judy estimates her opportunity cost on investments at 12%, compounded annually. Which of the following is the best investment alternative?

    a. To receive $50,000 today

    b. To receive $250,000 at the end of 14 years

    c. To receive $40,000 at the end of four years and $120,000 8 years later

    d. To receive $5,000 at the beginning of each 6-month period for 9 years, compounded semiannually

    e. To receive $60,000 at the end of 3 years

Example 10 Analysis

Step 1	Read each option and identify the topic(s): present value.				
Step 2	Read question.				
Step 3	Analysis of answer choices:				

	a	b	c	d	e
FV		$250,000.00	$120,000.00		$60,000.00
n		14	12	18	3
i		12	12	6	12
PMT				$5,000 AD	
Objective $\Rightarrow$ PV	$50,000.00	$51,154.95	$30,801.01	$57,386.30	$42,706.81
FV			$40,000.00		
n			4		
i			12		
PV			$25,420.72		
Total			$56,221.73		

Step 4   Select Choice d.

Answer: d

PMT = $5,000

i = 6 (12 ÷ 2)

n = 18 (9 × 2)

PV_{AD} = $57,386.30

SOLVING K-TYPE QUESTIONS

EVALUATE EACH K-TYPE STATEMENT

Example 11

Which of the following transactions is(are) permissible regarding an IRA?

1. A nonspouse IRA beneficiary must distribute the balance of an IRA, where distribution had begun, over a period not exceeding 5 years.

2. A nonspouse IRA beneficiary may distribute the balance of an IRA, where distribution had not begun, over the life expectancy of the beneficiary.

3. A beneficiary spouse of a deceased owner of an IRA can delay any distribution of such IRA until April 1 following the year in which such heir or beneficiary is 70½.

4. A spouse beneficiary of a deceased owner IRA can roll such IRA balance into her own IRA, even if distributions had begun to the owner prior to death.

Example 11 Analysis

Step 1	Read last line and identify the topic. Note: positive/are or negative/are not. IRA/Distributions.
Step 2	Read question.
Step 3	Analysis of statements:
	1. False
	2. True
	3. True
	4. True
Step 3	Read answers.
Step 4	Select Choice d.

    a. 1 and 2

    b. 2 and 3

    c. 1, 2, and 3

    d. 2, 3, and 4

    e. 1, 2, 3, and 4

Answer: d

Statement 1 is incorrect. The option is to pay at least as fast as the original payment schedule. For K-type questions, anchor yourself in certainty. Include the answers that are certainly correct and exclude any answer with a statement that is certainly incorrect.

Example 12

Which of the following is(are) deductible for adjusted gross income?

1. Alimony paid to the taxpayer's former spouse

2. Capital losses

3. Ordinary and necessary expenses incurred in a business

4. A deductible individual retirement account (IRA) contribution

Example 12 Analysis

Step 1	Read last line and identify the topic: Note: is/are versus are not/AGI.
Step 2	Read question.
Step 3	Analysis of statements:
	1. True
	2. Let's suppose I don't know
	3. Let's suppose I don't know
	4. True
Step 4	Evaluate answers.
	a. 1 only (definitely incorrect)
	b. 4 only (definitely incorrect)
	c. 1 and 4 (possible answer)
	d. 1, 3, and 4 (possible answer)
	e. 1, 2, 3, and 4 (possible answer)
Step 5	Evaluate statements 2 and 3 above.
Step 4	Select Choice e.

---

    a. 1 only

    b. 4 only

    c. 1 and 4

    d. 1, 3, and 4

    e. 1, 2, 3, and 4

Answer: e

All are deductible for adjusted gross income.

Example 13

Which of the following would best describe the action of a fiscal policy economist?

1. Increase in government spending
2. Decrease in the money supply
3. Decrease in income taxes
4. Increase in the inflation rate

Example 13 Analysis

Step 1	Read last line and identify the topic: fiscal policy.
Step 2	Read question and make notes:
	• Fiscal is taxation and spending; monetary is interest rates.
Step 3	Analysis of statements:
	1. Yes, fiscal
	2. Do not know
	3. Yes, fiscal
	4. Do not know
Step 4	Evaluate answers.
	a. Possible answer
	b. Possible answer
	c. No
	d. No
	e. No
Step 5	Reevaluate statements: statement 4 is incorrect, therefore Choice a is incorrect.
Step 4	Select Choice b.

a. 1, 2, 3, and 4
b. 1 and 3
c. 2 only
d. 2 and 4
e. 1 only

Answer: b

Fiscal policy economists believe that the economy can be controlled through the use of government spending and income tax adjustments. Choice c is the answer to describe economists who believe that economic activity is controlled through the use of the money supply. Choice a is incorrect since that answer describes all the choices that include both fiscal policy as well as monetary policy economists. Choice d is incorrect because inflation is determined by market factors. Choice e partially describes the actions of a fiscal policy economist.

YOUR COMMENTS FOR VOLUMES I–VI

Our goal is to provide a high-quality product to you and other CFP® candidates. With this goal in mind, we hope to significantly improve our texts with each new edition. We welcome your written suggestions, corrections, and other general comments. Please be as detailed as possible and send your written comments to:

Kaplan Financial
143 Mallard Street, Suite E
St. Rose, Louisiana 70087
(504) 461-9860 Fax

	Volume	Page	Question	Comments (please be as specific as possible)
1.				
2.				
3.				
4.				
5.				
6.				
7.				
8.				
9.				
10.				
11.				
12.				
13.				
14.				
15.				

Name

Address

Phone   (Work)   (Home)   (Fax)

Email_____   Do you require a response? _____YES   _____NO

TABLE OF CONTENTS

I.   The Financial Planning Process
    A.   Establishing Client-Planner Relationships...3
    B.   Gathering Client Data and Determining Goals and Expectations..............................3
    C.   Determining the Client's Financial Status by Analyzing and Evaluating Various
        Client Information 3
    D.   Developing and Presenting the Financial Plan 5
    E.   Implementing the Financial Plan 6
    F.   Monitoring the Financial Plan 6

II.   Personal Financial Statements
    A.   Statement of Financial Position (Balance Sheet) 7
    B.   Statement of Cash Flows (for Past Year and Pro Forma for Next Year) 7

III. Analysis of Financial Statements and Identification of Strengths and Weaknesses
    A.   Described 11
    B.   Ratio Analysis 11

IV. Budgeting
    A.   Described 13
    B.   Steps in Preparing a Budget 13
    C.   Saving and Consumption Habits 13
    D.   Discretionary versus Nondiscretionary Expenses...14
    E.   Savings Strategies..14

V.   Internal Analysis
    A.   Life Cycle Positioning...16
    B.   Financial Planning for Special Circumstances 17
    C.   Life Cycle Phases and Characteristics 22
    D.   Risk Tolerance Levels 23

VI. Personal Use—Assets and Liabilities
    A.   Financing Strategies 24
    B.   Debt...25
    C.   Home Mortgages...26

VII. Economic Environment—Basic Concepts
    A.   Demand 30
    B.   Supply 31
    C.   Supply and Demand Interaction..32
    D.   Price Elasticity of Demand 32
    E.   Inflation 32
    F.   Measures of Inflation 33

VIII. **Monetary and Fiscal Policy**
    A. Monetary Policy 35
    B. Fiscal Policy 36
    C. The Nature of Interest Rates 36

IX. **Business Cycle Theories**
    A. Described 37

X. **Financial Institutions**
    A. Described 40
    B. Banks and Similar Institutions 40
    C. FDIC Insurance 41

XI. **Time Value of Money**
    A. Time Value of Money Concepts 46
    B. Future Value of a Single-Sum Deposit 46
    C. Present Value 47
    D. Solving for Time and Interest Rates 48
    E. Future Value of an Annuity 50
    F. Present Value of an Annuity 52
    G. Serial Payments 53
    H. Net Present Value 56

XII. **Educational Funding**
    A. Introduction 57
    B. Needs Analysis 57
    C. Educational Savings Calculation 57
    D. Education Tax Credits and Deductions 57
    E. Qualified Tuition Program (Section 529 Plans; Formerly Qualified State Tuition Programs) 59
    F. Coverdell Education Savings Accounts (Formerly Education IRAs) 63
    G. Savings Bonds 65
    H. Government Grants and Loans (Financial Aid) 66
    I. Other Sources 68

XIII. **Contracts**
    A. Nature and Types of Contracts 72
    B. Agreement 73
    C. Consideration 73

XIV. **Agency Relationships**
    A. The Nature of Agency 75
    B. Agency Distinguished from Other Relationships 75
    C. Formation of Agency Relationship 75
    D. Agent's Duties to Principal 76
    E. Principal's Duties to Agent 76

XV. **Negotiable Instruments**
    A. Described 78
    B. Types of Commercial Paper 78
    C. Liability of Parties 79

XVI. Property
    A. Personal Property 81
    B. Real Property.. 83

XVII. Consumer Protection
    A. Credit Protection.. 86
    B. Debt Collection.. 87

XVIII. Bankruptcy and Reorganization
    A. The Bankruptcy Reform Act of 1978, as Amended.. 88
    B. Bankruptcy Abuse Prevention and Consumer Protection Act (BAPCPA) of 2005 88
    C. Liquidation—Ordinary or Straight Bankruptcy (Chapter 7)........................... 88
    D. Reorganization (Chapter 11) 90
    E. Adjustment of Debts of an Individual with Regular Income (Chapter 13) 90

XIX. Torts
    A. Introduction 91
    B. Intentional Torts 91
    C. Negligence... 93
    D. Strict Liability 94

XX. Professional Liability—Financial Planners
    A. Introduction 95
    B. Potential Common Law Liability to Clients 95
    C. Potential Common Law Liability to Third Persons 96
    D. Potential Statutory Liability.. 96

XXI. Regulatory Requirements
    A. Introduction 98
    B. Federal Securities Regulation 98
    C. NASD 101

XXII. Investment Advisers' Regulation and Registration
    A. Introduction 103
    B. Regulation 103
    C. Reform of Previous Acts 105
    D. Investment Adviser Registration Depository 105

XXIII. CFP Board's Standards of Professional Conduct.. 106

Fundamentals Supplement

I.   **Financial Institutions** **145**
     A.   Mutual Savings Banks and Similar Institutions.. 145
     B.   Money Market Mutual Funds 146
     C.   Stock Brokerage Firms.. 146
     D.   Financial Services Companies 146

II. **Time Value of Money**...**147**
     A.   Future Value of a Single Sum Deposit—An Alternative Method 147
     B.   Present Value.. 147
     C.   Present Value of an Annuity 149

III. **Educational Funding**..**151**
     A.   Government Grants and Loans (Financial Aid) 151
     B.   Other Sources.. 152

IV. **Contracts**...**154**
     A.   Nature and Types of Contracts.. 154
     B.   Agreement 154
     C.   Consideration... 156
     D.   Capacity... 158
     E.   The Statute of Frauds 161
     F.   Discharge and Performance 163
     G.   Remedies 166

V.   **Agency Relationships** **168**
     A.   Agent's Duties to Principal 168
     B.   Principal's Duties to Agent 168
     C.   Termination of Agency Relationship 168

VI. **Negotiable Instruments** **170**
     A.   Requirements 170
     B.   Ambiguities 170
     C.   Negotiation 171
     D.   Liability of Parties... 172
     E.   Banks... 172

VII. **Consumer Protection** **174**
     A.   Public Policy Issues... 174
     B.   Advertising 174
     C.   State Laws... 175

QUESTIONS

The Financial Planning Process 179
Personal Financial Statements 181
Analysis of Financial Statements and Identification of Strengths and Weaknesses 183
Budgeting 186
Internal Analysis 187
Personal-Use Assets and Liabilities 188
Economic Environment—Basic Concepts 189
Monetary and Fiscal Policy 198
Business Cycle Theories 202
Financial Institutions 203
Time Value of Money 204
Educational Funding 215
Contracts 219
Agency 221
Negotiable Instruments 222
Property 223
Consumer Protection 225
Bankruptcy and Reorganization 226
Torts 228
Professional Liability—Financial Planners 229
Regulatory Requirements 230
Investment Adviser Regulation and Registration 233
CFP Board's Standards of Professional Conduct 234

SOLUTIONS

Answer Summary 247
The Financial Planning Process 248
Personal Financial Statements 249
Analysis of Financial Statements and Identification of Strengths and Weaknesses 251
Budgeting 253
Internal Analysis 254
Personal-Use Assets and Liabilities 255
Economic Environment—Basic Concepts 256
Monetary and Fiscal Policy 262
Business Cycle Theories 266
Financial Institutions 267
Time Value of Money 268
Educational Funding 282
Contracts 287
Agency 288
Negotiable Instruments 289
Property 290
Consumer Protection 292
Bankruptcy and Reorganization 293
Torts 294
Professional Liability—Financial Planners 295
Regulatory Requirements 296
Investment Adviser Regulation and Registration 298
CFP Board's Standards of Professional Conduct 299

TABLE OF EXHIBITS

Exhibit 1: Statement of Financial Position Example...9

Exhibit 2: Statement of Cash Flow Example 10

Exhibit 3: Life Cycle Phases and Characteristics...22

Exhibit 4: The Demand Curve...30

Exhibit 5: The Supply Curve 31

Exhibit 6: Business Cycles (General) 37

Exhibit 7: Hypothetical Business Cycle...38

Exhibit 8: Timeline for an Ordinary Annuity..51

Exhibit 9: Highlights of Tax Benefits for Higher Education for 2007 71

Exhibit 10: Qualifications/Registration Requirement Chart for Registered Representatives......................102

TABLE OF EXHIBITS—SUPPLEMENT

Exhibit 1: Present Value of $1 Due at the End of n Periods. 149

TABLE OF APPENDICES

Appendix 1: Future Value Table 140

Appendix 2: Future Value of an Ordinary Annuity 141

FUNDAMENTALS

Outline

Fundamentals

I. THE FINANCIAL PLANNING PROCESS

The financial planning process is an excerpt from the "Topic List for CFP® Certification Examination" and has been reprinted with permission of CFP Board.

A. ESTABLISHING CLIENT-PLANNER RELATIONSHIPS

1. Explain issues and concepts related to the overall financial planning process, as appropriate to the client

2. Explain services provided, the process of planning, and documentation required

3. Clarify client's and CFP® practitioner's responsibilities

B. GATHERING CLIENT DATA AND DETERMINING GOALS AND EXPECTATIONS

1. Obtain information from client through interview/questionnaire about financial resources and obligations

2. Determine client's personal and financial goals, needs, and priorities

3. Assess client's values, attitudes, and expectations

4. Determine client's time horizons

5. Determine client's risk tolerance level

6. Collect applicable client records and documents

C. DETERMINING THE CLIENT'S FINANCIAL STATUS BY ANALYZING AND EVALUATING VARIOUS CLIENT INFORMATION

1. General
   a. Current financial status (e.g., assets, liabilities, cash flow, and debt management)
   b. Capital needs
   c. Attitudes and expectations
   d. Risk tolerance
   e. Risk management
   f. Risk exposure

2. Special needs
   a. Divorce/remarriage considerations
   b. Charitable planning
   c. Adult dependent needs
   d. Disabled child needs
   e. Education needs
   f. Terminal illness planning
   g. Closely held business planning

3. Risk management

   a. Life insurance needs and current coverage

   b. Disability insurance needs and current coverage

   c. Health insurance needs and current coverage

   d. Long-term care insurance needs and current coverage

   e. Homeowners insurance needs and current coverage

   f. Auto insurance needs and current coverage

   g. Other liability insurance needs and current coverage (e.g., umbrella, professional, errors and omissions, and directors and officers)

   h. Commercial insurance needs and current coverage

4. Investments

   a. Current investments

   b. Current investment strategies and policies

5. Taxation

   a. Income and gift tax returns

   b. Current tax strategies

   c. Tax compliance status (e.g., estimated tax)

   d. Current income and gift tax liabilities

6. Employee benefits

   a. Available employee benefits

   b. Current participation in employee benefits

7. Retirement

   a. Current retirement plan tax exposures (i.e., premature distribution tax)

   b. Current retirement plans

   c. Social Security benefits

   d. Retirement strategies

8. Estate planning

   a. Estate planning documents

   b. Estate planning strategies

   c. Estate tax exposures

D. DEVELOPING AND PRESENTING THE FINANCIAL PLAN

1. Developing and preparing a client-specific financial plan tailored to meet the goals and objectives of the client, commensurate with client's values, temperament, and risk tolerance

    a. Financial position (net worth)

        1.) Current statement

        2.) Projected statement

        3.) Projected statement with recommendations

    b. Cash flow

        1.) Projections

        2.) Recommendations

        3.) Projection with recommendations

    c. Estate tax

        1.) Projections

        2.) Recommendations

        3.) Projection with recommendations

    d. Capital needs at retirement

        1.) Projections

        2.) Recommendations

        3.) Projection with recommendations

    e. Capital needs projections at death

        1.) Recommendations

        2.) Projection with recommendations

    f. Capital needs: disability

        1.) Recommendations

        2.) Projection with recommendations

    g. Capital needs: special needs

        1.) Recommendations

        2.) Projection with recommendations

    h. Income tax

        1.) Projections

        2.) Recommendations

        3.) Projection with strategy recommendations

    i. Employee benefits

        1.) Projections

       2.) Recommendations

  j. Asset allocation

       1.) Investment policy statement

       2.) Strategy recommendations

       3.) Statement with recommendations

  k. Investment

       1.) Recommendations

       2.) Policy statement

       3.) Policy recommendations

       4.) Policy statement with recommendations

  l. Risk

       1.) Assessment

       2.) Recommendations

  m. List of prioritized action items

2. Presenting and reviewing the plan with the client

3. Collaborating with the client to ensure that plan meets the goals and objectives of the client, revising as appropriate

E. IMPLEMENTING THE FINANCIAL PLAN

1. Assist the client in implementing the recommendations

2. Coordinate as necessary with other professionals, such as accountants, attorneys, real estate agents, investment advisers, stockbrokers, and insurance agents

F. MONITORING THE FINANCIAL PLAN

1. Monitor and evaluate soundness of recommendations

2. Review the progress of the plan with the client

3. Discuss and evaluate changes in client's personal circumstances (e.g., birth/death, age, illness, divorce, and retirement)

4. Review and evaluate changing tax laws and economic circumstances

5. Make recommendations to accommodate new or changing circumstances

> **Note:** See section, "CFP Board's Financial Planning Practice Standards" on page 116 for additional information

II. PERSONAL FINANCIAL STATEMENTS

A. STATEMENT OF FINANCIAL POSITION (BALANCE SHEET)

See Exhibit 1 at the end of this section

1. Assets and liabilities should be presented at fair market value (FMV)

2. Statement needs to be appropriately dated (i.e., "As of January 1, 20XX")

3. Net worth should be indicated

4. Footnotes should be used to describe details of both assets and liabilities

5. Property should be identified with owner (e.g., JTWROS, H for husband, or W for wife)

6. Categories of assets—depends on type and use of asset

   a. Cash and cash equivalents

   b. Invested assets (investment portfolio)

   c. Personal use assets (residence, furniture, and autos)

   d. Assets should be listed in order of liquidity (the ability to convert to cash quickly), from most liquid to least liquid

7. Liabilities should be categorized according to maturity date

   a. Current liabilities—due within one year

   b. Long-term liabilities—generally mortgages and notes

8. Net worth = assets – liabilities

B. STATEMENT OF CASH FLOWS (FOR PAST YEAR AND PRO FORMA FOR NEXT YEAR)

See Exhibit 2 at the end of this section

1. May be referred to as the income and expense statement

2. Indicate period covered (i.e., "For the period January 1, 20XX, to December 31, 20XX")

3. Inflows

   a. Gross salaries

   b. Interest income, regardless of reinvestment

   c. Dividend income, regardless of reinvestment

   d. Rental income

   e. Refunds due (tax)

   f. Other incoming cash flows

   g. Alimony received

4. Outflows

   a. Savings and investment—by item

   b. Fixed outflows—nondiscretionary

      1.) House payments

        2.) Auto payments

        3.) Taxes

    c. Fixed outflows—discretionary

        1.) Club dues

        2.) Utilities (a portion may be a variable outflow)

    d. Variable outflows—nondiscretionary

        1.) Food

    e. Variable outflows—discretionary

        1.) Vacations

        2.) Entertainment

5. Net discretionary cash flow = inflows – outflows

6. Footnotes should be used to explain details of income and expenses

EXHIBIT 1: STATEMENT OF FINANCIAL POSITION EXAMPLE

Dennis and Denise Smith
Statement of Financial Position
As of December 31, 20XX

ASSETS[1]

Cash/Cash Equivalents

JT	Cash (money market)	$40,000
	Total cash/cash equivalents	$40,000

Invested Assets

W	Publications, Inc.	$300,000
W	Denise's bakery	100,000
W	Denise's investment portfolio	90,000
H	SPDA	110,000
H	Dennis' investment portfolio (IRA)	200,000
H	Defined benefit plan (vested)	400,000
	Total investments	$1,200,000

Personal Use Assets

JT	Primary residence	$300,000
JT	Vacation home	180,000
JT	Personal property and furniture	100,000
H	Auto 1	20,000
W	Auto 2	22,000
	Total personal use	$622,000

Total Assets $1,862,000

LIABILITIES AND NET WORTH[2]

Liabilities

Current:

H	Bank credit card 1	$5,000
W	Bank credit card 2	7,000
W	Bank credit card 3	8,000
H	Auto 1 note balance	10,000
W	Auto 2 note balance	10,000
	Current liabilities	$40,000

Long-Term:

Mortgage—primary residence	$150,000
Mortgage—vacation home	120,000
Long-term liabilities	$270,000

Total liabilities	$310,000
Net Worth	$1,552,000

Total Liabilities and Net Worth $1,862,000

Notes to financial statements:*

[1] All assets are stated at fair market value.

[2] Liabilities are stated at principal only.

Titles and Ownership Information
H = Husband
W = Wife
JT = Joint husband and wife (with survivorship rights)—JTWROS

* Always pay special attention to the footnotes that appear on any financial statement.

EXHIBIT 2: STATEMENT OF CASH FLOW EXAMPLE

Charles and Vicki Jones
Statement of Cash Flow
For the year ended December 31, 20XX

Inflows—Annual

Charles' self-employment income	$42,000	
Vicki's salary	55,000	
Dividend income	1,220	
Interest income	1,110	
		$99,330

Outflows—Annual
Savings and investments

IRAs	$4,000	
Dividends	1,220	
Interest	1,110	
		$6,330

Fixed Outflows—Annual

Mortgage (P&I)	$11,592	
Property taxes	3,000	
Homeowners insurance	720	
Utilities	1,200	
Telephone	1,200	
Auto (P&I) payment	9,000	
Auto insurance	1,800	
Gas/oil/maintenance	3,600	
Credit card payments	7,200	
		$39,312

Variable Outflows

Taxes[1]	$26,142	
Food	8,490	
Medical/dental	2,400	
Clothing/personal care	3,600	
Child care	3,000	
Entertainment/vacation	3,000	
Discretionary	6,564	
		$53,196
		$98,838
Discretionary Cash Flow*		$492

[1]Notes on taxes

SE Tax—Charles	$5,934
FICA—Vicki	4,208
Est. Pmts—Charles	5,000
Fed. W/H—Vicki	11,000
	$26,142

* The difference between cash inflows and outflows.

III. ANALYSIS OF FINANCIAL STATEMENTS AND IDENTIFICATION OF STRENGTHS AND WEAKNESSES

A. DESCRIBED

1. Information on financial statements provides useful information to financial planners

---

Examples

For a given asset, there may be a corresponding liability and a payment, which should be shown or is shown on the cash flow statement.

For any given liability, generally there should be a corresponding asset.

B. RATIO ANALYSIS

1. Ratio analysis will give the planner a good idea or starting point in analyzing the client's financial situation

   a. Current ratio = current assets ÷ current liabilities. It also examines the relationship between the current assets and current liabilities (one year or less). It also indicates the ability to meet short-term obligations. The target for this ratio is 1.0–2.0.

      1.) Current assets consist of cash, cash equivalents (e.g. money markets, CDs), accounts receivable, and inventory (for businesses)

      2.) Current liabilities consist of accounts payable, current debts (e.g. annual amounts due on credit cards, home mortgages, auto/boat loans, etc.) and taxes

   b. Emergency ratio = liquid assets ÷ nondiscretionary monthly expenses. Most planners suggest 3–6 months' worth of coverage of fixed and variable outflows.

   c. Housing payment ratio = all monthly nondiscretionary housing costs* ÷ monthly gross income ≤ 28%

      *Includes principal, interest, taxes, insurance, and any condominium fee (if a renter, then the ratio is: rent + insurance ÷ monthly gross income ≤ 28%)

   d. Total payments ratio = all monthly debt payments and housing costs from above ÷ gross monthly income ≤ 36%. The 28% and 36% thresholds are common mortgage lender standards and are healthy targets for most clients.

   e. Solvency ratio = total assets ÷ total debt ≥ 1.1

   f. Savings ratio = savings per year ÷ gross income. The savings ratio should be 8–25% depending on age (e.g., a savings ratio of 8% for a younger individual and a savings ratio of 25% for a moderate net worth individual who is approaching retirement).

   g. Debt-to-income ratio = annual debt payment ÷ gross income ≤ 30%

2. The cash flow statement should be analyzed using a month-to-month comparison, calculating each outflow as a percentage of total income. The objective is to develop a predictive model for each expenditure (e.g., savings is 10% of gross income).

3. Emergency fund

    a. The emergency fund assists the client with the ability to withstand a sudden negative financial disruption of income

    b. It comprises cash and cash equivalents with short-term maturities (three to six months)

    c. It should generally be three to six months' worth of nondiscretionary cash flows to accommodate unemployment, loss of significant assets, or other unexpected major expenditures

        1.) Three months is generally used when there are two working spouses or a second source of income

        2.) Six months is generally used when the client is single or married with only one working spouse

4. Typical client strengths and weaknesses

STRENGTHS	WEAKNESSES
• Adequate savings	• Inadequate savings
• Appropriate investments	• Inappropriate investments
• Appropriate risk coverage	• Uncovered catastrophic risks:
• Appropriate net worth	*Life, Health, Disability, Property,*
• Appropriate emergency fund	*Liability, and Umbrella*
• Valid and appropriate will and transfer plan	• Inadequate net worth
• Well-articulated goals	• Inadequate emergency fund
• Excellent cash flow management	• No will or invalid will
• Knowledge about investments	• Inadequately defined financial goals
	• Poor budget—improper use of cash flow
	• Lack of knowledge about investments

IV. BUDGETING

A. DESCRIBED

1. Budgeting requires planning for the expected, the recurring, and the sometimes unexpected

2. Budgeting is a process of projecting, monitoring, adjusting, and controlling future income and expenditures

3. Budgeting may be used to determine the wage replacement ratio for capital needs analysis for retirement where the client is sufficiently close to retirement to be able to estimate the retirement budget

B. STEPS IN PREPARING A BUDGET

1. Start with a year of bank statements, checks, and check stubs. Create a spreadsheet of all expenditures by month by category. If needed, retrieve a year's copies of credit card expenditure information to assist in determining the amounts and categories of expenditures.

2. Once the dollar amounts are determined per category per month, calculate these as a percentage of gross income. Analyze each category, looking for consistent percentage expenditures, to develop a predictive model for that particular expenditure.

3. Identify which costs are sensitive to general inflation and which are fixed (e.g., home mortgage)

4. Forecast next year's income on a monthly basis

5. Determine how much expenditures will amount to and in which months the expenditure will occur. Often, insurance bills are paid annually or semiannually. If they arrive at the wrong time, they can play havoc with cash flows.

6. Project the budget for the next 12 months

7. Compare actual expenditures for the month to expected expenditures. Adjust the next 11 months accordingly.

8. Continue to analyze, picking out specific expenditure categories that you can control. Entertainment expenses are an example of a cost that can be managed. Some utilities, such as long distance telephone bills, may be reduced by changing carriers.

C. SAVING AND CONSUMPTION HABITS

1. Information about a client's saving and consumption habits assists the planner in developing a successful strategic financial plan for the client

2. If the client does not have a history of saving money consistently, it is wise to develop a strategy in which money is directed into savings before the client receives a check from his employer. Similarly, if the client has a history of making large dollar purchases impulsively, it would be wise to encourage investments in assets with early withdrawal penalties or for which withdrawal is difficult.

3. Withdrawal penalties or delays may discourage the client from making such impulse purchases. Historical behavior is the best indicator of future behavior. Therefore, a good way to collect information about the client's saving and consumption habits is by asking the client about previous saving and consumption habits.

D. DISCRETIONARY VERSUS NONDISCRETIONARY EXPENSES

1. A discretionary expense is a recurring or nonrecurring expense for an item or service that is either nonessential or more expensive than necessary

    a. Fixed discretionary expenses can include the following

        1.) Club dues

        2.) Cable television

        3.) Holiday and birthday gifts

        4.) Magazine subscriptions

    b. Variable discretionary expenses can include the following

        1.) Vacations

        2.) Entertainment costs

        3.) Club dues

        4.) Pet costs

        5.) Alcohol

2. A nondiscretionary expense is a recurring or nonrecurring expense that is essential for an individual to maintain his life

    a. Fixed nondiscretionary expenses can include the following

        1.) Rent or mortgage

        2.) Auto and health insurance premiums

        3.) Loan repayments

    b. Variable nondiscretionary expenses can include the following

        1.) Utilities

        2.) Taxes

        3.) Food

        4.) Clothing (this could potentially be discretionary)

        5.) Repairs

3. Both discretionary expenses and nondiscretionary expenses must be considered when preparing a budget

    a. Discretionary expenses plus nondiscretionary expenses equals the individual's total budgeted expenses for the budgeting period

    b. Any excess of income over budgeted expenses can be used as a cushion for unforeseen expenses

E. SAVINGS STRATEGIES

1. Developing a budget is one of the more important ways to help in the savings process

    a. The budget can both reveal problem spending areas and help an individual fine-tune the cash flow

    b.   The process of gathering information to begin or maintain a budget can help an individual control spending and free up cash to save, invest, or pay off debt

2.   Other savings strategies

    a.   Automatic payments to investment accounts are a great way to have money transferred to investment (or savings) accounts on a regular monthly basis

    b.   401(k) contributions through automatic payroll drafts are a great way to accumulate money for retirement on a pretax basis

    c.   Paying off accumulated credit card balances can be a good strategy before implementing a savings plan

V. INTERNAL ANALYSIS

A. LIFE CYCLE POSITIONING

Life cycle positioning information is needed because it plays a significant role in affecting the goals and behaviors of individuals. It also suggests which financial risks currently exist. To identify the client's life cycle positioning, the planner needs to have information about the client's age, marital status, dependents, income level, and net worth.

1. Age

    a. Age is one of the most important factors in financial planning. Generally, youth gives little thought or consideration to retirement goals or wealth-transfer goals. As people age, they become aware that adequate retirement income requires funding. At some time, they begin to seriously plan for this financial goal.

    b. In the recent past, it was common for persons to become conscious about their retirement reality as late as age 40, or even age 50. Today, it seems that clients are beginning to become more aware of this issue at a much younger age. Perhaps this phenomenon is due primarily to the increased amount of readily available information on the cost of retirement and the necessity to plan early.

2. Marital status

    a. The second factor that affects goal determination is marital status. The desire to provide for one's dependents creates a host of goals to achieve and risks to avoid. For example, it is common for married persons to combine their future economic resources to jointly purchase such assets as a house by jointly committing to indebtedness. The purchase of a personal residence through indebtedness, which can only be afforded by combining both incomes, creates an interdependency of one spouse on the other.

    b. In the event one spouse was to suffer unemployment, untimely death, disability, or some other catastrophic event, the commitment to the repayment of the debt may not be met.

3. Dependents

    a. The third factor affecting the creation of goals is dependents and their ages. Dependents may be children, grandchildren, or elderly parents. Persons with children quite commonly have goals of providing education for their children. Education is an expensive goal that requires substantial expenditures made over a finite period.

    b. Grandchildren may also be considered dependents. A person may have grandchildren as early as in their 30s but more commonly in their 50s or older. The significance of grandchildren as a factor is not that they are actual dependents, but rather that grandchildren may signal the initial phase of wealth transfer. Grandparents may find themselves with more assets and income than they feel is necessary. They then begin to help provide financially for their grandchildren.

    c. Other examples of dependencies that affect goals are caring for an aging parent or providing special care to a handicapped person. It is important for the planner to realize that not only married persons with children have dependents. Single childless persons may have financial dependents by taking on the obligations of aging parents or other loved ones.

4. Income and net worth

    a. Income and net worth are the last two factors concerning life cycle positioning. Substantial income suggests an opportunity to achieve financial goals as long as the goals are realistic relative to the income.

    b. Lower income presents greater challenges in achieving financial security and financial independence. Persons with a low income and low net worth generally have a more difficult time overcoming financial setbacks.

    c. A person with substantial net worth is generally less likely to suffer catastrophic consequences as a result of a single financial setback. However, substantial net worth also implies a need for increased management of assets and planning, and an increasing emphasis and concern about the avoidance of all taxes.

B. FINANCIAL PLANNING FOR SPECIAL CIRCUMSTANCES

1. Special circumstances include divorce, terminal illness, nontraditional families, and job loss. Careful analysis of internal factors should be reviewed and closely monitored.

2. Divorce

    a. A divorce can be traumatic, as well as very expensive, for the parties involved

        1.) After a divorce, each person's financial picture will be changed drastically

        2.) Each spouse may suffer a decline in their standard of living

    b. Financial planners should gather the following information from a client who has gone through a divorce

        1.) Personal and business income tax returns

        2.) Insurance policies

        3.) Retirement plan benefit statements

        4.) Investment information

        5.) Income and expense information

        6.) Debt information

    c. Budgeting after a divorce

        1.) Former spouses must adequately plan future income and expenses after a divorce, including the effects of alimony and child support payments paid and received

        2.) A new postdivorce budget should be created, taking into account the revised living expenses and sources of income that will occur after a divorce

        3.) A revised net worth statement should be created after a divorce, reflecting the property division of the divorce

        4.) Often spouses must change their investment philosophy after a divorce

            a.) A lower risk tolerance may occur after a divorce, because certain investments are earmarked for specific purposes, such as education

            b.) Property division after a divorce usually results in a much smaller investment portfolio, which may actually require a higher degree of risk tolerance to achieve a higher rate of return

5.) Insurance coverage must be revised after a divorce

    a.) Each spouse must obtain a separate automobile insurance policy, as well as a separate homeowners (or renters) policy

    b.) Beneficiary designations of life insurance policies may need to be changed, unless prohibited by court order

    c.) Availability of COBRA continuation coverage for a nonworking spouse should be determined. Generally, a nonworking spouse is eligible for up to 36 months of continued coverage in the group plan sponsored by the working spouse's employer.

6.) Income tax ramifications of a divorce

    a.) Alimony payments are deductible by the payor and are includible in the gross income of the payee

      • Several conditions must be met for alimony to be deductible for income tax purposes

      • If there is more than a $15,000 decrease in alimony payments between any of the first three years, there may be alimony recapture

      • These conditions are discussed in the Income Tax section

    b.) Money received for child support is not includible in income by the payee and is not deductible by the payor

      • Distinguishing alimony from child support is not always obvious

      • If payments are reduced when the child reaches a certain age, marries, or dies, the amount of the reduction is presumed to be considered child support

    c.) Property settlements received pursuant to a divorce are not includible in income by the recipient and are not deductible by the transferor

3. Terminal illness

    a. The terminal illness, and eventual death, of a spouse, life partner, or other family member can be a difficult emotional period for caretakers

      1.) During the period of terminal illness, emotional and financial considerations must be balanced so the terminally ill person does not unduly suffer

      2.) After the death of a loved one, surviving family members will need to revised their financial plan

      3.) When a person is terminally ill, he is very aware that his declining health is leading him toward death

    b. A financial planner must ascertain the following information to assist in planning for a terminally ill patient

      1.) Life and health insurance policies

      2.) Availability of Medicare

      3.) Potential for stay in nursing home

      4.) Titling of assets and other probate concerns

      5.) Income and expense information

      6.) Debt

   c. Hospice care

      1.) A hospice cares for people who are terminally ill. The focus is on caring, not curing.

      2.) A hospice has a team of specially trained professionals who provide unique expert care, pain management, and emotional and spiritual support that are tailored to the individual patient's needs and wishes

      3.) A hospice is available to anyone regardless of illness, culture, age, gender, or financial status

          a.) The patient must have a terminal illness

          b.) The patient must have been certified by a medical professional as having a prognosis of six months or less to live

          c.) The patient does not wish to pursue curative treatment

      4.) The hospice offers a wide range of services (at a nursing home, hospice facility, or at the patient's home)

          a.) Physician services

          b.) Regular home visits by registered and licensed practical nurses

          c.) Home health aides to assist in activities of daily living

          d.) Social work and counseling services

          e.) Medical equipment and supplies

          f.) Volunteer support to assist exhausted caregivers and family members

          g.) Specialized services, such as physical therapy, speech therapy, occupational therapy, and nutritional counseling

      5.) Medicare Part A pays for certain hospice costs. Many other types of health plans, including health maintenance organizations (HMOs) and preferred provider organizations (PPOs), also cover costs related to hospice care.

   d. Viatical settlements

      1.) A viatical settlement is an arrangement in which an insured (usually terminally ill) sells his life insurance contract to a viatical settlement provider (VSP) for cash

          a.) The VSP will receive the death benefit when the insured dies

          b.) Often times the terminally ill person is a victim, because the policy is discounted so deeply that the ill person gets very little cash for the insurance policy

      2.) Amounts received from a VSP are income tax free to the insured, if the insured is terminally or chronically ill

          a.) A terminally ill individual is an individual who has been certified by a physician as having an illness or condition that can reasonably be expected to result in death within 24 months of the date of certification

          b.) A chronically ill individual is generally a person who is unable to perform at least two activities of daily living (e.g., eating or bathing) for a period of at least 90 days. If the individual is chronically ill, the benefits will be excluded from income only to the extent they are used for long-term care services.

4. Nontraditional families

  a. Millions of responsible, well-adjusted people are seeking out and living new ways of relating that don't embrace the traditional one man-one-woman marriage model

    1.) Recognizing the demonstrated problems of legal marriage at a young age, many people are postponing marriage, or forgoing it altogether in favor of cohabitation in record numbers

    2.) Millions of senior citizens choose not to marry legally for a host of valid financial, tax, and emotional reasons

    3.) Millions of same-sex unions, both sexually exclusive and nonexclusive, exist and thrive

  b. Estate issues for nontraditional families

    1.) Nontraditional families need to plan their estates, maybe even more so than married couples

      a.) Any nontraditional family, including single parents or unmarried men and women living together, should consider the unique estate planning challenges presented to them

        • Legally married couples can transfer unlimited wealth to each other during their lifetimes and at death with no estate tax, income tax, or gift tax implications

        • Unmarried people cannot take advantage of the gift or estate tax marital deduction

      b.) A good estate-planning attorney can help nontraditional families design an estate plan and legal documents that can eliminate or reduce these tax burdens

    2.) Unmarried couples, either same sex or opposite sex, can still own property together, and share parenting responsibilities as much as any husband and wife

      a.) Nontraditional families can face a disadvantage in the area of property ownership if they don't know the law

      b.) People not legally married can jointly own property as tenants in common

        • If one person dies, that person's share of the property will be passed to his heirs or closest living relative if there is no will

        • The surviving person may not receive decedent's portion of the property

      c.) People not legally married can jointly own property as joint tenancy with right of survivorship

        • The surviving tenant will automatically receive the decedent's share of the property

        • Will or having to go to court is not necessary

    3.) Estate planning for nontraditional relationships

      a.) Create a will leaving specific bequests to the partner

      b.) Make lifetime gifts to partner

      c.) Convert property owned outright into joint tenancy with right of survivorship (JTWROS) or tenancy in common d.) Name the other cohabitant as the beneficiary of qualified plans and IRAs

         e.) Obtain life insurance policy with the other cohabitant as beneficiary

         f.) Make charitable bequests at death to take advantage of the estate tax charitable deduction

         g.) Make use of POD (pay on death) and TOD (transfer on death) beneficiary designations for bank and investment accounts

5. Job loss

   a. Job loss can be a very difficult experience for individuals. Many options are pursued after a job loss.

      1.) Flat-out financial survival, a stopgap measure until the individual can get back on his feet

      2.) A plan to jump back into a company, industry, or situation similar to one the individual just left

      3.) A career change, starting a business, returning to school, or arranging for a better work-life balance

   b. The most common moves after a job loss

      1.) Maintaining career continuity

      2.) Ensuring financial survival by seeking contract or part-time work

   c. Financial planning concerns after a job loss

      1.) Financial planners should assist a client in preparing a cash flow and net worth statement after a job loss

         a.) Planner should help determine which discretionary expenses can be reduced or eliminated

         b.) Planner should ensure that client has filed for unemployment benefits

      2.) Client could lose a large amount of employer benefits after losing a job

         a.) Nonvested retirement plan balance is lost

         b.) Group insurance coverage may be lost

            • COBRA continuation coverage may apply

            • Individual will be required to pay premiums

      3.) Client may want to start a new business

         a.) Financial planner can assist client in the creation of a business plan

         b.) Financial planner can assist the client in choosing a business entity, as well as assist in the filing of tax forms

         c.) Employment contracts, tax returns, retirement plans, and lease agreements need to be filed and considered

C. LIFE CYCLE PHASES AND CHARACTERISTICS

1. As people progress through the life cycle, there is a tendency to move subtly but surely among financial objectives as the result of changes in personal financial circumstances. We have identified and labeled these life cycle phases and characteristics as the asset accumulation phase of life, the conservation/protection phase of life, and the distribution/gifting phase of life.

2. Although not all people move through these phases at the same rate, a sufficient percentage of people do. Financial planners can gain valuable insight into their client's objectives and concerns by identifying which phase or phases their client is in at a particular point in time. Exhibit 3 illustrates the life cycle phases and the typical characteristics of each.

EXHIBIT 3: LIFE CYCLE PHASES AND CHARACTERISTICS

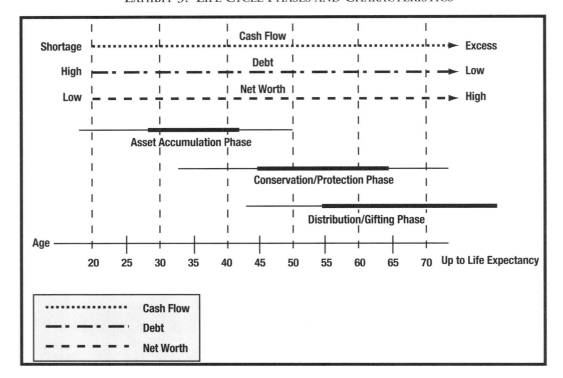

   a. Asset accumulation phase

      1.) The asset accumulation phase is described as beginning somewhere between the ages of 20 and 25 and lasting until somewhere around age 50 for many persons. The beginning of the phase is characterized by limited excess funds for investing, high degree of debt to net worth, and low net worth.

      2.) At the beginning of the phase, there generally is a low appreciation for the risks that exist. As the person moves through the asset accumulation phase, cash for investments generally increases, there is less use of debt as a percentage of total assets, and there is an increase in net worth.

   b. Conservation/protection phase

      1.) The conservation/protection phase begins when one has acquired some assets, usually in late 30s or 40s and may last throughout his working life, and depending on the nature of the person, may last all the way to the end of his life. It is also characterized by an increase in cash flow, assets, and net worth with some decrease in the proportional use of debt.

   2.) People generally become more risk averse as more assets are acquired. Therefore, from an investment planning viewpoint, they are more concerned about losing what they have acquired than acquiring more. They become aware and concerned with many of the risks they ignored at the beginning of the asset accumulation phase, including an increased awareness of life's risks (e.g., untimely death, unemployment, or disability).

 c. Distribution/gifting phase

   1.) The distribution/gifting phase begins subtly when the person realizes that he can afford to spend on things he never believed possible. The asset accumulation and conservation/ protection phases make this phase possible. It is quite common that at the beginning of this phase the person remains in both the asset accumulation and conservation/protection phases. (Yes, there is a period for many people when they are being influenced by all three phases simultaneously, although not necessarily to the same degree.)

   2.) When parents purchase new cars for adult children, pay for a grandchild's private school tuition, or treat themselves to expensive vacations relative to their tradition, they are likely to be in the distribution/gifting phase

D. RISK TOLERANCE LEVELS

 1. Knowledge of risk tolerance levels is needed to assist the financial planner in determining the types of investments and the style of risk management best suited for the client. The style of risk management refers to the issue of self-insuring reasonable risks versus overinsuring in an attempt to mitigate even small losses.

 2. Essentially, it is the choice of balancing lower premiums with self-reliance for smaller losses, or alternatively, higher premiums with less loss exposure. However, risk tolerance levels are subject to misinterpretation because they are so subjective. The statement, "I am not very risk tolerant," may mean something different to each client. Therefore, additional questioning is needed to ensure understanding.

VI. PERSONAL USE—ASSETS AND LIABILITIES

A. FINANCING STRATEGIES

1. Buying versus leasing

    a. The effect on cash flow when buying a home

    1.) Income – expenses = discretionary cash flow

    2.) Down payment, closing costs, mortgage insurance, property insurance and taxes, maintenance, and operating expenses are all costs associated with purchasing a home. Families often purchase more life insurance when they own a home, in the event of one of the spouse's deaths.

    3.) Upfront charges place a heavy burden on the homeowner

    4.) Interest on mortgage is deductible

    5.) There are different types of mortgage payments to choose from (variable rate, fixed rate, or balloon payment) that can change both short-term and long-term cash flow

    b. The effect on cash flow when renting living quarters

    1.) Cost is fixed in the short term, and there is no long-term commitment

    2.) There is no property tax associated with renting

    3.) Maintenance and repair costs are usually grouped with the rental fee

    4.) Cost of insurance is substantially lower than for a homeowner

    5.) It is a good time to start saving toward the purchase of a house

    c. The following two cash flow statements compare and contrast sample homeowner's and a renter's cash flows

Statement of Cash Flow (Renter)		Statement of Cash Flow (Homeowner)	
Gross salary	$55,500	Gross salary	$55,500
Interest/dividend income	$1,000	Interest/dividend income	$1,000
Total Inflows	**$56,500**	**Total Inflows**	**$56,500**
After-tax savings investment	$5,250	After-tax savings investment	$1,750
Renters insurance	$150	Homeowners insurance	$350
Term life insurance	$200	Term life insurance premiums	$350
Taxes (income, emp.)	$10,000	Taxes (inc., emp., prop.)	$12,000
401(k) contribution	$2,350	401(k) contribution	$2,350
Annual rent	$8,400	Mortgage principal and interest	$7,200
Total Financial Outflows	**$26,350**	**Total Financial Outflows**	**$24,000**
Food	$3,200	Food	$3,200
Transportation with insurance	$4,000	Transportation with insurance	$4,000
Utilities	$2,400	Home maintenance	$3,700
Medical	$1,200	Utilities	$3,700
Vacation	$4,200	Medical	$1,200
Clothing	$4,900	Vacation	$4,200
Miscellaneous	$7,600	Clothing	$4,900
		Miscellaneous	$7,600
Total Living-Expense Outflows	**$27,500**	**Total Living-Expense Outflows**	**$32,500**

B. DEBT

1. Debt is appropriate when matched properly with the economic life of the asset and the ability to repay

---

Example

The purchase of an automobile that is expected to be used for three years (36 months) has a maximum realistic economic life of five years (60 months). It should probably be financed over 36 months but certainly no longer than 60 months.

---

2. The issues

    a. There are a number of risks to consider

        1.) A shortened economic life

        2.) Increasing cash outflows for repairs as the asset ages

        3.) The changing of the initial utility curves of the purchaser during the holding period unexpectedly reducing the overall utility of the asset

    b. Matching debt repayment cash flows to economic life

        1.) Generally, the considered cash flows are not just the principal and interest to retire the debt

        2.) Also included are the cash flows associated with the increase in repairs and maintenance due to asset aging (both real and personal property) as well as the prospect of higher executory costs (insurance and taxes)

    c. Cost of replacement

        1.) The cost of the replacement asset will have to either be borne entirely by future cash flows, or the current asset value will help to offset replacement costs

        2.) One question is whether the cost of the new asset is increasing in price faster than that of the old asset

        3.) Another question is whether the value of the old asset (exchange value to another buyer) is diminishing faster than the debt is being extinguished

            a.) If so, the purchasers of such an asset may find that they are in a negative equity position

            b.) This is the primary reason that lenders insist on down payments and generally establish a repayment schedule to ensure that the borrower will always be in a positive equity position

            c.) Such a position will reduce the likelihood that the borrower will abandon the property

C. HOME MORTGAGES

1. Types

    a. 30-year fixed mortgage

    b. 15-year fixed mortgage

    c. Variable mortgage

    d. Balloon mortgage

    e. Interest only mortgage

2. Issues in the selection of mortgages

    a. Length of time expected to stay in the house

    b. Cash flow capacity

    c. Tolerance for risk

    d. The spread between yields after a quantitative analysis comparison of fixed-to-fixed rates and fixed-to-variable rates

    e. If the time expected to be in the house is short, the more likely it is that an adjustable rate mortgage (ARM) is the mortgage of choice. This is simply because most ARMs have a 2–3% lower interest rate than a 30-year fixed-rate mortgage and have 2/6 caps (i.e., 2% maximum interest rate increase per year and 6% life of loan).

    f. The downside risk to an ARM is the prospect of the interest rate increasing periodically causing the payment to increase proportionally

g. Another advantage of an ARM is that, because of the low initial interest rate, the principal and interest (P&I) payments are low relative to a 30-year fixed-rate mortgage. It is easier to qualify for a mortgage using the traditional lender hurdle rates of 28%/36%.

h. When comparing a 15-year to a 30-year fixed-rate mortgage, the interest rates will usually be about .5% different assuming the same down payment. The cash flows will differ depending on the interest rate and the size of the mortgage.

Example

	Sales Price	Down Payment	Paid Closing Costs	Mortgage Amount	Term Months	Interest Rate	P&I Payment
Fixed 30-Year	$180,000	$36,000	$5,760	$144,000	360	5.5%	$818
Fixed 15-Year	$180,000	$36,000	$5,760	$144,000	180	5.0%	$1,139
ARM 30-Year	$180,000	$36,000	$5,760	$144,000	360	3.0%	$607

i. Although the ARM has the current lowest payment, the risk is that at some point in the life of the ARM the interest rate will be 9.0%, assuming a 2%/6% cap, at which time the monthly P&I payment would be $1,158.66 over a 30-year period. It should be pointed out that in this particular example, qualifying for a loan would be easier using the ARM because the initial payment is lower (assuming $200 per month taxes and $75 per month insurance).

1.) 30-year fixed rate: total monthly housing costs = $818 + $200 + $75 = $1,093; monthly gross income needed to qualify for loan = $1,093 ÷ .28 = $3,903.57

2.) 15-year fixed rate: total monthly housing costs = $1,139 + $200 + $75 = $1,414; monthly gross income needed to qualify for loan = $1,414 ÷ .28 = $5,050

3.) ARM: total monthly housing costs = $607 + $200 + $75 = $882; monthly gross income needed to qualify for loan = $882 ÷ .28 (Housing ratio threshold) = $3,150

3. Tolerance for risk

a. If a client has a low tolerance for fluctuating payments, a fixed mortgage should be selected. Assuming a higher risk tolerance, the planner will have to consider the length of expected ownership (shorter term will mitigate risk) and the opportunity cost of alternative investments. The client may consider an ARM.

b. It is generally not appropriate to select an ARM (using the first-year teaser rate) simply to qualify for a loan and hope that cash flows will be sufficient to pay for any interest increases

4. Savings due to mortgage selection

a. The savings is a result of (1) the 15-year mortgage causing earlier retirement of the principal indebtedness and (2) the slightly lower interest rate. However, many 30-year loans are selected simply as a necessity to meet lender qualification requirements. If no prepayment penalties exist, most of the savings can be achieved by paying a 30-year loan according to a 15-year amortization schedule.

Example (See previous example)

	Number of Payments	Monthly Payment	Total Payment	Loan	Interest Paid
30-Year Fixed	360	$818	$294,341.80	$144,000	$150,341.80
15-Year Fixed	180	$1,139	$204,973.71	$144,000	$60,973.71
Savings			$89,368.09	$0	$89,368.09

    b. The total interest paid is determined by multiplying the amount of the payment by the number of payments and then subtracting the principal borrowed

5. Calculating mortgage payments

    a. Mortgages can be calculated using the time value of money concepts discussed later in this section

---

Example

Sara purchased a house for $200,000. She made a $10,000 down payment and took out a 30-year loan for the remainder at 6%. Sara's monthly loan payment will be $1,139.15. It can be calculated using the following keystrokes on your financial calculator.

PV	=	190,000 (200,000 − 10,000)
FV	=	0
n	=	360 (30 × 12)
i	=	0.5 (6 ÷ 12)
PMT_{OA}	=	$1,139.15

Note: This is discussed in more depth later in this section. Also, the payment is an ordinary annuity because the payments are in arrears.

---

6. A reverse mortgage is a special type of home loan for which the payment stream is reversed. In regular home loans, the borrower makes payments to the lender.

    a. With a reverse mortgage, the opposite takes place

    b. The lender makes payments to the homeowner on the basis of the value of the home and holds legal title to it

    c. Once the homeowner no longer occupies the property, the lender sells it in order to recover the money that was paid out

    d. Reverse mortgages are primarily used to provide financial security to seniors in their retirement years

7. Federal Housing Administration (FHA)—The government may guarantee loans through various FHA programs for individuals from lower and middle income households who would not be able to secure a conventional home loan, under normal circumstances, because of a lack of certain loan requirements (i.e. insufficient down payment)

8. Veterans Administration (VA)—Same as FHA, but for veterans

9. A home equity loan (i.e., second mortgage) is a conventional loan secured by the homeowner's equity. The loan is based on the fair market value of the homeowner's equity. The interest payments may also be tax deductible.

10. A taxpayer can claim itemized deductions on a qualified residence up to $1,000,000 for acquisition debt, and up to $100,000 of home equity debt. Anything above these amounts would be subject to excess qualified residence limitations.

11. For 2007, homeowners will be able to take an itemized deduction on paid mortgage insurance premiums

    a. This deduction applies only to those mortgages closed (or refinanced) in 2007

    b. The phaseout for this deduction is $100,000–$110,000 for married, filing jointly, and $50,000–$55,000 for single taxpayers

VII. ECONOMIC ENVIRONMENT—BASIC CONCEPTS

A. DEMAND

1. The amount of a commodity people buy depends on its price

2. The relationship between price and quantity bought is called the demand curve

    a. Downward sloping demand—if the price of a commodity is raised (all other things equal), buyers tend to buy less of the commodity

    b. The demand curve (see Exhibit 4) measures price on the vertical axis and quantities demanded on the horizontal axis

EXHIBIT 4: THE DEMAND CURVE

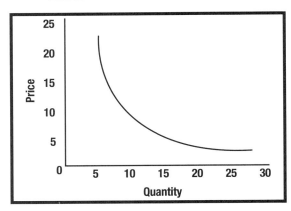

    c. When the price is lowered (all other things equal), quantity demanded increases

3. Quantity demanded tends to fall as price rises for two reasons

    a. Substitution effect—when the price of a good rises, consumers substitute other similar goods for it

    b. Income effect—when the price rises, consumers curb consumption

4. The average income of consumers is a key determinant of demand. As incomes rise, individuals tend to buy more.

5. The size of the market clearly affects the market demand

6. The prices and availability of related goods influence the demand for a commodity

7. Factors affecting demand

    a. The price of the good affects quantity demanded

    b. Average income

    c. Population

    d. The prices of related goods

    e. Tastes

    f. Special influences, such as expectations about future economic conditions, particularly prices, may affect demand

8. Demand curve shift—influences, other than the price of the good, change

B. SUPPLY

1. Supply means the quantity of a good that businesses willingly produce and sell

2. The supply curve for a commodity shows the relationship between its market price and the amount of that commodity producers are willing to produce and sell. The supply curve (see Exhibit 5) measures price on the vertical axis and quantities supplied on the horizontal axis.

EXHIBIT 5: THE SUPPLY CURVE

3. Behind the supply curve—the main force operating on supply is profit. A key element affecting supply decisions is the cost of production.

4. Another element influencing supply is the price of related goods. Related goods are goods that can be readily substituted for one another in the production process. If the price of one good rises, the supply of another substitute good is likely to decrease.

5. A reduction in tariffs and quotas on foreign goods will open the market to foreign producers and will tend to increase supply. If a market becomes monopolized, the price at each level of output will increase.

6. Factors affecting supply

   a. The price of the good affects quantity supplied

   b. Technology

   c. Input prices

   d. Prices of related goods

   e. Target organization

   f. Special influences

7. Competition

   a. Pure competition exists when there are many competitors selling a product or service with very little difference

   b. An oligopoly occurs when you have a small number of companies that control the market for a given type of product or service

   c. A monopoly occurs when a single company owns all or nearly all of the market for a given type of product or service

C. SUPPLY AND DEMAND INTERACTION

1. The market equilibrium comes at the price and quantity where the supply and demand forces are in balance

2. Supply and demand can do more than tell us about the equilibrium price and quantity. They can be used to predict the impact of changes in economic conditions on prices and quantities.

3. When factors underlying demand or supply change, these lead to shifts in demand or supply and to changes in the market equilibrium of price and quantity

4. Care must be taken not to confuse a change in demand, denoted by a shift of the demand (supply) curve, with a change in the quantity demanded (supplied), denoted by movement to a different point on the same demand curve after a price change

5. Rationing by prices—by determining the equilibrium prices and quantities of all inputs and outputs, the market allocates (rations) the scarce goods of the society among the possible uses

D. PRICE ELASTICITY OF DEMAND

1. The price elasticity is the responsiveness of the quantity demanded of a good to changes in the good's price, other things held constant

2. The percentage change in quantity demanded is divided by the percentage change in price

3. Elastic and inelastic demand—goods differ in their elasticities. Demand for necessities (e.g., food) responds little to price changes, whereas luxuries are generally highly price sensitive.

4. A good is elastic when its quantity demanded responds greatly to price changes and is inelastic when its quantity demanded responds little to price changes

5. Unit-elastic demand occurs when the percentage change in quantity is exactly the same size as the percentage change in price

6. The slope is not the same as the elasticity because the demand curve's slope depends on the changes in price and quantity, whereas the elasticity depends on the percentage changes in price and quantity

7. Elasticity and revenue—elasticity helps to clarify the impact of price changes on the total revenue of producers

8. Total revenue

    a. When demand is price inelastic, a price decrease reduces total revenue

    b. When demand is price elastic, a price decrease increases total revenue

    c. In the case of unit-elastic demand, a price decrease leads to no change in total revenue

9. Economic factors determine the magnitude of price elasticities for individual goods, the degree to which a good is a necessity or a luxury, the extent to which substitutes are available, the time available for response, and the relative importance of a commodity in the consumer's budget

10. The price elasticity of supply measures the percentage change in quantity supplied in response to a 1% change in the good's price

E. INFLATION

1. Inflation denotes an increase in the general level of prices. The rate of inflation is the rate of change in the general price level.

2. The opposite of inflation is deflation, which is a decline in general price levels and is often caused by a reduction in the supply of money

3. Disinflation denotes a decline in the rate of inflation (a reduction in the rate at which prices rise)

4. Moderate inflation is characterized by slowly rising prices

5. Galloping inflation occurs when money loses its value very quickly, and real interest rates can be minus 50% or 100% per year

    1.) People hold only the bare minimum amount of money needed for daily transactions

    2.) Financial markets wither away, and funds are generally allocated by rationing rather than by interest rates

    3.) People hoard goods, buy houses, and never lend money at the low, nominal interest rate

6. Impact of inflation—during periods of inflation, some, but not all, prices and wages move at the same rate

7. Effects of inflation

    a. A redistribution of income and wealth occurs among different classes. The major redistributive impact of inflation occurs through its effect on the real value of people's wealth. In general, unanticipated inflation redistributes wealth from creditors to debtors (that is, unanticipated or unforeseen inflation helps those who have borrowed money and hurts those who have lent money). An unanticipated decline in inflation has the opposite effect.

    b. Changes are created in the relative prices and outputs of different goods, or sometimes in output and employment for the economy as a whole

8. Real interest rate adjustment—inflation persists for a long time, and markets begin to adapt. An allowance for inflation is generally built into the market interest rate.

9. Inflation affects the real economy in two specific areas: total output and economic efficiency

10. There is no necessary relationship between prices and output

11. Inflation may be associated with either a higher or a lower level of output and employment

12. Generally, the higher the inflation rate, the greater are the changes in relative prices

13. Distortions occur when prices get out of line relative to costs and demands

F. MEASURES OF INFLATION

1. A price index is a weighted average of the prices of numerous goods and services. The most well known price indexes are the Consumer Price Index (CPI), the Gross Domestic Product (GDP) deflator, and the Producer Price Index (PPI)

    a. The Consumer Price Index (CPI) measures the cost of a market basket of consumer goods and services, including prices of food, clothing, shelter, fuels, transportation, medical care, college tuition, and other commodities purchased for day-to-day living

        1.) A price index is constructed by weighting each price according to the economic importance of the commodity in question

        2.) Each item is assigned a fixed weight proportional to its relative importance in consumer expenditure budgets, as determined by a survey of expenditures in the 1982–1984 period

b. GDP deflator is a broader price index than the CPI

   1.) It is designed to measure the change in the average price of the market basket of goods included in GDP

   2.) In addition to consumer goods, the GDP deflator includes prices for capital goods and other goods and services purchased by businesses and governments

   3.) It also separates increases in productivity from inflation increases

c. The Producer Price Index (PPI) is the oldest continuous statistical series published by the Labor Department. It measures the level of prices at the wholesale or producer stage. It is based on approximately 3,400 commodity prices, including prices of foods, manufactured products, and mining products.

d. Index-number problems—the cost of living may be overestimated because consumers substitute relatively inexpensive goods for relatively expensive ones. The CPI does not accurately capture changes in quality of goods. Although the CPI is modified from time to time, the CPI is not corrected for quality improvements.

VIII. MONETARY AND FISCAL POLICY

A. MONETARY POLICY

1. The Federal Reserve Bank (Fed) controls the supply of money, enabling it to significantly affect interest rates. The Fed will follow a loose, or easy, monetary policy when it wants to increase the money supply to expand the level of income and employment. In times of inflation and when it wants to constrict the supply of money, the Fed will follow a tight monetary policy.

   a. Expansionary (easy) monetary policy—the supply of money increases resulting in the circulation of more money. This leads to more funds available for banks to lend and ultimately to a decline in interest rates.

   b. Restrictive (tight) monetary policy—the supply of money is restricted resulting in less money available for banks to lend. This leads to an increase in interest rates.

2. The Fed has several methods of controlling the money supply

   a. Reserve requirements—the reserve requirement for a member bank of the Federal Reserve Bank is the percentage of deposit liabilities that must be held in reserve. As this requirement is increased, less money is available to be loaned to customers, resulting in a restriction of the money supply.

   b. Federal Reserve discount rate

      1.) This is the rate at which member banks can borrow funds from the Federal Reserve to meet reserve requirements

      2.) When the Fed raises the discount rate, it increases the borrowing cost and discourages member banks from borrowing funds, resulting in a contraction of the money supply

      3.) The Fed will lower the discount rate when it wants to increase the money supply. Banks are able to borrow funds at lower rates and lend more money, which increases the supply.

   > **Note:** The discount rate is the borrowing rate from the Federal Reserve, and the Fed Funds Rate is the overnight lending rate between member banks

   c. Open market operations

      1.) This is the process that the Federal Reserve follows to purchase and sell government securities in the open market

      2.) The Fed will buy government securities to cause more money to circulate, thus increasing lending and lowering interest rates

      3.) The Fed will sell government securities to restrict the money supply. As investors purchase government securities, more money leaves circulation, which decreases lending and increases interest rates.

      4.) It is important to note that the Federal Open Market Committee (FOMC) is in charge of open market operations. The FOMC is made up of a rotation membership of Federal Reserve banks with the Federal Reserve Bank of New York, which is a permanent member.

B. FISCAL POLICY

1. Taxation, expenditures, and debt management of the federal government is called fiscal policy. Economic growth, price stability, and full employment are goals that may be pursued by changes in fiscal policy.

    a. Expansionary (easy) fiscal policy—when the government increases purchases of good and services while holding its revenues constant, it creates a budget deficit and stimulates aggregate demand

    b. Restrictive (tight) fiscal policy—when the government either reduces its expenditures of goods and services or raises taxes, which causes a budget surplus or a reduction in the budget deficit

2. Changes in taxation will affect corporate earnings, disposable earnings, and the overall economy

    a. As tax rates increase, corporations' after-tax income declines, which reduces their ability to pay dividends. This may cause the price for equities to decrease.

    b. Tax increases also reduce individuals' disposable income and limit the amount of money entering the economy

    c. The demand for tax-free investments is also influenced by changes in taxation levels. As increases in taxes occur, the attractiveness of tax-free instruments also increases.

3. Government expenditures—corporate earnings benefit from increases in government expenditures

4. Deficit spending—deficit spending occurs when expenditures exceed revenues of the government. By selling securities to the public to finance deficits, Treasury securities compete with other securities. This drives the prices down. The decrease in price causes the yields to rise.

C. THE NATURE OF INTEREST RATES

1. The price of money is the interest rate

2. The nominal interest rate measures the yield in dollars per year per dollar invested

3. The return on investments in terms of real goods and services is a real interest rate measure. The return in terms of dollars is an absolute measure. The real interest rate measures the quantity of goods we get tomorrow for goods forgone today. The real interest rate is obtained by correcting nominal, or dollar, interest rates for the rate of inflation and is calculated as follows:

$$\left(\frac{1 + \text{nominal rate}}{1 + \text{inflation rate}} - 1 \right) \times 100 = \text{real rate}$$

This is a key component in the calculation of educational, retirement needs, and serial payments.

IX. BUSINESS CYCLE THEORIES

A. DESCRIBED

1. Business cycles consist of swings in total national output, income, and employment marked by widespread expansion or contraction in many sectors of the economy

2. Business cycles generally occur as a result of shifts in aggregate demand. The cycle consists of two phases, expansion and contraction, and two points, peak and trough.

    a. The expansion phase comes to an end and goes into the contraction phase at the upper turning point, or peak

    b. Similarly, the contraction phase gives way to that expansion at the lower turning point, or trough. The emphasis here is not so much on high or low business activity as on the dynamic aspects of rising or falling business activity.

EXHIBIT 6: BUSINESS CYCLES (GENERAL)

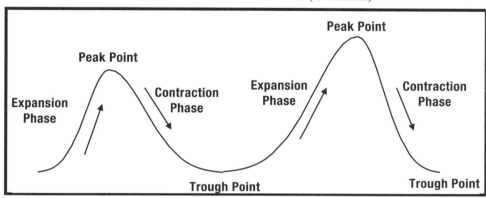

3. Definitions

    a. Peak point—the point at the end of the expansion phase when most businesses are operating at capacity and gross domestic product (GDP) is increasing rapidly. The peak is the point at which GDP is at its highest point and exceeds the long-run average GDP. Usually, employment peaks here.

    b. Trough point—the point at the end of the contraction phase where businesses are operating at their lowest capacity levels. Unemployment is rapidly increasing and peaks because sales fall rapidly. GDP growth is at its lowest or negative.

    c. Contraction phase—leads to trough. Business sales fall. Unemployment increases. GDP growth falls.

    d. Expansion phase—leads to peak. Business sales rise. GDP grows. Unemployment declines. Also called recovery phase.

    e. Recession—a decline in real GDP for two or more successive quarters characterized by the following:

        1.) Consumer purchases decline

        2.) Business inventories expand

        3.) GDP falls

        4.) Capital investment falls

     5.) Demand for labor falls

     6.) Unemployment is high

     7.) Commodity prices fall

     8.) Business profits fall

     9.) Interest rates fall as a result of reduced demand for money

  f. Depression—persistent recession and a severe decline in economic activity.

EXHIBIT 7: HYPOTHETICAL BUSINESS CYCLE

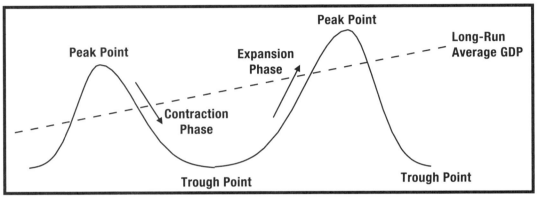

GDP trend line assumes expansion at 3% annually.

> **Note:** The business cycle is not symmetrical as drawn. The pattern of the business cycle is irregular and unpredictable.

4. Each phase of the cycle passes into the next. Each is characterized by different economic conditions.

5. Capital formation—certain economic variables always show greater fluctuations than others do in the business cycle

6. Durable goods (leader) are subject to violently erratic patterns of demand. It is the durable or capital goods sector of the economy that shows, by far, the greatest cyclical fluctuations.

7. Leading indicators—these indicators are used to predict changes in the business cycle, because they tend to precede and anticipate the change. Bond yields, housing starts, investor sentiment, and durable goods orders are examples of leading indicators.

8. Coincident indicators—these indicators occur simultaneously during the business cycle in order to confirm the current state of the economy or cycle. Examples include unemployment, consumer income, industrial production and profits.

9. GDP vs. GNP

  a. Gross Domestic product (GDP)—GDP (or nominal GDP) is the total monetary value of goods and services produced within a country's border over the course of a year. It is used to measure the health of a country's economy and standard of living. Real GDP is an inflation adjusted GDP figure in constant dollars.

b. Gross National Product (GNP)—Gross National Product (GNP) includes income generated by domestic individuals both domestically and internationally; however, unlike GDP, it does not include income generated domestically by a foreign firm. It is measured with constant dollars.

Note: The main purpose of the study of economic cycles is to understand which investment classes behave best in various economic times. For example, in an expansion phase, inflation and interest rates rise, generally depressing financial assets.

X. FINANCIAL INSTITUTIONS

A. DESCRIBED

1. Providers of financial services include banks, money market mutual funds, financial services companies, financial planners, brokerage firms, and insurance companies

2. The primary providers of cash management services are banks and similar institutions, money market mutual funds, stock brokerage firms, and financial services companies

B. BANKS AND SIMILAR INSTITUTIONS

1. There are several financial institutions that offer various forms of checking and savings accounts

   a. Commercial banks

   b. Savings and loan associations

2. Commercial banks

   a. Commercial banks are chartered under federal and state regulations. Commercial banks offer numerous consumer services, such as checking, savings, loans, safe-deposit boxes, investment services, financial counseling, and automatic payment of bills.

   b. Approximately 8,000 commercial banks exist nationwide with over 70,000 branch offices

   c. Each nonretirement account in a federally chartered bank is insured against loss up to $100,000 in principal and interest per account by the Bank Insurance Fund (BIF) of the Federal Deposit Insurance Corporation (FDIC), an agency of the federal government, subject to an aggregate limit of $100,000 for each person's accounts at that bank titled similarly (see discussion below)

   d. Coverage for retirement accounts (e.g., IRAs and self-directed Keoghs) that an individual has on deposit at a FDIC Insured Institution is $250,000

3. Savings and loan associations (thrifts)

   a. The main purpose of S&Ls is to accept savings and provide home loans. S&Ls are also called thrift institutions.

   b. S&Ls also make installment loans for consumer products (e.g., automobiles and appliances)

   c. S&Ls are not permitted to provide demand deposits (such as checking accounts with a commercial bank); however, they can offer interest-bearing NOW accounts, which are similar to demand deposit accounts

   d. The FDIC insures accounts in all federally chartered S&Ls up to $100,000 in principal and interest per account through its Savings Association Insurance Fund (SAIF) as well as some state-chartered institutions

   e. S&Ls are either mutual or corporate. The mutual savings and loans, which are more common, have the depositors as the actual owners of the association (shareowners). Corporate savings and loans operate as corporations and issue common and preferred stock to denote ownership.

C. FDIC INSURANCE

1. Any person or entity can have FDIC insurance on a deposit. A depositor does not have to be a US citizen, or even a resident of the United States.

2. The FDIC insures deposits in some, but not all, banks and savings associations

3. Federal deposit insurance protects deposits that are payable in the United States. Deposits that are only payable overseas are not insured.

4. Securities, mutual funds, and similar types of investments are not covered by FDIC insurance

   a. Creditors (other than depositors) and shareholders of a failed bank or savings association are not protected by federal deposit insurance

   b. Treasury securities (bills, notes, and bonds) purchased by an insured depository institution on a customer's behalf are not FDIC insured

5. All types of deposits received by a qualifying financial institution in its usual course of business are insured

   a. For example, savings deposits, checking deposits, deposits in NOW accounts, Christmas club accounts, and time deposits (including certificates of deposit, or CDs), are all FDIC insured deposits

   b. Cashiers' checks, money orders, officers' checks, and outstanding drafts are also insured

   c. Certified checks, letters of credit, and travelers' checks for which an insured depository institution is primarily liable are also insured, when issued in exchange for money or its equivalent, or for a charge against a deposit account

6. Deposits in different qualified institutions are insured separately

   a. If an institution has one or more branches, however, the main office and all branch offices are considered to be one institution

   b. Thus, deposits at the main office and at branch offices of the same institution are added together when calculating deposit insurance coverage

   c. Financial institutions owned by the same holding company but separately chartered are separately insured

7. The FDIC presumes that funds are owned as shown on the deposit account records of the insured depository institution

8. The basic FDIC insured amount of a depositor is $100,000

   a. Accrued interest is included when calculating insurance coverage

   b. Deposits maintained in different categories of legal ownership are separately insured. Accordingly, a depositor can have more than $100,000 of insurance coverage in a single institution if the funds are owned and deposited in different ownership categories.

   c. The most common categories of ownership are single (or individual) ownership, joint ownership, and testamentary accounts

   d. Separate insurance is also available for funds held for retirement and business purposes

      1.) FDIC coverage for retirement accounts (e.g., IRAs and self-directed Keoghs) that an individual has on deposit at a FDIC-insured institution is $250,000

9. Federal deposit insurance is not determined on a per-account basis

   a. A depositor cannot increase FDIC insurance by dividing funds owned in the same ownership category among different accounts within the same institutions

   b. The type of account (whether checking, savings, certificate of deposit, outstanding official checks, or other form of deposit) has no bearing on the amount of insurance coverage

10. Single ownership accounts

    a. A single (or individual) ownership account is an account owned by one person. Single ownership accounts include accounts in the owner's name; accounts established for the benefit of the owner by agents, nominees, guardians, custodians, or conservators; and accounts established by a business that is a sole proprietorship.

    b. All single ownership nonretirement accounts established by, or for the benefit of, the same person are added together and the total is insured up to a maximum of $100,000

    c. If an individual owns and deposits funds in his own name but then gives another person the right to withdraw funds from the account, the account will generally be insured as a joint ownership account

    d. Example of insurance for single ownership accounts

Depositor	Type of Deposit	Amount Deposited
A	Savings account	$25,000
A	CD	100,000
A	NOW account	25,000
A's restaurant (a sole proprietorship)	Checking	25,000
Total deposited		$175,000
Maximum amount of insurance available		(100,000)
Uninsured amount		$75,000

    e. The Uniform Gift to Minors Act is a state law that allows an adult to make an irrevocable gift to a minor. Funds given to a minor under the Uniform Gift to Minors Act are held in the name of a custodian for the minor's benefit. The funds are added to any other single ownership accounts of the minor, and the total is insured up to a maximum of $100,000.

11. Joint accounts

    a. A joint account is an account owned by two or more individuals

    b. Joint accounts are insured separately from single ownership account if each of the following conditions are met

       1.) All co-owners must be natural persons. This means that legal entities such as corporations or partnerships are not eligible for joint account deposit insurance coverage.

       2.) Each of the co-owners must have a right of withdrawal on the same basis as the other co-owners. For example, if one co-owner can withdraw funds on his signature alone, but the other co-owner can withdraw funds only on the signature of both co-owners, then this requirement has not been satisfied; the co-owners do not have equal withdrawal rights.

Likewise, if a co-owner's right to withdraw funds is limited to a specified dollar amount, the funds in the account will be allocated between the co-owners according to their withdrawal rights and insured as single ownership funds. So, for example, if $100,000 is deposited in the names of Anne and Betty, but Anne has the right to withdraw only up to $5,000 from the account, $5,000 is allocated to Anne and the remainder is allocated to Betty. The funds, as allocated, are then added to any other single ownership funds of Anne or Betty, respectively.

3.) Each of the co-owners must have personally signed a deposit account signature card. The execution of an account signature card is not required for certificates of deposit, deposit obligations evidenced by a negotiable instrument, or accounts maintained by an agent, nominee, guardian, custodian, or conservator, but the deposit must in fact be jointly owned.

c.   The interests of each individual in all joint accounts he owns at the same FDIC-insured depository institution are added together and insured up to $100,000 maximum. Each person's interest (or share) in a joint account is deemed equal unless otherwise stated on the deposit account records.

d.   Example

Nonretirement account	Owners	Balance
#1	A and B	$100,000
#2	B and A	25,000
#3	A, B, and C	75,000
#4	D and A	80,000

A's Ownership Interest	
Account #1 (A and B)	$50,000
Account #2 (B and A)	12,500
Account #3 (A, B, and C)	25,000
Account #4 (D and A)	40,000
Total deposited:	$127,500

A's ownership interest in the joint account category is limited to $100,000, so $27,500 is uninsured.

B's Ownership Interest	
Account #1 (A and B)	$50,000
Account #2 (B and A)	12,500
Account #3 (A, B, and C)	25,000
Total deposited:	$87,500

B's ownership interest in the joint account category is $87,500. That amount is less than the $100,000 maximum, so it is fully insured.

C's Ownership Interest	
Account #3 (A, B, and C)	25,000
Total deposited:	$25,000

C's ownership interest in the joint account category is $25,000. That amount is less than the $100,000 maximum, so it is fully insured.

D's Ownership Interest	
Account #4 (D and A)	40,000
Total deposited:	$40,000

D's ownership interest in the joint account category is $40,000. That amount is less than the $100,000 maximum, so it is fully insured.

e. Community property laws do not affect deposit insurance coverage. In states recognizing this form of ownership, an account in the sole name of one spouse will be insured as the single ownership account of that spouse. Separately, a qualifying joint account in the names of both spouses will be insured as a joint account.

f. A deposit account held in two or more names that does not qualify for joint account deposit insurance coverage is treated as being owned by each named owner as an individual, corporation, partnership, or unincorporated association, as the case may be, according to each co-owner's actual ownership interest. As such, each owner's interest is added to any other single ownership accounts or, in the case of a corporation, partnership, or unincorporated association, to other accounts of such entity, and the total is insured up to $100,000.

12. Business accounts

a. Funds deposited by a corporation, partnership, or unincorporated association are FDIC insured up to a maximum of $100,000. Funds deposited by a corporation, partnership, or unincorporated association are insured separately from the personal accounts of the stockholders, partners, or members. To qualify for this coverage, the entity must be engaged in an independent activity. *Independent activity* means that the entity is operated primarily for some purpose other than to increase deposit insurance.

b. Funds owned by a business that is a sole proprietorship are treated as the individually owned funds of the person who is the sole proprietor. Consequently, funds deposited in the name of the sole proprietorship are added to any other single ownership accounts of the sole proprietor, and the total is insured to a maximum of $100,000.

13. Retirement accounts

a. Retirement accounts established at FDIC-insured institutions also qualify for FDIC insurance. The total amount insured across all retirement accounts held at a single institution is limited to $250,000. This is provided that the accounts are in bank investments, and not securities, and are not securities secured from the bank's investment arm.

XI. TIME VALUE OF MONEY

A. TIME VALUE OF MONEY CONCEPTS

1. Time value of money (TVM) is one of the most useful and important concepts in finance and personal financial planning

   a. The concept of time value of money is that money received today is worth more than the same amount of money received sometime in the future

   b. A dollar received today is worth more than a dollar received one year from today because the dollar received today can be invested and will be worth more in one year

   c. Alternatively, a dollar to be received a year from now is currently worth less than a dollar today

2. There are two time periods and two values for time value of money analysis: future and future value and present and present value

   a. Future value is the future dollar amount to which a sum certain today will increase compounded at a defined interest rate and a period of time

   b. Present value is the current dollar value of a future sum discounted at a defined interest rate and a period of time

B. FUTURE VALUE OF A SINGLE-SUM DEPOSIT

1. A dollar in hand today is worth more than a dollar to be received next year. If you had one dollar now, you could invest, earn interest, and end up next year with more than one dollar.

Example

Calculation:

Connie has an account of $100 that pays 10% interest compounded annually. At the end of year 1, Connie will have:

PV = $100 = present value of her account, or the beginning amount.

i = 10% = interest rate per period. Expressed as a decimal, *i* = 0.10.

FV_n = future value, or ending amount, of Connie's account at the end of *n* years.

Although PV is the value now, at the present time FV_n is the value *n* years into the future, after compound interest has been earned. Note also that FV_0 is the future value zero years into the future, which is the present, so FV_0 = PV.

n = number of periods, often years, involved in the transaction.

n = 1, so FV_n = FV_1, calculated as follows:

The future value, FV, at the end of 1 period is the present value multiplied by 1 plus the interest rate. The equation can now be used to find how much Connie's $100 will be worth at the end of 1 year at a 10% interest rate:

FV_1 = $100(1 + 0.10) = $100(1.10) = $110

Connie's account will earn $10 of interest; therefore, she will have $110 at the end of the year.

---

2. Solve future value problems in one of three ways

   a. Regular calculator—Use a regular calculator, either by multiplying $(1+i)$ by itself $n-1$ times or by using the exponential function to raise $(1+i)$ to the nth power

   b. Compound interest tables—There are many appropriate interest tables available to find the proper interest factor. For example, find the correct interest factor for the 5-year, 10% problem addressed in the previous example. Look down the first column to Period 5 and across the row to the 10% column to find the interest factor, 1.6105. Using this interest factor, multiply it by the $100 initial investment:

   $$FV_5 = PV\ (FV_{10\%,\ 5\ years}) =\ \$100\ (1.6105) = \$161.05.$$

   c. Financial calculator—Financial calculators are programmed to solve most discounted cash flow problems. The calculators generate the $FVIF_{i,n}$ factors for a specified pair of i and n values, then multiply the computed factor by the PV to produce the FV. In the illustrative problem, enter PV = 100, i = 10, and n = 5, and press the FV key. The answer, $161.05, rounded to two decimal places, is displayed. The FV will appear with a minus sign on some calculators. The logic behind the negative value is that the initial amount is an investment (the PV) and the ending amount is a disinvestment (the FV), so one is an inflow and the other is an outflow. Some calculators may require pressing the Compute key before pressing the FV button. Financial calculators permit you to specify the number of decimal places. Use at least two places for problems where the answer is in dollars or percentages and four if the answer is an interest rate in decimal form.

C. PRESENT VALUE

1. This calculation is used to determine what a sum of money to be received in a future year is worth in today's dollars on the basis of a specific discount rate

2. A financial calculator could be used to find the PV of the $161.05 calculated in the previous example of future value. Just enter n = 5, i = 10, and FV = $161.05, and press the PV button to find PV = $100. On some calculators, the PV will be given as –$100, and, on some calculators, you must press the Compute key before pressing the PV key.

Example

- A client invested $10,000 in an interest-bearing promissory note earning an 11% annual rate compounded monthly. At the end of 7 years, the note will be worth $21,522.04, assuming all interest is reinvested at the 11% rate.

  PV = $10,000
  i = 0.91666 (11÷12)
  n = 84 (7 × 12)
  FV = $21,522.04

- Bill purchased $60,000 worth of silver coins 8 years ago. The coins have appreciated 7.5% compounded annually over the last 8 years. Today, the coins are worth $107,008.67.

  PV = $60,000
  i = 7.5
  n = 8
  FV = $107,008.67

D. SOLVING FOR TIME AND INTEREST RATES

1. So far, only one equation has been used, Equation 1, and its transformed version, Equation 2

$$(1) \quad FV_n \quad = \quad PV(1+i)^n \quad = \quad PV(FV_{i,n})$$

$$(2) \quad PV \quad = \quad \frac{FV_n}{(1+i)^n} \quad = \quad FV_n(PV_{i,n})$$

2. There are four variables in the equations

    a. PV = present value = $100 in the examples

    b. FV = future value = $161.05 after 5 years at 10%

    c. i = interest (or discount) rate = 10% in the examples

    d. n = number of years = 5 in the examples

3. If the values of three of the variables are known, the fourth can be determined. Thus far, the interest rate (i) and the number of years (n) as well as either the PV or the FV have been given. In many situations, however, the unknown will be either n or i.

4. Periods (n)—Example

    a. Calculation 1

        Assume the following: PV = $100, FV = $161.05, and i = 10%. Determine the number of periods, n, involved.

FV_n	=	$PV(FV_{i,n})$
$161.05	=	$100\ (FV_{10\%,n})$
$FV_{10\%,n}$	=	$161.05 ÷ $100
$FV_{10\%,n}$	=	$1.6105

        The interest rate of 10% is given, and the future value interest factor is the unknown (refer to Exhibit 9). In Exhibit 9, the 10% column is used to find the future value interest factor of $1.6105 (row 5). The number of time periods for $100 to accumulate to $161.05 is equal to 5.

    b. Calculation 2

        The problem could also be solved using Equation 2, solving for the length of time it takes $100 to grow to $161.05 at a 10% interest rate

PV_n	=	$FV(PV_{i,n})$
$100	=	$161.05\ (PV_{10\%,n})$
$PV_{10\%,n}$	=	$100 ÷ $161.05
$PV_{10\%,n}$	=	$0.6209

        The interest rate of 10% is given, and the present value interest factor is the unknown (refer to Exhibit 10). In Exhibit 10, the 10% column is used to find the present value interest factor of 0.6209 (row 5). Thus, the number of time periods for $100 to accumulate to $161.05 is equal to 5.

c. Calculation 3

The easiest way to solve the problem is by using a financial calculator. Input i = 10, PV = 100, FV = $161.05 (or –$161.05), and then press the n key to find n = 5 years.

> **Note:** Be cautious when solving for term n because some financial calculators (i.e., HP 12c) treat n as a whole number; therefore, your answer is not always precise when calculating for term. Anytime you calculate for n, you may need to find the answer by trial and error. Recalculate one of the other known factors (i.e., FV or PV) using the whole numbers n. The recalculated known factor will likely be too high or low using the whole number n. You will then have to continue using different values for n until you have correctly recalculated the known factor.

Pay close attention to this example.	Example		Correct Calculation	
	FV	= $400	FV	= $400
	i	= 4.5	i	= 4.5
	PV	= $250	PV	= $250
	n	= 11	n	= 10.678

Once you have finished the calculation using a financial calculator, reenter the n and calculate the FV to assure yourself that the n calculated is correct to the precise degree that you require (e.g., two decimal places).

5. Interest Rate—Example

a. Calculation 1

Assume the following: PV = $100, FV, = $161.05, and n = 5. The interest rate that $100 would grow to $161.05 over 5 periods must be determined.

$$FV_5 = PV\ (FV_{i,n})$$
$$\$161.05 = \$100\ (FV_{i,5})$$
$$FV_{i,5} = \$1.6105$$

The number of time periods, 5, is given; the future value interest factor is the unknown (refer to Exhibit 9). Period 5 row is used to find the future value interest factor of $1.6105 (10% column). Thus, $100 accumulates to $161.05 at an interest rate equal to 10%.

b. Calculation 2

Alternatively, the equation could be set up as follows

$$PV = FV_5(PV_{i,5})$$
$$\$100 = \$161.05\ (PV_{i,5})$$
$$PV_{i,10\%} = \$0.6209$$

The number of time periods, 5, is given; the present value interest factor is the unknown (refer to Exhibit 10). The Period 5 row is used to find the present value interest factor of 0.6209 (10% column). Thus, $100 accumulates to $161.05 at an interest rate equal to 10%.

c.   Calculation 3

The easiest way to solve the problem is with a financial calculator. Input PV = 100, FV = $161.05 (or – $161.05), and *n* = 5. Press the *i* key to find *i* = 10%.

Example

- Joe purchased 10 shares of an aggressive growth mutual fund at $90 per share 7 years ago. Today, he sold all 10 shares for $4,500. His average annual compound rate of return on this investment before tax was 25.8499%.

  PV = $900
  FV = $4,500
  n = 7
  i = 25.8499

- Leslie borrowed $800 from her father to purchase a mountain bike. Leslie paid back $1,200 to her father at the end of 5 years. The average annual compound rate of interest on Leslie's loan from her father was 8.4472%.

  PV = $800
  FV = $1,200
  n = 5
  i = 8.4472

E. FUTURE VALUE OF AN ANNUITY

An annuity is a series of equal payments at fixed intervals for a specified number of periods. Payments are given the symbol PMT. If the payments occur at the end of each period, they are referred to as an ordinary annuity, sometimes called a deferred annuity. If the payments are made at the beginning of each period, they are referred to as an annuity due (e.g., lease or rent payment). Both ordinary annuities and annuities due are common in financial planning.

Example—Ordinary Annuity

- A promise to pay $1,000 a year for 3 years is a 3-year annuity. If each payment is made at the end of the year, it is an ordinary annuity. Patty receives such an annuity and deposits each annual payment into a savings account that pays 10% interest. How much will Patty have at the end of 3 years?

Calculation 1
The answer is shown graphically as a timeline (Exhibit 11). The first payment is made at the end of Year 1, the second at the end of Year 2, and the third at the end of Year 3. The first payment is compounded for 2 years, and the last payment is not compounded at all. When the future values of each of the payments are summed, the total is the future value of the annuity. Patty's total is $3,310.00.

EXHIBIT 8: TIMELINE FOR AN ORDINARY ANNUITY

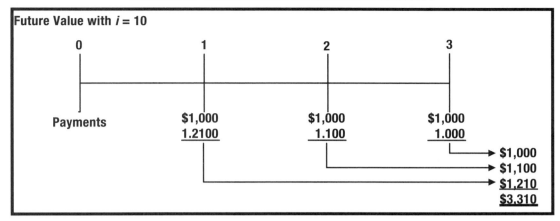

Calculation 2

Annuity problems can also be solved using a financial calculator. To solve Patty's problem, key in $n = 3$, $i = 10$, and PMT = 1,000, and then press the FV key to produce the correct answer, $3,310.00.

Example—Annuity Due

- Had Patty's three $1,000 payments in the above example been made at the beginning of each year, the annuity would have been an annuity due.

Calculation 1

In terms of the timeline, each payment would have been shifted one period to the left, so there would have been $1,000 under Period 0 and a zero under Period 3; thus, each payment would be compounded for one extra year. The equation is modified to handle annuities due as follows:

$$FVA_n \text{ (annuity due)} = PMT(FV_{i,n})(1 + i)$$

Since payment is compounded for one extra year, multiplying the term $PMT(FVA_{i,n})$ by $(1 + i)$ solves the extra compounding. Applying this equation to the previous example:

$$FVA_n \text{ (annuity due)} = \$1,000(3.3100)(1.10) = \$3,641.00.$$

$3,641.00 is the future value for the annuity due versus $3,310.00 for the ordinary annuity. Since the payments are received faster, the annuity due is more valuable at the end of 3 years.

Calculation 2

Annuity due problems can also be solved with financial calculators, most of which have a switch or key marked Due or Beg that permits conversion from ordinary annuities to annuities due.

Example

Christine has been dollar cost averaging into a mutual fund by investing $2,000 at the beginning of every quarter for the past 7 years. She has been earning an average annual compound return of 11% compounded quarterly on this investment. Today, the fund is worth $84,996.80.

$PMT_0 = \$2,000$
$i = 2.75\ (11 \div 4)$
$n = 28\ (7 \times 4)$
$FV_{AD} = \$84,996.80$

F. PRESENT VALUE OF AN ANNUITY

1. The difference between the present value of an annuity due and the present value of an ordinary annuity is that the annuity due's payments are made at the beginning of each period rather than at the end, as for an ordinary annuity
2. This makes the present value of an annuity due always larger than the present value of an ordinary annuity with the same payments
3. This calculation is quite common in financial planning and is most often used for educational funding and for retirement capital needs analysis

---

Example

Amanda is offered the following alternatives: (1) a 3-year annuity with payments of $1,000 at the end of each year, or (2) a lump-sum payment today. She has no current need for the money during the next 3 years, and if she accepts the annuity, she would deposit the receipts in a savings account that pays 10% interest. Similarly, the lump-sum receipts would be deposited in an account paying 10%. How large must the lump-sum payment be to make it equivalent to the annuity?

Calculation 1

The present value of the first payment is $PMT[1 \div (1 + i)]$, the PV of the second is $PMT[1 \div (1 + i)]^2$, and so on. The PV of annuity due will always be greater than the PV of an ordinary annuity. To equate the two calculations, multiply the PV of the ordinary annuity by $(1 + i)$:

$PVA_n(\text{annuity due}) = PMT(PVA_{i,n})(1+i)$

If payments were made at the end of each year, Amanda's 10%, 3-year annuity has a present value of $2,486.85.

$PVA = \$1,000\ (2.48685) = \$2,486.85$

Calculation 2

Again, a financial calculator can be used to solve the problem.

Ordinary Annuity

n	=	3
i	=	10
PMT_{OA}	=	$1,000
PV_{OA}	=	$2,486.85

Therefore, the lump-sum payment must be equal to or greater than $2,486.85 if the $1,000 is paid at the end of each year.

Example

Jane wants to withdraw $4,000 at the beginning of each year for the next 7 years. She expects to earn 10.5% compounded annually on her investment. The lump sum Jane should deposit today is $21,168.72.

$PMT_{AD} = \$4,000$

$i = 10.5$

$n = 7$

$PV_{AD} = \$21,168.72$

G. SERIAL PAYMENTS

1. A serial payment is a payment that increases at some constant rate (usually inflation) on a regular basis. There are many situations where it is more affordable to increase payments on an annual basis since the payor expects to have increases in cash flows or earnings to make those increasing payments (e.g., life insurance, educational needs, or retirement needs).

2. Serial payments differ from fixed annuity payments (both ordinary and annuity due payments) in that serial payments are not a fixed amount per year. The result is that the initial serial payment is less than its respective annuity due or ordinary annuity payment. The last serial payment will obviously be greater than the last respective fixed annuity payment but will have the same purchasing power as the first serial payment.

AMORTIZATION SCHEDULE 1
Schedule of Equal Annuity Payments (Annuity Due)

Payment	Deposit (Beginning of Year)	Account Balance (Year-End)	Target	Date
1	$18,462.43	$20,493.29	$100,000.00	1/1/07 (TODAY)
2	18,462.43	43,240.84	105,000.00	1/1/08
3	18,462.43	68,490.63	110,250.00	1/1/09
4	18,462.43	96,517.89	115,762.50	1/1/10
5	18,462.43	127,628.15	121,550.63	1/1/11
6	0	127,628.15	127,628.16	1/1/12

AMORTIZATION SCHEDULE 2
Schedule of Equal Ordinary Annuity Payments

Payment	Payment (End of Year)	Account Balance (Year-End)	Target	Date
1	$0	$20,493.29	$100,000.00	Today 1/1/07
2	20,493.29	22,747.55	105,000.00	1/1/08
3	20,493.29	47,997.33	110,250.00	1/1/09
4	20,493.29	76,024.59	115,762.50	1/1/10
5	20,493.29	107,134.85	121,550.63	1/1/11
6	20,493.29	127,628.14	127,628.16	1/1/12

$$
\begin{array}{llll}
n & = 5 & n & = 5 \\
i & = 11 & i & = 5 \\
FV & = \$127,628.16 & PV & = \$100,000 \\
PMT_{OA} & = \$20,493.29 & FV & = \$127,628.16
\end{array}
$$

The calculation of the initial serial payment will depend on when it is to be made (today or one year from today at the first year-end). If it is to be made today and the payment is an annuity due, the calculation is shown below:

$$
\begin{array}{ll}
FV & = \$100,000 \\
n & = 5 \\
i & = 5.7142857, \text{ or } [(1.11 \div 1.05) - 1] \times 100 \\
PMT_{AD} & = \$16,876.75
\end{array}
$$

Each successive period serial payment will increase by 5% (the inflation rate). An amortization table is provided (Amortization Schedule 3) to demonstrate the deposits, account balance, and the target account balance. The future value is stated in real terms ($100,000) for purposes of the calculation.

AMORTIZATION SCHEDULE 3

Schedule of Annuity Due Serial Payments

Payment	Deposit (Beginning of Year)	Account Balance (Year-End)	Target Balance (Beginning of Year)
1	$16,876.75	$18,733.19	$100,000.00
2	17,720.58	40,463.69	105,000.00
3	18,606.61	65,568.03	110,250.00
4	19,536.94	94,466.52	115,762.50
5	20,513.79	127,628.14	121,550.63
6	0	—	127,628.16

FV = $100,000 (real dollars) n = 5
i = 5.7142857 (real rate of earnings) PMT_{AD} = $16,876.75

The calculation of the serial payment made in arrears (Amortization Schedule 4) is a little odd. Because the payment is to be made at year-end, the calculated ordinary annuity payment must be inflated by the appropriate inflation rate to determine the first payment to be made at the end of year one. This is consistent with the year-end value in year one for Amortization Schedule 3.

n = 5
i = 5.7142857
FV = $100,000
PMT = $17,841.13 today
   × 1.05
   $18,733.19 at year-end

AMORTIZATION SCHEDULE 4

Deposits Made in Arrears (OA)

Payment	Deposit (End of Year)	Interest	Account Balance (Year-End)	Target Balance	Year
1	$0	$0	$18,733.19	$100,000.00	2002
2	18,733.19	2,060.65	20,793.84	105,000.00	2003
3	19,669.85	4,451.01	44,914.70	110,250.00	2004
4	20,653.34	7,212.48	72,780.52	115,762.50	2005
5	21,686.01	10,391.32	104,857.85	121,550.63	2006
6	22,770.31	0	127,628.16	127,628.16	2007

FV = $100,000
n = 5
i = 5.7142857
PMT_{OA} = $17,841.13 (today)

3. One difficulty in using serial payments is determining exactly how much to deposit and when to make those deposits. The second difficulty is having confidence that the calculation is accurate.

H. NET PRESENT VALUE

1. Net present value (NPV) analysis is a common technique used by businesses and investors to evaluate capital projects and capital expenditures, generally in the capital budgeting area

2. The model assumes the following

   a. Information is known about the future (e.g., cash flows and life)

   b. All reinvestments in nonlike life assets are made at the weighted average cost of capital of the firm (this is a more conservative assumption than the internal rate of return [IRR] method, which assumes the reinvestment rate is the IRR calculated)

3. NPV is considered a superior model to IRR, when comparing investment projects of unequal lives; it helps a company decide whether to buy a particular piece of equipment or make a particular investment

4. The resultant of the analysis is in dollars

5. NPV equals the difference between the initial cash outflow (investment) and the present value of discounted cash inflows

> If NPV > 0, then IRR > required rate of return
>
> If NPV = 0, then IRR = required rate of return
>
> If NPV < 0, then IRR < required rate of return

Example

If the present value of a series of cash flows is $200 and the initial outflow is $150, then the NPV equals $50 ($200 − $150). An NPV greater than zero implies that the IRR of the cash flows is greater than the discount rate used to discount the future cash flows. An NPV of zero implies that the discount rate used is equal to the IRR for the cash flows. A negative NPV implies that the discount rate used is greater than the true IRR of the cash flows. As a general rule, you should look for investments that have a positive NPV.

---

6. Multiple IRRs

Example

Bobby is considering buying a machine for his factory. It will initially cost $100,000, but projections show that its use will generate an additional $150,000 in revenue. However, projections also show that by the second year, it will need an upgrade that typically costs $20,000.

If you were to calculate the IRR for this series of cash flows, you would get 35.2%. If you use 35.2% as the interest rate, your NPV would be zero, so this would seem like the correct answer and method. However, if you were to use certain computer models, they would provide you with a more accurate IRR of −85.2%, which would also give you an NPV of zero. So both IRR figures could possibly be suitable IRR solutions. This is why NPV is a better overall measure.

XII. EDUCATIONAL FUNDING

A. INTRODUCTION

1. One of the most common financial planning goals of parents is to provide an education for their children

2. Over the past 15 years, tuition at colleges and universities throughout the country has increased at an annual rate of 7%, whereas the Consumer Price Index (CPI) has only averaged 3% increases

3. There are many ways an individual can save for future education costs or pay for current ones

   a. The most significant consideration is how much time exists before the student enters college

   b. There are many funding options available for parents of very young children who are years away from entering college

   c. Those parents with children nearing college age or currently entering college, or individuals paying for their own education, do not have as many options and savings methods

B. NEEDS ANALYSIS

1. Before creating an educational funding plan, individuals should first determine the estimated needs

2. Examples of needs

   a. Tuition and tuition-related expenses

   b. Books, school supplies, and equipment (e.g., calculator and computer)

   c. Lodging

   d. Meals

   e. Transportation

   f. Entertainment (school sporting events) and leisure (health club)

   g. Travel expenses

   h. Tutoring (if necessary)

   i. Extracurricular (fraternity/sorority dues)

   j. Clothing and attire

   k. Other considerations particular to the student or family

C. EDUCATIONAL SAVINGS CALCULATION

See the Educational Funding section in *Understanding Your Financial Calculator, 4th Edition*, Dalton, James F., published by Kaplan Financial

D. EDUCATION TAX CREDITS AND DEDUCTIONS

1. General

   a. Education credits

      1.) Hope Scholarship Credit

      2.) Lifetime Learning Credit

  b. Deductions for education

    1.) Employer Educational Assistance Program Deduction

    2.) Qualified Higher Education Expense Deduction

2. Hope Scholarship Credit

  a. The Hope Scholarship Credit equals 100% of the first $1,100 of qualified expenses paid in the tax year, plus 50% of the next $1,100

  b. The maximum credit allowed in a given year is $1,650 per student, if there are $2,200 of qualifying expenses

  c. Requirements

    1.) This tax credit is available for qualified tuition and related expenses incurred and paid in the first two years of postsecondary education for the taxpayer, spouse, or dependent

    2.) A student must be enrolled no less than half time to be eligible

    3.) The credit is subject to a phaseout based on the taxpayer's adjusted gross income

      a.) Married filing jointly, $94,000–$114,000 for 2007

      b.) All other taxpayers, $47,000–$57,000 for 2007

3. Lifetime Learning Credit

  a. Benefits

    1.) The Lifetime Learning Credit provides annual per taxpayer reimbursement for qualified tuition and related expenses per family in the amount of $2,000 per year (2007)

    2.) The taxpayer must spend $10,000 annually on qualified expenses in 2007 in order to qualify for the full credit; however, a partial credit can be obtained with lower levels of education expense

    3.) This credit is based on a 20% factor of the qualified expenses; in other words, to obtain the full $2,000 credit in 2007, there must be qualified education expenses of at least $10,000

  b. Requirements

    1.) This tax credit is available for tuition and enrollment fees for undergraduate, graduate, or professional degree programs

    2.) Half-time enrollment or more is required; however, if the courses taken are geared toward the acquisition or improvement of job skills, the student may be enrolled less than half time

    3.) The Lifetime Learning Credit can be claimed for an unlimited number of years

    4.) The credit is subject to a phaseout based on the taxpayer's adjusted gross income

      a.) Married filing jointly, $94,000–$114,000 (for 2007)

      b.) All other taxpayers, $47,000–$57,000 (for 2007)

    c. Coordination of the Hope Scholarship Credit and the Lifetime Learning Credit

        1.) If two or more children in the same household incur qualified expenses in the same year, the parents may claim a Lifetime Learning Credit for the family, a Hope Scholarship Credit for each child, or a Lifetime Learning Credit for one child and a Hope Scholarship Credit for the other

        2.) Only one credit is allowed per child per year

  4. Employer's Educational Assistance Program

    a. Under the Employer's Educational Assistance Program, an employer can reimburse an employee's tuition (both graduate and undergraduate), enrollment fees, books, supplies, and equipment, and these benefits are excluded from the employee's income up to $5,250 per year (for 2007)

    b. The employer or employee cannot, however, also claim an educational credit (Hope Scholarship or Lifetime Learning Credit) for the same expenses. If the employee has expenses greater than $5,250, then the employee will be permitted to claim an educational credit for the expenses over $5,250 (assuming the employee also meets the requirements for the educational credits).

  5. Deduction for qualified higher education expenses

    a. This above-the-line deduction applies to qualified tuition and related expenses through December 31, 2007

E. QUALIFIED TUITION PROGRAM (SECTION 529 PLANS; FORMERLY QUALIFIED STATE TUITION PROGRAMS)

  1. Plan sponsors

    a. States are allowed to enact qualified tuition programs (QTPs) in accordance with IRC Section 529

        1.) Each state can use its own statutory language, but the plan must be in conformity with Section 529 to be an eligible plan

        2.) Although state plans may differ, they must all contain the required provisions under IRC Section 529

    b. Eligible educational institutions can also create plans

        1.) An eligible educational institution is generally an accredited postsecondary educational institution

        2.) To be an eligible educational institution the plan must receive a ruling of determination from the IRS

  2. Types of QTPs

    a. Prepaid tuition plans

        1.) Allow the contributor to prepay tuition today at a particular school for an individual in the future

        2.) The plan will lock in today's prices but subjects the participant to many risks

        3.) The main risks are that the beneficiary may choose a school different from the one named in the plan or may not accepted into the school named in the plan

        4.) Before investing in this type of plan, the participant will want to investigate the details of the particular plan as they relate to the above factors

   b. Savings plan

        1.) This plan allows an individual to make contributions today into a savings fund

        2.) The earnings grow tax deferred

        3.) If the proceeds are used for higher educational expenses, the distributions are tax free

3. Qualified Tuition Program rules

   a. Contributions must be made in cash

        1.) Cash, check, money order, credit cards, and so forth are acceptable

        2.) Property is not an allowed contribution

   b. Plans must use separate accounting for each beneficiary

   c. Direction of investments

        1.) A plan can permit the contributor to select among different investment strategies designed exclusively for the program when the initial contribution is made to establish the account

        2.) The IRC states that neither the contributor nor the beneficiary can direct the investment. However, Notice 2001-55 announced that the final regulations are expected to state that the individual can change the investments one time per year. Until the final regulations are issued, taxpayers can rely on this notice.

   d. The account cannot be pledged as security for a loan

4. Plan advantages

   a. Tax-deferred growth

   b. Tax-free distributions if used for education

   c. Generally, removes assets from taxable estate

   d. Generally, low commission and management fees

   e. Many states offer state income tax deductions for contributions (e.g., NY allows an annual state income tax deduction of up to $5,000 for contributions)

   f. The contributor can change the beneficiary at any time

   g. The contributor decides when and how expenses are paid

   h. The amount deposited varies by state but can be as much as is reasonable to fund educational costs; some states have maximum contributions exceeding $200,000

   i. For gift tax purposes, contributions can be treated as though they were made ratably over a five-year period

   j. Contributions are not phased out, even at higher AGI levels

   k. Can be coordinated with other educational plans, but no double dipping is allowed (i.e., if the beneficiaries claim the Lifetime Learning Credit or Hope Scholarship Credit, then no tax advantages are allowed for the same expenses)

5. Qualified expenses

   a. Tuition

   b. Fees

   c. Books

   d. Supplies

   e. Equipment

   f. Certain room and board expenses (requires at least half-time status)

     1.) Normally assessed fee, if school lodging

     2.) School determines reasonable amount for other locations

6. Estate and gift tax consequences

   a. The contributions are removed from the contributor's gross estate (even though he still has the power to change the beneficiary)

   b. Contribution can be a split gift (e.g., half made by the donor, and half by the donor's spouse as available under IRC Section 2513)

   c. Contribution is considered a completed gift of a present interest, allowing it to qualify for the annual exclusion

   d. Favorable gift tax rules at contribution—five-year averaging can be elected, allowing an individual to use five years' worth of annual exclusions on an initial contribution

---

Example

In Year 1, when the annual exclusion is $12,000, Polly makes a contribution of $65,000 to a QTP for the benefit of her child, Cindi. Polly elects to account for the gift ratably over a five-year period beginning with the calendar year of contribution. Polly is treated as making an excludible gift of $12,000 in each of Years 1 through 5 and a taxable gift of $5,000 in Year 1.

Assuming in Year 3 the annual exclusion is increased to $13,000, Polly makes an additional contribution for the benefit of Cindi in the amount of $7,000. Polly is treated as making an excludible gift of $1,000; the remaining $6,000 is a taxable gift in Year 3.

---

   e. If contributor dies within the five-year period, then the deferred portion for calendar years after the date of death is included in the gross estate

---

Example

In Year 1, when the annual exclusion is $12,000, Polly makes a contribution of $60,000 to a QTP for the benefit of her child, Cindi. Polly elects to account for the gift ratably over a five-year period beginning with the calendar year of contribution.

Assume Polly dies in Year 2. The gross estate will include $36,000 of the deferred portion (Years 3, 4, and 5).

Assume, instead, Polly only made a $20,000 contribution in Year 1 and again elected to account for the gift ratably over the five-year period. Polly is treated as making an excludible gift of $4,000 in each of Years 1 through 5, because the 5-year averaging, if elected, must be ratable over the 5-year period. Under the assumption that Polly dies in Year 2, the gross estate will include $12,000 of the deferred portion (Years 3, 4, and 5).

---

      f.   Generation-skipping transfer tax (GSTT) does not apply on the gift as long as it does not exceed the exclusion amount

7.   Change of beneficiary

      a.   Allowed at any time

      b.   Rollovers will not be considered a taxable distribution if the funds are transferred to one of the following within 60 days of the distribution

          1.)   To another qualified tuition program for the benefit of the designated beneficiary (as long as a previous transfer to a qualified tuition program for the benefit of the designated beneficiary has not occurred within the last 12 months)

          2.)   To the credit of another designated beneficiary under a qualified tuition program who is a member of the family of the designated beneficiary with respect to which the distribution was made

      c.   Any change in the designated beneficiary of an interest in a qualified tuition program will not be a taxable distribution if the new beneficiary is a member of the family of the previous beneficiary

      d.   A transfer that occurs by reason of a change in the designated beneficiary, or a rollover of credits or account balances from the account of one beneficiary to the account of another beneficiary, will be treated as a taxable gift by the previous beneficiary to the new beneficiary if the new beneficiary is assigned to a lower generation than the previous beneficiary, whether or not the new beneficiary is a member of the family of the previous beneficiary. The transfer will be subject to the generation-skipping transfer tax if the new beneficiary is assigned to a generation two or more levels lower than the generation assignment of the previous beneficiary.

Example

In Year 1, a parent makes a contribution to a QTP on behalf of his child. In Year 4, the parent directs that a distribution from the account for the benefit of the child be made to an account for the benefit of a grandchild. The rollover distribution is treated as a taxable gift by the child to the grandchild, because the grandchild is assigned to a generation below the generation assignment of the child.

---

8. Funds used for nonqualified expenses

    a. The distribution is included in the gross income of the distributee

    b. A 10% additional tax will be applied to any distribution that is includible in gross income, on the basis of the above rules

    c. The penalty is waived if the distribution is:

        1.) Made to a beneficiary (or to the estate of the designed beneficiary) on or after the death of the designated beneficiary

        2.) Attributable to the designed beneficiary's being disabled

        3.) Made on account of a scholarship, allowance, or payment being received by the account holder to the extent that the amount of the payment or distribution does not exceed the amount of the scholarship, allowance, or payment

9. Distribution of funds

    a. Distributions are prorated between contributions and earnings

---

Example

Assume the contributor deposits $100, has $10 of earnings, and has a distribution of $11. The $11 distribution will be composed of $10 return of contribution and $1 earnings.

---

10. Limits to amounts contributed

    a. State sets limit

    b. Contributions cannot exceed reasonable cost

F. COVERDELL EDUCATION SAVINGS ACCOUNTS (FORMERLY EDUCATION IRAs)

1. Introduction

    a. Coverdell ESAs are designed to offer tax benefits to individuals who wish to save money for a child or grandchild's qualified education expenses

    b. A Coverdell ESA is an investment account established with contributions of cash, which are not deductible

2. Benefits

    a. The contributions grow tax free within the account

    b. Money withdrawn from the account is free from tax or penalty if the funds are used for qualified educational expenses

    c. If the funds are used for anything other than higher education expenses, the earnings are generally subject to income tax and a 10% penalty

    d. Generally, the parent (responsible individual) maintains the right to change the beneficiary to another family member at any time

3. Requirements

    a. A Coverdell ESA can be established for any child under the age of 18 by a parent, grandparent, other family members or friends, or even by the child, as long as the contributor who establishes the account does not have income over $220,000, if filing married, or $110,000, if filing single

    b. Annual contributions can be made up to $2,000 for each beneficiary. This includes contributions from all sources, including parents, grandparents, and so forth.

    c. The definition of qualified education expenses (beyond undergraduate or graduate level courses) that may be paid tax free from a Coverdell ESA include qualified elementary and secondary school expenses, including the following

        1.) Tuition, fees, academic tutoring, special need services, books, supplies, and other equipment incurred in connection with the enrollment or attendance of the beneficiary at a public, private, or religious school providing elementary or secondary education (kindergarten through grade 12) as determined under state law

        2.) Room and board, uniforms, transportation, and supplementary items or services (including extended-day programs) required or provided by such a school in connection with such enrollment or attendance of the beneficiary

        3.) The purchase of any computer technology or equipment or Internet access and related services, if such technology, equipment, or services are to be used by the beneficiary and the beneficiary's family during any of the years the beneficiary is in school

    d. When the beneficiary attains age 30 (unless the beneficiary has special needs or dies), the account must be distributed to the beneficiary within 30 days. The distribution will be subject to income tax and the 10% penalty as discussed within this section.

        1.) The Coverdell ESA may be rolled over (tax and penalty free) into a Coverdell ESA for a family member of the original beneficiary. If the new beneficiary is a generation below the generation of the original beneficiary the distribution is treated as a taxable gift.

        2.) If the beneficiary dies and the account has not been distributed during the 30-day period, the remaining balance is considered distributed to the beneficiary and included in the beneficiary's estate

        3.) No contributions can be made to the account once the beneficiary turns 18 years of age

4. Estate and gift tax consequences

    a. The contributions are removed from the contributor's gross estate (even though he still generally has the power to change the beneficiary)

    b. Contribution can be a split gift (i.e., half made by the donor, and half by the donor's spouse, as available under IRC Section 2513)

    c. Contribution is considered a completed gift of a present interest, allowing it to qualify for the annual exclusion

    d. Favorable gift tax rules at contribution—five-year averaging can be elected, allowing an individual to use five years' worth of annual exclusions on an initial contribution. Although this is allowed by statute, the $2,000 limit will prevent it from ever coming into play.

5. Distributions and withdrawals

   a. Distributions or withdrawals from Coverdell ESAs are composed of principal and earnings

   b. The designated beneficiary of a Coverdell ESA can take withdrawals at any time; distributions are always paid to the beneficiary (or beneficiary's estate) and will not be repaid to the contributor

   c. The principal is always excluded from taxation, whereas earnings are excluded if they are used to pay for qualified educational expenses

   d. Withdrawals are tax free whether the student is enrolled full time, half time, or less than half time as long as the withdrawals do not exceed the student's qualified educational expenses

6. Penalty on certain distributions

   a. A 10% additional tax will be applied to any distribution that is includible in gross income, on the basis of the above rules

   b. The penalty is waived if the distribution is:

      1.) Made to a beneficiary (or to the estate of the designated beneficiary) on or after the death of the designated beneficiary

      2.) Attributable to the designated beneficiary's being disabled

      3.) Made on account of a scholarship, allowance, or payment being received by the account holder to the extent that the amount of the payment or distribution does not exceed the amount of the scholarship, allowance, or payment

7. Coordination with other tax benefits

   a. A taxpayer can claim a Hope Scholarship Credit or Lifetime Learning Credit for a taxable year and can exclude from gross income amounts distributed (both the contributions and the earnings portions) from a Coverdell ESA on behalf of the same student as long as the distribution is not used for the same educational expenses for which a credit was claimed

G. SAVINGS BONDS

1. Series EE United States savings bonds (EE bonds)

   a. The face values of EE bonds start as low as $50 and increase up to $10,000

   b. EE bonds are purchased at one-half of their face value

   c. EE bonds have varying interest rates, but face value must be reached within 20 years

   d. They must be purchased after 1989 to be a qualified educational savings bond

   e. Bonds purchased after May 2005 will earn a fixed rate of interest, and rates for these issues will be adjusted each May 1 and November 1, with each new rate effective for all bonds issued through the following six months

   f. If used to pay for qualified higher education expenses at an eligible institution, EE bonds bestow significant tax savings—that is, there is no federal income tax on the interest

   g. Qualified higher education expenses include rolling over proceeds from the savings bonds into a Qualified Tuition Program (IRC Section 529 Plan) or a Coverdell ESA (formerly known as an Education IRA)

h. To attain tax-free status, EE bonds must be purchased in the name of one or both parents of the student/child

i. The parent(s) are considered the owners of the bond and must be at least 24 years old before the first day of the month of the issue date of the bond

j. Also, the owners must redeem the bonds in the same year that the student/child's qualified higher education expenses are paid

k. The exclusion is subject to a phaseout in the years in which the bonds are cashed and the tuition is paid. The phaseouts for 2007 are $98,400–$128,400 for joint returns and $65,600–$80,600 for other returns.

l. Series I bonds have the same tax benefits as EE bonds for purposes of qualified higher education expenses (see Investment Planning section of this text for further discussion)

H. GOVERNMENT GRANTS AND LOANS (FINANCIAL AID)

1. Types of financial aid

    a. Federal Pell Grants

        1.) Federal Pell Grants are outright gifts from the government based on the student's need and the cost of attending the chosen school

        2.) Only undergraduate students who have not previously received a bachelor's degree are eligible for the grants

        3.) The maximum amount of award ranges each year depending on program funding

        4.) The Federal Pell Grant Program is the largest need-based student aid program

    b. Federal Supplemental Educational Opportunity Grant (SEOG) Program

        1.) The Federal Supplemental Educational Opportunity Grant (SEOG) Program is another grant program for undergraduates with exceptional financial need

        2.) This program is managed by colleges instead of the federal government

        3.) Students are automatically considered when they submit a FAFSA form

    c. Federal Perkins Loan Program

        1.) The Federal Perkins Loan Program is a federally funded program administered by colleges

        2.) This program provides loans of up to $4,000 per year for an undergraduate program (up to a total of $20,000 per student if student completes two years of undergraduate work; otherwise, the total a student can borrow is $8,000)

        3.) Graduate students and professional study students may borrow up to $6,000 per year

        4.) The total loan amount may reach $40,000 if a student pursues graduate and professional studies (the total includes any loans as an undergraduate)

        5.) Characteristics of a Perkins Loan include a 5% fixed interest rate, deferred repayment, a nine-month grace period, and a maximum of ten years to repay the loan. Students are automatically considered if they complete a FAFSA.

d. Federal College Work-Study Program

   1.) Although the Federal College Work-Study Program is sponsored by the government, it is administered through colleges

   2.) Students work 10–15 hours per week at a job that is typically on campus, to earn a portion of their financial aid package

e. Federal PLUS Loans

   1.) Federal PLUS Loans allow the parents of undergraduate students to borrow up to the total cost of education less other financial aid awards

   2.) The interest rate is variable, is based on the 91-day T-Bill rate plus 3.1%, and is capped at 9%

   3.) Loans are not made on the basis of financial need, but borrowers must show that they do not have unsatisfactory credit history

   4.) Repayment of the loan must begin within 60 days of disbursement

   5.) Graduate and independent undergraduate students may defer the principal, but must pay the interest on the loan immediately

f. Subsidized Federal Stafford Loans

   1.) Subsidized Federal Stafford Loans are based on financial need

   2.) The interest is variable, is based on the 91-day T-bill rate plus 2.3%, and is capped at 8.25%

   3.) The government pays the interest while the student is enrolled in college

   4.) Repayment of the loan may take up to ten years and is deferred until six months after the student graduates, leaves school, or drops below half-time status

   5.) Borrowers are charged a 3% origination fee and a guaranty fee of up to 1%; both are deducted from the face value of the loan before disbursement

g. Unsubsidized Federal Stafford Loans

   1.) Unsubsidized Federal Stafford Loans are available for students who do not qualify for subsidized loans or require additional funds

   2.) For unsubsidized loans, the government does not pay the interest during the college years, and repayment begins almost immediately after disbursement

   3.) While the student is in school, in deferment, or in a grace period, the interest is variable, is based on the 91-day T-bill rate plus 1.7%, and is capped at 8.25%

   4.) The interest during repayment or forbearance is the same as that for the subsidized Federal Stafford Loan (91-day T-bill rate plus 2.3%, capped at 8.25%)

   5.) Both types of Stafford loans are available to undergraduate and graduate students

I. OTHER SOURCES

1. Traditional IRA

   a. Generally speaking, if a taxpayer withdraws funds from a traditional IRA before age 59½, the taxpayer is required to pay a 10% early withdrawal penalty on all or part of the amount withdrawn

   b. The 10% penalty does not apply if a taxpayer withdraws funds from a traditional (or Roth) IRA to pay for qualified higher educational expenses for the taxpayer, the taxpayer's spouse, or the child or grandchild of the taxpayer or taxpayer's spouse

   c. Unlike a Coverdell Education Savings account or a QTP, the taxpayer will owe federal income tax on the amount withdrawn

2. Roth IRA

   a. Contributions

      1.) The Roth IRA does not provide for tax-deductible contributions

      2.) Contributions grow tax free within the IRA

      3.) Contributions to Roth and traditional IRAs are $4,000 for 2007 and $5,000 in 2008 and thereafter

      4.) Contributions to Roth IRAs are limited to the lesser of the annual limit or earned income

      5.) Contributions can be made as late as the due date of the individual's tax return for the previous tax year

      6.) Contributions to a Roth IRA can be made for years beyond the age of 70½, whereas traditional IRAs prevent contributions after the attainment of age 70½

      7.) Allowed contributions to Roth IRAs are phased out for joint filers with an adjusted gross income of $156,000–$166,000 and for single taxpayers with an adjusted gross income of $99,000–$114,000

   b. Distributions

      1.) A distribution from a Roth IRA is not includible in the owner's gross income if it is a qualified distribution, or to the extent that it is a return of the owner's contributions to the Roth IRA

      2.) Qualified distributions are those that occur after a five-year holding period and for one of the following four reasons

         a.) Death

         b.) Disability

         c.) Attainment of age 59½

         d.) First-time house purchase (limit of $10,000)

      3.) If a distribution is not a qualified distribution and it exceeds contribution (and conversions) to Roth IRAs, then the distribution will be subject to income tax and may be subject to the 10% penalty

      4.) Excess distributions can avoid the 10% penalty if the proceeds are used for qualified higher education costs

          5.) The taxpayer is always able to withdraw amounts up to the total contribution without income tax or penalty

   c.   Requirements

          1.) Qualified higher educational expenses are tuition, fees, and room and board

   d.   Benefits

          1.) Roth IRAs may be an even more attractive vehicle for education savings than Coverdell ESAs because the age of the student is irrelevant (versus the 30-year-old requirement) and because contribution limits are higher

          2.) Funds in a Roth IRA not used for education can be used for retirement of the parent (contributor)

3.   Home equity lines of credit

   a.   A home equity loan or line of credit is yet another vehicle that can be used to fund college-related expenses

   b.   Because home equity loans are secured by a house, the interest rate on a home equity loan may be lower than rates for an unsecured student loan

   c.   Many state schools do not consider the value of the home when determining eligibility for financial aid, but numerous private colleges take equity in the home into account

   d.   If equity in the home is considered in the financial aid equation, a home equity loan could decrease home equity and possibly improve one's eligibility for financial aid

   e.   Furthermore, the interest on home equity loans is normally deductible as an itemized deduction

   f.   As a general rule, using home equity loans and lines of credit to pay for higher education expenses should be a last resort, or at least done after researching all other options, rates, and conditions for alternative funding

   g.   Borrowing too much against the home could result in foreclosure or other difficult situations

4.   Uniform Gift to Minors Act/Uniform Transfers to Minors Act

   a.   The Uniform Gift to Minors Act (UGMA) or Uniform Transfers to Minors Act (UTMA) allows parents the option to put assets in a custodial account for a child

   b.   If the child is younger than 18 years, the child's unearned income (i.e., interest and dividends) may be taxed at the income tax rate of the parents

   c.   If the child is 18 years old or older, the child's unearned income (i.e., interest and dividends) is taxed at the tax rate for the child

   d.   Custodial account assets are considered an asset of the child and are considered in determining financial aid

5.   Interest on educational loans

   a.   Interest paid on student loans for undergraduate and graduate education may be deducted as an adjustment to the taxpayer's AGI

   b.   The deduction is $2,500

    c.   The loaned funds must have been spent on tuition and enrollment fees, books, supplies, equipment, room and board, transportation, or other necessary expenses

    d.   For 2007 there is a phaseout of this deduction for taxpayers filing jointly with an AGI of $110,000–$140,000 and for single filers with an AGI of $55,000–$70,000

6. Highlights of tax benefits for higher education

The following exhibit provides a glance at the highlights and attributes of the various vehicles covered in this section

EXHIBIT 9: HIGHLIGHTS OF TAX BENEFITS FOR HIGHER EDUCATION FOR 2007

	HOPE Scholarship Credit	Lifetime Learning Credit	Coverdell Education Savings Account[1]	Traditional, Roth, SEP & SIMPLE IRAs[1]	Student Loan Interest	Qualified Tuition Programs[2] (Section 529 Plans)	Education Savings Bond Program[1]	Employer's Educational Assistance Program[1]
What is your benefit?	Credits can reduce the amount of tax you must pay		Earnings are not taxed	No 10% additional tax on early withdrawal	You can deduct the interest	Earnings are not taxed	Interest is not taxed	Employer benefits are not taxed
What is the annual limit?	Up to $1,650 per student	Up to $2,000 per family	$2,000 contribution per beneficiary	Amount of qualifying expenses	$2,500	Determined by Sponsor	Amount of qualifying expenses	$5,250
What expenses qualify besides tuition and required enrollment fees?	None		Books Supplies Equipment Room & board if at least a half-time student Payments to state tuition program	Books Supplies Equipment Room & board if at least a half-time student	Books Supplies Equipment Room & board Transportation Other necessary expenses	Books Supplies Equipment Room & board if at least a half-time student	Payments to Coverdell ESAs Payments to qualified tuition program	Books Supplies Equipment
What education qualifies?	1st 2 years of under-graduate	All undergraduate and graduate[3]						
What are some of the other conditions that apply?	Can be claimed only for 2 years Must be enrolled at least half-time in a degree program		Can contribute to Coverdell Education Savings Accounts and qualified tuition program in the same year Must withdraw assets by age 30		Must have been at least half-time student in a degree program	Distribution is excluded from gross income HOPE and Lifetime Learning Credit are permitted in the same year but not for the same expenses	Applies only to qualified series EE bonds issued after 1989 or series I bonds	
In what income range do benefits phase out?	2007: $47,000 - $57,000; $94,000 - $114,000 for joint returns		$95,000 - $110,000; $190,000 - $220,000 for joint returns	No phaseout[4]	$55,000 – $70,000 $110,000 – $140,000 for joint returns	No phaseout	2007: $65,600 - $80,600; $98,400 - $128,400 for joint returns	No phaseout

[1] Any nontaxable withdrawal is limited to the amount that does not exceed qualifying educational expenses.

[2] Exclusion is extended to distributions from Qualified Tuition programs established by an entity other than a State after December 31, 2003.

[3] For Coverdell Education Savings Accounts, qualified elementary and secondary school expenses are also permitted (Grades K-12).

[4] Phaseouts exist at the time of contribution. They are not relevant for withdrawals.

XIII. CONTRACTS

> **Note:** Only a basic understanding of these concepts is usually tested on the exam

A. NATURE AND TYPES OF CONTRACTS

1. A contract is an agreement made by two or more parties that contains a promise or set of promises to perform or refrain from performing some act or acts that can be enforced by a court

2. Elements of a contract

   To have a contract, certain elements must be present

   a. Agreement—the mutual assent and agreement of the parties must be evidenced by an offer and an acceptance

   b. Consideration—legally sufficient and bargained-for consideration must be exchanged for contractual promises

   c. Contractual capacity—there must be two or more parties who have contractual capacity

   d. Legality—the purpose and subject matter of the contract must not be contrary to law or public policy

   e. Genuineness of assent—the assent of the parties must be real, genuine, and voluntarily given

   f. Form—the agreement must be in the form that is required by law, if one is prescribed. If real estate is involved or if non-real estate is involved above certain thresholds, then the Statute of Frauds requires that the agreement be in writing.

3. Types of contracts and distinctions between them

   a. Based on the manner in which the assent of the parties is given

      1.) Express contract—the terms of the agreement are stated in words used by the parties

      2.) Implied—the terms of the agreement are inferred from the conduct of the parties even though nothing is said

      3.) The parties must objectively have the intention of entering into a contract

   b. Based on the nature of the promises made

      1.) Bilateral contract—reciprocal promises are exchanged by the parties (i.e., the promise of one party is exchanged for the promise of the other)

      2.) Unilateral contract—one party makes a promise in exchange for the other party's actually performing some act or refraining from performing some act

   c. Based on legal validity and enforceability

      1.) Valid and enforceable contract—all elements of a contract are present

      2.) Void contract—agreement has no legal effect (it was not really a contract)

      3.) Voidable contract—one of the parties has the option of avoiding contractual obligations

      4.) Unenforceable contract—contract that cannot be proven in the manner required by law, and/or fails to meet a procedural or formal requirement

B. AGREEMENT

1. An agreement must have the manifestation of apparent mutual assent by parties to the agreement

   a. Only present, objective intent of the parties, which they have manifested by such words or conduct as would indicate to a reasonable person an intention to be bound by the same terms, is recognized in law

   b. This concept is referred to as objective assent

2. The offer—the offeror shows assent when he communicates a proposal (the offer) to the offeree that sets forth with reasonable clarity, definiteness, and certainty the material terms under which he is presently, objectively agreeing and intending to be bound

3. Acceptance—the offeree accepts the offer when he unequivocally manifests his assent to the terms of the offer

   a. Requisites

      1.) Offeree has knowledge of the terms of the offer

      2.) Offeree's overt conduct manifests willingness and intention to be bound

      3.) Offeree complies with conditions, if any, stated in the offer (acceptance must be in the proper manner, at the proper place, and at the proper time)

      4.) Acceptance must be made by the party to whom the offer was directed

      5.) Acceptance must positively, unequivocally accord to the terms of the offer

   b. Manner of acceptance

      1.) If a bilateral contract is contemplated, the offeree makes a promise

      2.) If a unilateral contract is contemplated, the offeree performs required act or forbears from acting

      3.) Silence, generally, will not be considered to be an acceptance unless:

         a.) There was a similar, prior course of dealings, or

         b.) The offeree accepted the benefits, or

         c.) The offeree exercised dominion over the subject matter

C. CONSIDERATION

1. The concept of legally sufficient consideration

   a. Parties to a contract

      1.) Promisor—the party who makes a promise to do or refrain from doing something

      2.) Promisee—the party who receives a promise

      3.) Unilateral contract—only one party (A) is the promisor; the other party (B) is the promisee

A ————— promise made by A —————▶ B

4.) Bilateral contract—promises are exchanged by the parties. Each party is, therefore, a promisor as to the promise that he makes and a promisee as to the promise he receives. Each promise must be supported by consideration.

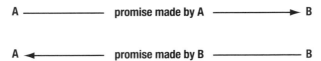

b. There must be a presently bargained-for exchange between the parties. Consideration may be thought of as the price paid by the promisee for a promise so that mutual obligations are present.

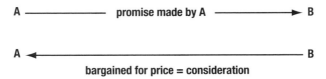

c. Legally sufficient consideration exists when either the promisee incurs a legal detriment or the promisor receives a legal benefit, or both

1.) A legal detriment is incurred by a promisee if the promisee does one of the following

a.) Actually gives up something that he has a legal right to keep, in the case of a unilateral contract

b.) Actually refrains or forbears from doing something that he has a legal right to do, in the case of a unilateral contract

c.) Promises to surrender something that he has a right to retain, as in a bilateral contract

d.) Promises to forbear from doing something that he has a right to do, as in a bilateral contract

2.) A legal benefit is received by a promisor if the promisor receives something to which he is not entitled, except under the contract

3.) It is not necessary that an economic or material loss be incurred by the promisee or benefit received by the promisor; all that is necessary is a surrender or receipt of a legal right

XIV. AGENCY RELATIONSHIPS

A. THE NATURE OF AGENCY

1. By using a representative or agent, one person may conduct multiple business operations

2. A corporation can function by using agents exclusively

B. AGENCY DISTINGUISHED FROM OTHER RELATIONSHIPS

1. Principal-agent relationship

   a. An agent acts on behalf of and instead of a principal to engage in business transactions

   b. An agent may bind his principal in contract with a third person

   c. An agent has a degree of independent discretion

2. Employer-employee relationship

   a. To determine whether a relationship is one of employment, one must examine the surrounding circumstances

      1.) An employer controls, or has the right to control, the employee in the performance of physical tasks

      2.) Employees have little or no independent discretion

      3.) Employees are paid for time rather than results

   b. The rights and duties of an employee differ from those of an agent. Today, the distinction is important for purposes of applicability of legislation, such as tax, Social Security, unemployment, workplace safety, and workers' compensation statutes.

3. Independent contractor

   a. An independent contractor engages to bring about some specified end result and is normally paid at the completion of performance

   b. The person employing an independent contractor does not exercise control over the details of the performance

   c. An independent contractor cannot bind the person employing him in a contract with a third party

   d. An independent contractor usually uses his own material, equipment, and employees

C. FORMATION OF AGENCY RELATIONSHIP

1. In general

   a. An agency may be formed for any legal purpose

   b. An agency is a consensual relationship but not necessarily a contractual one; consideration need not be given by a principal

   c. Generally, no special formalities are required to create an agency

      1.) Unless required by the Statute of Frauds or other statute, a writing is not necessary

      2.) If the appointment of an agent is in a writing, the writing is called a power of attorney

    d. Capacity

        1.) A principal must have legal (contractual) capacity because contracts entered into by his agent are treated as contracts of the principal; if a principal lacks capacity, such contracts are voidable by the principal but not the third party

        2.) An agent need not have legal (contractual) capacity in order to act as an agent, but the contract of agency may be avoided by the agent, who lacks capacity (but not the principal)

  2. Agency created by agreement

    a. The agent and principal affirmatively indicate that they consent to the formation of the agency

    b. The agreement may be expressed or implied on the basis of the conduct of the parties

  3. Agency created by ratification

    a. The principal's consent to the agency is given after the purported agent acted on behalf of the principal

    b. Ratification may be expressed or implied

    c. Ratification relates back to the time that the agent acted without authorization

  4. Agency created by estoppel—a person may be estopped to deny the existence of an agency if he caused a third party to reasonably believe that a person was his agent because it appeared that an agency relationship existed (apparent authority)

D. AGENT'S DUTIES TO PRINCIPAL

  1. Duty to perform—an agent is required to follow instructions, use reasonable skill and diligence in performing agency obligations, and use special skills that the agent possesses, if they are applicable

  2. Duty to notify—an agent has the duty to notify a principal of material information that relates to the subject matter of the agency

  3. Duty of loyalty

    a. An agent may neither compete with his principal nor act for another principal unless full disclosure is made to the principal and the principal consents

    b. After termination of an agency, the agent may not disclose trade secrets, confidential information, customer lists, and so forth acquired in the course of his employment as an agent

    c. Conflicts of interest—any secret profits or benefits received by an agent, acting adversely to his principal, belong to the principal, who may recover them from the agent

  4. Duty to account—an agent must account to his principal for any monies or property rightfully belonging to the principal that have come into the agent's hands. An agent should not commingle such property with his own property or that of others.

E. PRINCIPAL'S DUTIES TO AGENT

  1. A principal has an obligation to perform in accordance with his contract with an agent

  2. Duty to compensate, indemnify, and reimburse agent

     a.   A principal is required to pay any agreed compensation to his agent

     b.   If no compensation is specified, a principal is required to pay expenses, losses, and reasonable compensation for services rendered by the agent. An exception exists when the agency is a gratuitous one or there are circumstances, such as a family relationship, that indicate compensation was not intended.

     c.   There is no duty to pay compensation to an agent who has failed to perform his duties

3.   Duty of cooperation—a principal is required to assist an agent in performing his duties and to do nothing to prevent such performance

4.   Duty to provide safe working conditions

XV. NEGOTIABLE INSTRUMENTS

A. DESCRIBED

1. Two important functions

    a. Extension of credit

    b. Substitute for money

2. If an instrument is nonnegotiable, ordinary contract law applies. Assignees of contractual rights can get only the rights given by the assignor and, therefore, are burdened by any defenses between prior parties.

3. Whether an instrument is negotiable is determined by analyzing its form and content on the face of the instrument

    a. Individuals accepting such instruments can determine whether they are negotiable

    b. If a holder of a negotiable instrument is a holder in due course, that holder may collect on the instrument despite most contractual defenses

B. TYPES OF COMMERCIAL PAPER

1. A draft has three parties: one person or entity (drawer) orders another (drawee) to pay a third party (payee) a sum of money

---

Example

The following example is a draft in which Donna Jones is the drawer, Acme Publications is the drawee, and Allison Krauss is the payee.

August 29, 2007

On August 29, 2007, pay to the order of Allison Krauss $1,000 plus 6% annual interest from August 29, 2008.

To: Acme Publications, Inc.

(signed) **Donna Jones**

---

2. A check is a special type of draft that is payable on demand; the drawee must be a bank, and the check writer is the drawer

3. A promissory note is a two-party instrument

    a. Party A (the maker) promises to pay a specified sum of money to Party B (the payee)

b. The following example is a promissory note in which Jean Smith is the maker and Kristin Fourroux is the payee

---

August 29, 2006

I promise to pay to the order of Kristin Fourroux $1,000 plus 6% annual interest on August 29, 2007.

To: Acme Publications, Inc.

(*signed*) **Jean Smith**

---

c. May be payable on demand or at a definite time

4. A certificate of deposit is an acknowledgment by a financial institution of receipt of money and a promise to repay it; it is actually a special type of promissory note in which the maker is the financial institution

C. LIABILITY OF PARTIES

1. Two general types of warranties on negotiable instruments

   a. Contractual liability

   b. Warranty liability

2. Contractual liability

   a. Refers to liability of any party who signs a negotiable instrument as a maker, drawer, drawee, or endorser

   b. A maker of a note has that primary liability; this means that the maker has absolute liability to pay according to the note's terms until it is paid or until the statute of limitations has run

   c. No party of a draft (or check) initially has primary liability because the drawee has only been ordered to pay by the drawer

   d. Drawer has secondary liability on draft and is liable only if the drawee fails to pay

   e. Endorsers of the note or draft have secondary liability; the holder can hold the endorser liable if the primary parties obligated to make payment fail to pay

   f. Drawers and endorsers may avoid secondary liability by signing without recourse

   g. Upon certification of the check, the drawer and all previous endorsers are discharged from liability because the bank has accepted the check and agreed to pay it

3. Warranty liability

   a. Two types under which holder can seek payment from secondary parties

      1.) Transfer warranties

      2.) Presentment warranties

   b. Transfer warranties—the transferor gives these transfer warranties whenever a negotiable instrument is transferred for consideration

      1.) Transferor has good title

2.) All signatures are genuine or authorized

3.) Instrument has not been materially altered

4.) No defense of any party is good against the transferor

5.) Transferor has no notice of insolvency of the maker, drawer, or the acceptor

c. Transfer warranties generally give the loss to the parties who dealt face to face with the wrongdoer and were in the best position to prevent or avoid forged, altered, or stolen instruments

d. If not endorsed by the transferor, the transferor makes all five warranties only to the immediate transferee; if endorsed by the transferor, the transferor makes them to all subsequent holders taking in good faith

e. To recover under warranty liabilities (either transfer or presentment warranties), a party does not have to meet conditions of proper presentment, dishonor, or timely notice of dishonor that are required under contractual liability against endorsers

XVI. PROPERTY

A. PERSONAL PROPERTY

1. Personal property (personalty) includes rights and interests associated with ownership in things, other than real property, capable of being possessed and movable. Personal property may be tangible or intangible.

    a. Tangible personal property—rights in movable property, subject to physical possession

    b. Intangible personal property—rights in a thing that lacks physical substance (e.g., patents, copyrights, and royalties)

    c. Fixtures—personal property attached to real property

2. Property rights

    a. Right to possession and enjoyment

    b. Right to make disposition by sale, gift, or conveyance

3. Title to property may be held

    a. Fee simple—the total collection of ownership rights held by one person

    b. Concurrent ownership by two or more persons

        1.) Tenancy in common—two or more persons own an undivided share, which may be unequal, in property that is transferable during their lifetimes and by inheritance, without rights of survivorship among the cotenants

        2.) Joint tenancy with right of survivorship

            a.) Two or more persons own equal undivided interests, acquired simultaneously, and have equal rights to use, enjoy, and so forth and rights of survivorship

            b.) The transferor must have clearly indicated an intention to create a joint tenancy

            c.) A joint tenant may sever and transfer his interest during his lifetime (right of partition)

        3.) There is a presumption that a cotenancy is a tenancy in common

        4.) Tenancy by the entirety—a joint tenancy existing between spouses cannot be transferred by either spouse without the consent of the other (survivorship rights)

        5.) Community property—generally includes all property acquired during marriage in a community property state

            a.) Each spouse is considered to own half of the community property

            b.) Exceptions to community property

                • Property acquired before marriage

                • Property received as a gift or inheritance by one spouse

            c.) Community property states are Arizona, California, Idaho, Louisiana, Nevada, New Mexico, Texas, Washington, and Wisconsin

            d.) Moving between states

- When moving between states, the character of property (community or separate) is generally not changed

- Effect of moving from a community property state to a separate property state

    — The property will generally remain community property

    — The spouses may choose to divide the property upon arrival in a common law state

        - Property can be divided by having one spouse gift their interest in the community property to the other spouse

        - Will not result in gift tax because of the unlimited gift tax marital deduction

        - If the property is divided, when one spouse dies, the benefits of a stepped-up basis of both halves of the property will be lost

- Effect of moving from a separate property state to a community property state

    — The property will generally remain separate property

    — Upon death, a surviving spouse typically has no claim against the separate property

        - Several states have statutes preventing a spouse from being disinherited by a deceased spouse

        - Spouse can elect against the will in some states

    — In most community property states, a couple can voluntarily change the titling of the assets to convert them to community property

        - Spouses can convert separate property to community property by registering the assets in both spouses' names as community property, or by creating a written agreement declaring all assets as community property

        - Written agreement can exclude certain assets, thus preserving their character as separate property

        - Converting separate property to community property may not be a desirable option if the marriage is troubled

    — If property is converted to community property, favorable community property step-up in basis rules will apply

        - Only one-half of the property is included in the gross estate of the first spouse to die

        - However, both halves of property will receive a step-up in basis at the death of the first spouse

        - Because of the gift tax marital deduction, separate property can be converted into community property without wasting either spouses' gift tax applicable credit

c. Uniform Transfers to Minors Act (UTMA) and Uniform Gift to Minors Act (UGMA)

    1.) The Uniform Gift to Minors Act allows parents the option to put assets in a custodial account for a child. If the child is younger than 18 years, all income earned by the assets (above the kiddie tax threshold) are taxed at the income tax rate of the parents. If the child is 18 years of age or older, the income earned by the assets is taxed at the rate for the child. Notably, this is considered an asset of the child and is considered in determining financial aid.

    2.) Starting in the mid 1980s, states started adopting the Uniform Transfers to Minors Act, which is similar to the UGMA, except that it expanded the types of properties legally transferable to a minor. Nearly all states have adopted the UTMA, but many people still refer to it as UGMA.

B. REAL PROPERTY

1. Real property refers to rights associated with ownership or possessory interests in land and things of a permanent nature on or affixed to land or contained above or below the surface

2. Nature of real property

    a. The land or soil itself, bodies of water contained on the land, natural and artificial structures attached to it, and plant life and vegetation growing on the land

    b. Fixtures—personal property affixed to real property

        1.) Fixtures that are attached or affixed to real property are included in the sale of realty unless the contract for sale provides otherwise

        2.) The objective intention of the party who placed the item determines whether the item is a fixture

3. Ownership interest in real property

    a. Freehold estates—estates for indefinite time (possessory interest in land) are transferable during the owner's lifetime or as an inheritance

        1.) Fee simple absolute—the owner possesses all the rights that one may possess, convey, or inherit in land

        2.) Life estates—Duration is measured by the life of one or more persons

            a.) Measured by the life of a person to whom the estate is given or the life of another person

            b.) It may not be inherited but may be conveyed during the lifetime of the person by whose life it is measured

            c.) A life tenant has the right to possess, use, and convey specific interest in the property; the life tenant also has an obligation to pay taxes, make repairs, and not commit waste

            d.) May be created by voluntary acts of the parties or by operation of law

    b. Estates less than freehold—leaseholds for a determinable period of time in accordance with a contract of lease

        1.) Tenancy for a specified term

            a.) Generally, a lease is for a specified number of years

            b.) No notice of termination at the end of the term is needed

            c.) Upon the death of the tenant, the rights under the lease become part of the decedent's estate or personal property

        d.) Statutes may require that the lease be in writing in order to be enforceable (Statute of Frauds or state laws)

    2.) Periodic tenancy

        a.) Created by contracting to pay rent periodically without stating the duration of the lease or by tenant holding over after expiration of a lease for a specified term (month to month)

        b.) Terminated after giving one period's notice or as provided by statute

    3.) Tenancy at will—terminated upon death or, at common law, the will of either party, or after giving such notice as required by statute

4. Concurrent ownership—property may be held by two or more people simultaneously rather than individually

    a. Tenancy in common

        1.) Two or more persons own undivided shares (which may be equal or unequal) in property

        2.) Each tenant may transfer his interest during his lifetime, by will or by inheritance, without rights of survivorship among the other cotenants

    b. Joint tenancy with right of survivorship

        1.) Two or more persons own equal, undivided shares of an entire estate that they acquire simultaneously and have equal rights of enjoyment and rights of survivorship.

        2.) The transferor must have clearly indicated an intention to create a joint tenancy

        3.) A joint tenant may sever and transfer interest during lifetime

        4.) There is a presumption that a cotenancy is a tenancy in common unless there is a clear intention to create a joint tenancy

    c. Tenancy by the entirety—a joint tenancy existing between spouses cannot be severed by either spouse without the consent of the other

    d. Community property—in some states, spouses own undivided half interests in property acquired during their marriage (other than by gift or inheritance)

    e. Condominium ownership—each owner owns the unit that he occupies and is a tenant in common with others with respect to common areas

5. Future interests—a present, existing right to have possession of real property after the termination of a preceding estate

    a. Reversionary interests and powers of termination

        1.) Arise when a grantor makes a conveyance of less than all interests without disposing of the residue

        2.) The owner of the reversionary interest may transfer the future interest during lifetime

        3.) Upon the death of the owner of the reversionary interest, the interest vests in owning heirs or devisees

        4.) Reversion

a.) The interest retained by a grantor who transfers a life estate to another without making a disposition of the interest remaining after the death of the person who is the measuring life

b.) A vested, future interest

5.) Possibility of reverter

a.) It is the interest retained by a grantor who has conveyed a fee simple determinable

b.) It is contingent upon the happening of the event specified in the conveyance, which terminates the grantee's interest automatically

6.) Power of termination

a.) The interest retained by a grantor who has conveyed a fee simple subject to a condition subsequent is not automatically terminated upon the happening of the condition

b.) The grantor (or heirs) must affirmatively exercise right of entry

b. Remainders and executory interests

1.) Created by the same instrument that conveyed a present possessory interest

2.) May be conveyed and inherited

3.) Vested remainder—an absolute right to possession that exists at the end of a prior life estate or leasehold

4.) Contingent remainder—the right to possession depends on the termination of a preceding estate and the occurrence of a contingency or the existence and identification of some person

5.) Executory interest—the right to possession takes effect either before the natural termination of a preceding estate, upon the occurrence of some contingency (a shifting executory interest), or after the termination of the preceding estate (a springing executory interest)

XVII. CONSUMER PROTECTION

A. CREDIT PROTECTION

1. Federal Truth-in-Lending Act (Consumer Credit Protection Act) is administered by the Federal Reserve Board

   a. The act applies when a debtor is a natural person; the creditor in the ordinary course of its business is a lender, seller, or provider of services; and the amount being financed is less than $25,000

   b. Regulation Z uniform disclosure requirements provide consumers with means of comparing the terms and costs of credit

      1.) Financing charges (including interest; charges for loans and insurance; and finders, credit report, appraisal, financing, and service fees) must be stated in an annual percentage rate (APR)

      2.) The consumer must be informed of the number of payments, the dollar amount of each payment, the dates that payments are due, and prepayment provisions, including prepayment penalties

2. Credit card

   a. Fair Credit Billing Act amends the Truth-in-Lending Act

   b. A credit cardholder is given limited right to withhold payment if there is a dispute concerning goods that were purchased with a credit card

   c. Billing disputes—if a credit cardholder believes that an error has been made by the issuer:

      1.) The cardholder may suspend payment, but must notify and give an explanation to the card issuer concerning an error within 60 days of receipt of the bill (in writing)

      2.) The issuer of the credit card must acknowledge receipt of notification within 30 days and has 90 days to resolve the dispute

   d. A credit cardholder will not be liable for more than $50 (per card) if there was an unauthorized use of the card and notice thereof was given to the card issuer

   e. A credit card issuer may not bill a cardholder for unauthorized charges if a credit card is improperly issued

3. Fair Credit Reporting Act

   a. Upon request, one who is refused credit or employment because of information in a credit bureau report must be supplied with a summary of the information in the report, including the sources and recipients of the information. The individual must be given an opportunity to correct errors.

   b. Consumers have the right to be informed as to the nature and scope of a credit investigation, the kind of information that is being compiled, and the names of people who will receive a credit report

   c. The compiler of a credit report must exercise reasonable care in preparing a credit report

   d. Inaccurate or misleading data must be removed from a credit report, and the consumer has the right to add a statement regarding a disputed matter, not to exceed 100 words

   e. Fair and Accurate Credit Transactions Act of 2003 (FACTA)

1.) Consumers who report suspected identity theft or fraud to a consumer reporting agency must be provided with a summary of their rights at no charge. The rights must include information required by the Federal Trade Commission. The consumer may also request that the agency block reporting of information that the consumer has identified as resulting from identity theft. The agency may decline to comply with the request if the consumer materially misrepresents the information or has received goods or services as a result of the blocked information. The consumer must be notified of the refusal.

2.) Under FACTA, consumers will be entitled to receive on an annual basis a free copy of their credit report from each nationwide consumer reporting agency, regardless of being refused credit or employment on the basis of information contained within the report. The consumer will retain the opportunity to correct errors.

4. Equal Credit Opportunity Act—prohibits discrimination based on race, religion, national origin, color, sex, marital status, age, or receipt of certain types of income

B. DEBT COLLECTION

1. The Fair Debt Collection Practices Act prohibits debt collectors from engaging in certain practices

   a. Contacting a debtor at his place of employment if the employer objects

   b. Contacting a debtor at unusual or inconvenient times or, if the debtor is represented by an attorney, at any time

   c. Contacting third parties about the payment of the debt without court authorization

   d. Harassing or intimidating debtor or using false and misleading approaches

   e. Communicating with the debtor after receipt of notice that the debtor is refusing to pay the debt except to advise the debtor of action to be taken by the collection agency

2. Garnishment

   a. A state court may issue an order for garnishment of a portion of a debtor's wages in order to satisfy a legal judgment that was obtained by a creditor

   b. The Truth in Lending Act and Federal Bankruptcy Law provide that a certain minimum income and no more than 25% of a judgment debtor's after-tax earnings can be garnished

XVIII. BANKRUPTCY AND REORGANIZATION

A. THE BANKRUPTCY REFORM ACT OF 1978, AS AMENDED

1. Establishes Bankruptcy Courts with jurisdiction over all controversies affecting the debtor or the debtor's estate

2. Provides procedures for the following

   a. Voluntary and involuntary liquidation (bankruptcy) of bankruptcy estates of natural persons, firms, partnerships, corporations, unincorporated companies, and associations (Chapter 7)

   b. Reorganization of persons, firms, and corporations (Chapter 11)

   c. Adjustment of debts of individuals with regular income (Chapter 13)

B. BANKRUPTCY ABUSE PREVENTION AND CONSUMER PROTECTION ACT (BAPCPA) OF 2005

1. Makes abuse of bankruptcy protection more difficult for those debtors who have the capacity to pay; it forces many consumers to file under Chapter 13 (adjustment of debts) rather than Chapter 7 (discharge of debts)

   a. A means test is used to identify consumers who qualify for a discharge of debts (Chapter 7) and those who would qualify for an adjustment of debts (Chapter 13)

   b. This means test is imposed on would-be filers whose income (based on the six months before filing) is above the state's median income level

2. The law also increases creditor protection for retirement accounts to those who declare bankruptcy

   a. Under previous legislation, non-ERISA-protected plans (i.e., IRAs) were protected under state laws that varied state by state. With BAPCPA 2005, all retirement plans are protected in bankruptcy proceedings

   b. Roth and Traditional IRAs are protected only up to a $1,000,000 exemption amount; however, a ruling bankruptcy body may increase this exemption amount on a case-by-case basis. SEP, SIMPLE, and rollover accounts are not subject to this exemption amount. They have unlimited protection.

3. The law also outlines certain guidelines for credit counseling and financial education for those debtors whose debts consist primarily of consumer debts

C. LIQUIDATION—ORDINARY OR STRAIGHT BANKRUPTCY (CHAPTER 7)

1. Voluntary liquidation

   a. Commenced by any natural person, firm, association, or corporation (except certain organizations under other chapters)

   b. Petitioning debtor need not be insolvent unless it is a partnership

   c. The debtor will be granted an order for relief if the petition is proper and if the debtor has not been discharged in bankruptcy within the past six years

2. Involuntary liquidation

   a. Commenced against any debtor, except railroad, banking, insurance, or municipal corporations, building or savings and loan associations, credit unions, nonprofit organizations, ranchers, or farmers

    b.   Creditors who have noncontingent, unsecured claims in the amount of $5,000 or more may file a petition with the Bankruptcy Court

        1.) If there are 12 or more creditors, three of them must join in the petition

        2.) If there are fewer than 12 creditors, one must file the petition

        3.) If a party so requests, a temporary trustee may be appointed to take possession of the debtor's property to prevent a loss

3.   The debtor must file documents with the Bankruptcy Court

    a.   A list of secured and unsecured creditors with their addresses and the amounts owed

    b.   A schedule of assets

    c.   A statement of financial affairs

    d.   A list of current income and expenses

    e.   A schedule of exempt property if the debtor wishes to claim exemptions. The debtor has the option of taking exemptions provided by either the law of the state where the debtor is domiciled or the Federal Bankruptcy Act, which provides for the following exemptions:

        1.) Equity in a home and burial plot not exceeding $15,000

        2.) Interest in one motor vehicle up to $2,400

        3.) Interest in personal household goods, clothing, books, animals, and so forth up to $400 for any single item, but not exceeding a total of $8,000

        4.) Interest in jewelry up to $1,000

        5.) Other property worth up to $800 plus up to $7,500 of the unused part of the $15,000 exemption for equity in a home and/or burial plot

        6.) Items used in a trade or business, up to $1,500

        7.) Interests in life insurance policies

        8.) Professionally prescribed health aids

        9.) Federal and state benefits, such as Social Security, veterans' disability, and unemployment benefits

        10.)Alimony and child support, pensions, and annuities

            a.) The US Supreme court decided in *Patterson v. Shumate* that assets in qualified plans were outside the reach of creditors with regard to bankruptcy proceedings

        11.)Rights to receive certain personal injury and other awards

4.   Discharge of debtor from debts

    a.   Nondischargeable debts

        1.) Back taxes (three years)

        2.) Those based on fraud, embezzlement, misappropriation, or defalcation against the debtor acting in a fiduciary capacity

        3.) Alimony and child support

        4.) Intentional tort claims

5.) Secured debt

6.) Property or money obtained by the debtor under false pretenses or fraudulent representations

7.) All student loans are nondischargable, unless paying the loan will impose an undue hardship on the debtor and the debtor's dependents

8.) Unscheduled claims (not listed)

9.) Claims from prior bankruptcy action in which the debtor was denied a discharge for a reason other than the six-year limitation

10.) Consumer debts of more than $500 for luxury goods or services owed to a single creditor within 40 days of the order for relief

11.) Cash advances aggregating more than $1,000 as extensions of open-end consumer credit obtained by the debtor within 20 days of the order for relief

12.) Judgments or consent decrees awarded against the debtor for liability incurred as a result of the debtor's operation of a motor vehicle while intoxicated

   b. Denial of discharge of a debtor—assets are distributed, but the debtor remains liable for unpaid portion of the claims

D. REORGANIZATION (CHAPTER 11)

1. Any individual, business firm, or corporate debtor who is eligible for Chapter 7 liquidation (except stockbrokers, commodities brokers, and railroads) is eligible for Chapter 11 reorganization

2. A voluntary or involuntary petition may be filed; the automatic stay and entry or order for relief provisions apply

3. The debtor remains in possession and may continue to operate the debtor's business

E. ADJUSTMENT OF DEBTS OF AN INDIVIDUAL WITH REGULAR INCOME (CHAPTER 13)

1. An individual debtor who is a wage earner or engaged in business may voluntarily file a petition for adjustment of debts

   a. The debtor's noncontingent, liquidated, unsecured debts amount to less than $307,675, and secured debts amount to less than $922,975 (amounts increase every three years)

   b. The debtor remains in possession

   c. Automatic stay provisions apply

   d. The debtor submits a plan that may provide for a reduction in the amount of obligations or for additional time within which to pay debts or both

2. A reasonable plan that provides for timely payments and is made in good faith will be confirmed by the court. In most instances, the plan will have to be approved by all secured creditors. Approval by unsecured creditors is not necessary.

3. Most plans call for payments of all or a portion of future income or earnings to be made to a trustee for a five-year period

4. A Chapter 13 may be converted into a Chapter 7 liquidation or Chapter 11 reorganization

XIX. TORTS

A. INTRODUCTION

1. Tort law is concerned with wrongs committed against the person or property of another; in other words, a tort is a private wrong, whereas a crime is a public wrong

2. Unreasonable, wrongful conduct by one individual resulting in injury to the person or property of another for which the wrongdoer (tortfeasor) should compensate the injured party

3. Remedies for torts are obtained in civil actions; if a defendant's conduct is also criminally wrong, he may be prosecuted by the state for a crime as well

4. As a result of the defendant's breach of duty not to harm the plaintiff, the plaintiff is injured

5. Elements of a tort

   a. A duty was owed by the defendant

      1.) A private obligation other than an obligation arising out of contract

      2.) Defendant owed duty of not unreasonably causing harm to the person or property of the plaintiff

      3.) Plaintiff has a reciprocal right not to be wrongfully injured

   b. Breach of duty—defendant violated the duty owed to plaintiff because of some act or omission that was intentional, careless, or abnormally dangerous

   c. Injury to plaintiff—plaintiff incurred some loss, harm, or wrong to or invasion of a protected interest. It is not necessary that plaintiff be financially or physically harmed.

   d. Proximate causation—plaintiff's injury was caused by defendant's breach of duty

      1.) Factual cause

         a.) Injury would not have occurred without the defendant's wrongful act or omission

         b.) Defendant's conduct was a substantial factor in causing the injury

      2.) Proximate or legal cause—defendant's conduct was the immediate, foreseeable, direct cause, (rather than remote cause) of plaintiff's injury

B. INTENTIONAL TORTS

1. Defendant consciously desired (intended) to perform an act that resulted in harm to the plaintiff or the plaintiff's property. Additionally, if the defendant's actions were substantially certain to cause harm to the plaintiff or the plaintiff's property, the defendant's actions may be deemed intentional.

2. Wrongs against the person

   a. Battery

      1.) Intentional infliction of a harmful or offensive touching of the person, or what is usually close enough to be considered to be part of the person, that brings about harmful or offensive contact

      2.) Defenses

         a.) Privilege or consent

         b.) Reasonable force to defend oneself, other persons, or one's property

    b. Assault

        1.) Threat by defendant to inflict immediate bodily harm to plaintiff that intentionally creates reasonable apprehension of imminent harmful or offensive contact

        2.) Defenses

            a.) Privilege

            b.) Self-defense of others

            c.) Defense of property

    c. False imprisonment (false arrest)

        1.) Unreasonable, intentional confinement of a plaintiff without justification (there must be confinement)

        2.) Present interference with the freedom to move without restraint

        3.) Merchant protection statutes permit reasonable detention of a suspected shoplifter if there is justified or probable cause to believe that the suspect has taken or interfered with the merchant's property

        4.) Injury may include harm to one's reputation and mental distress

        5.) Defense—consent

    d. Infliction of mental distress—extreme and outrageous conduct that intentionally or recklessly results in severe emotional stress to another

    e. Defamation—harm to reputation and good name

        1.) Publication of statement to or within hearing of others that holds plaintiff up to contempt, ridicule, or hatred

        2.) Slander—false oral statement

        3.) Libel—false written statement

        4.) Defenses—truth or privilege

    f. Misrepresentation (fraud or deceit)

        1.) False representation of fact made by the defendant with knowledge of its falsity or reckless disregard for the truth

        2.) The defendant intended to induce the plaintiff to change his position; fraud or deceit may result from silence or inaction

        3.) The plaintiff reasonably relied on the representation

        4.) As a result of the misrepresentation, the plaintiff was damaged

        5.) In a commercial setting, a seller's overstatement of his abilities is distinguishable from actionable misrepresentation

3. Wrongs against property

    a. Trespass to land—wrongful interference with another person's real property rights even though there is no actual harm to the land; this includes direct or indirect breach of borders

        1.) Attractive nuisance—liability that stems from harm caused by a hazardous object or condition that is likely to attract individuals (usually children) who do not appreciate the risk posed by the object or condition. For example, a swimming pool or a lake located on a property would be considered an attractive nuisance and thus make the owner of the property liable for any harm caused.

    2.) Trespasser versus licensee versus invitee—a licensee is someone you have not invited on to your property but who has the right to enter (i.e., police officer); an invitee is someone you have invited on to your property

  b. Trespass to personal property—defendant unlawfully injures or interferes with plaintiff's right to exclusive possession and enjoyment of personal property

  c. Conversion—a wrongful taking and keeping of chattel to which one has no right, so serious as to constitute remedy as sale

C. NEGLIGENCE

1. Unintentional failure to exercise reasonable care under the circumstances so that a foreseeable risk to another person is created; an injury to the plaintiff results

2. Elements

  a. The defendant owed a duty to exercise reasonable care

  b. The defendant breached that duty

  c. The plaintiff suffered actual damages

  d. The plaintiff's injury was caused by the defendant's failure to exercise reasonable care

    1.) Causation in fact—a "but for" analysis or substantial factor in bringing about the harm

    2.) Proximate cause or legal cause

3. Defenses

  a. Contributory and comparative negligence—plaintiff's own negligence contributed to his own injury

    1.) Common law doctrine of contributory negligence—plaintiff cannot recover from defendant at all

    2.) Comparative negligence—the amount of damages is apportioned between the plaintiff and defendant, on the basis of the relative percentage of fault for each of the parties

    3.) A negligent plaintiff may be able to recover if a negligent defendant had the last clear chance to prevent injury to a helpless plaintiff

  b. Implied or expressed assumption of the risk—plaintiff, expressly or implicitly, knowingly and voluntarily placed self in a situation involving risk

4. Structured settlements—a plaintiff (injury victim) may receive compensation in form of a structured settlement, which involves installment payments over the course of a certain period or lifetime, rather than in a lump sum. Settlements may contain the following

  a. Compensatory damages—compensation for medical expenses and treatment (including psychological treatment) are generally tax free; however, interest accumulated on an award for compensatory damages are generally taxable

  b. Punitive damages—used to punish the defendant and are generally taxable, except in cases of wrongful death

D. STRICT LIABILITY

Liability without fault and without regard to defendant's intent or exercise of reasonable care

1. Abnormally dangerous activities

   a. The activity involves a high degree of risk that cannot be completely guarded against even with the exercise of reasonable or extraordinary care (blasting or crop dusting)

   b. The risk is one that involves potentially serious harm

   c. The activity is one that is not commonly performed in the geographic area

2. Employers are strictly liable to their employees for injuries sustained during the ordinary course of their employment under the workers' compensation statutes

3. Employers and principals are strictly liable for torts committed by employees and agents acting within the ordinary course of their employment

4. Manufacturers of products are held strictly liable for damages caused by their products in many states

5. Strict liability is liability without the need to prove negligence; in other words, strict liability has the same elements of negligence except that it is immaterial whether the strictly liable defendant knew or should have known of the injury-causing defect

XX. PROFESSIONAL LIABILITY—FINANCIAL PLANNERS

A. INTRODUCTION

1. As members of a profession, financial planners are expected to comply with standards of ethics and to perform their services in accordance with accepted principles and standards

2. Those financial planners who fail to perform these duties may be civilly liable to their clients, for whom they have agreed to provide services, and to third persons, who may have relied on statements, prepared by them

3. In addition, sometimes civil and criminal liability may be imposed on financial planners because of statutes, such as the federal securities laws

B. POTENTIAL COMMON LAW LIABILITY TO CLIENTS

1. Liability based on breach of contract

    a. The failure to perform one's contractual duties is a breach of contract for which one is liable to the party to whom the performance was to be rendered

    b. Thus, if a financial planner has agreed to perform certain services for a client and fails to honestly, properly, and completely perform those contractual duties, the financial planner will be civilly liable to the client for breach of contract

    c. In most cases, if there has been a breach of contract by a financial planner, courts will award compensatory damages as a remedy to the client

        1.) The measure of damages will be equal to the foreseeable losses that the client incurs as a result of the breach

        2.) Damages may include expenses that are incurred by a client to secure the services of another financial planner and penalties that are imposed on the client who failed to meet statutory deadlines

    d. In an action that is based on breach of contract, liability is not imposed because of the breach of a duty that existed as a result of tort law. It is, therefore, not a defense where the financial planner exercised reasonable care and conformed to accepted principles and standards; or the client's own negligence contributed to the client's injury.

2. Liability based on the tort of negligence

    a. A financial planner has a duty to exercise the same standard of care that a reasonably prudent and skillful financial planner in the community would exercise under the same or similar circumstances

    b. A violation of generally accepted principles and standards is prima facie evidence (i.e., evidence good and sufficient on its face) of negligence

    c. Although a financial planner may have complied with principles and standards, he may still be considered as not having acted with reasonable care

    d. A financial planner is not liable for errors of judgment

    e. A financial planner is liable for his negligence

f. If a financial planner is found to be liable for negligence, damages may be awarded to compensate the client for any reasonable, foreseeable injuries that were incurred

g. Defenses that may be asserted by a financial planner in an action that is based on negligence

    1.) Lack of negligence

    2.) Lack of proximate cause between the breach of the duty that was owed by the financial planner and the injury that was incurred by the client

    3.) The client's own negligence (or intentional acts) or the fault of a third party contributed to the client's loss

3. Financial planner's liability based on fraud—in an action based on fraud, the client must establish the following

    a. The financial planner made a false representation of a material fact

    b. The representation was made by the financial planner with knowledge that it was false (actual fraud) or with reckless disregard for its truth or falsity (constructive fraud)

    c. The financial planner intentionally made the misrepresentation to induce the client to act or not act

    d. The client was injured as a result of the client's reasonable reliance on the misrepresentation

C. POTENTIAL COMMON LAW LIABILITY TO THIRD PERSONS

Third persons are people who were not clients of the financial planner but who had knowledge of documents that were prepared by the financial planner

1. Contract liability

    a. Traditionally, in common law, a financial planner does not owe contractual duties to third persons unless they are direct parties to or third-party beneficiaries of a contract for the services of the financial planner

    b. This is so because there is lack of privity of contract between the financial planner and the other person

2. Tort liability

    a. Tort liability is based on negligence in failing to exercise ordinary, reasonable care

    b. Restatement of torts (second) position—a financial planner may be liable to a third person who has no privity of contract but who reasonably and foreseeably relied upon the documents prepared by the financial planner

D. POTENTIAL STATUTORY LIABILITY

1. Liability under Section 11 of the Securities Act of 1933

    a. Securities Act of 1933 relates to new issues of investment securities (i.e., going public)

    b. Registration statements, including financial statements, must be filed with the Securities and Exchange Commission (SEC) before investment securities can be offered for sale by issuer

2. Liability under the Securities Exchange Act of 1934

    a. The Securities Exchange Act of 1934 relates to the purchase and sale of investment securities in the market (i.e., being public)

    b. Section 18—a financial planner is liable for false and/or misleading statements of material facts that are made in applications, reports, documents, and registration statements that are prepared by the financial planner and filed with the SEC

    c. Section 10(b) and SEC Rule 10b-5

        1.) Liability is imposed on those (including financial planners) who, because of their inside positions, have access to material information that is not available to the public and that may affect the value of securities and who trade in the securities without making a disclosure

        2.) Section 10(b) provides that it is unlawful to use any manipulative or deceptive device in connection with the sale or purchase of securities

        3.) Rule 10b-5 provides that, "in connection with the purchase or sale of any security," the following actions are unlawful

            a.) To "employ any device, scheme, or artifice to defraud"

            b.) To "make any untrue statement of a material fact or to omit to state a material fact necessary in order to make the statements made, in the light of the circumstances under which they were made, not misleading"

            c.) To "engage in any act, practice, or course of business which operates or would operate as a fraud or deceit upon any person"

        4.) A financial planner may be liable to a person who purchased or sold securities when the following can be established

            a.) The statement or omission was material

            b.) The financial planner intended to deceive or defraud others

            c.) As a result of his reasonable reliance on the misrepresentation, the purchaser or seller incurred a loss

3. Criminal liability for willful conduct is imposed by the Securities Act of 1933, the Securities Exchange Act of 1934, the Internal Revenue Act, and other federal statutes, as well as state criminal codes

XXI. REGULATORY REQUIREMENTS

A. INTRODUCTION

1. The issuance and sale of corporate securities are extensively regulated by the Securities and Exchange Commission (SEC), a federal agency that administers the Securities Act of 1933, the Securities Exchange Act of 1934, and other federal statutes

2. A major objective of securities regulation is to protect the investing public by requiring full and correct disclosure of relevant information

3. Both the federal and state governments require a substantial amount of regulation; however, most regulation is from the federal government because the majority of trading is done across state borders

B. FEDERAL SECURITIES REGULATION

This legislation is based on the power of Congress to regulate interstate commerce

1. Federal regulatory statutes are administered by the SEC

2. Securities Act of 1933

   a. This securities act is primarily concerned with new issues of securities or issues in the primary market

   b. The term *investment security* is broadly defined

      1.) "Any note, stock, treasury stock, bond, debenture, evidence of indebtedness, certificate of interest or participation in any profit-sharing agreement ... investment contract ... or, in general, any interest or instrument commonly known as a 'security' or any certificate of interest or participation in ... receipt for ... or right to subscribe to or purchase, any of the foregoing"

      2.) Includes the following transactions

         a.) A person invests money or property in a common enterprise or venture

         b.) An investor reasonably expects to make a profit primarily or substantially as a result of the managerial efforts of others

   c. The 1933 Act requires full disclosure of material information that is relevant to investment decisions and prohibits fraud and misstatements when securities are offered to the public through the mail and/or interstate commerce

   d. A registration statement contains a thorough description of the securities; the financial structure, condition, and management personnel of the issuing corporation; and a description of material pending litigation against the issuing corporation. This statement is filed with the SEC.

   e. The 1933 Act also requires that a prospectus based on the information in the registration statement be given to any prospective investor or purchaser

   f. After registration, there is a 20-day waiting period

      1.) During the waiting period, an issuer can obtain underwriters and distributes a red herring prospectus

2.) The issuer may solicit revocable offers from prospective purchasers after filing the registration statement but may not sell securities until the effective date of the statement

g. After the waiting period, the registered securities can be bought and sold, and tombstone advertisements can be placed in newspapers and other publications

h. Securities that are exempt from registration requirements

    1.) Intrastate offerings for which all offerees and issuers are residents of the state in which issuer performs substantially all of its operations

    2.) The issuer is a governmental body or nonprofit organization

    3.) The issuer is a bank, savings institution, common carrier, or farmers' cooperative and is subject to other regulatory legislation

    4.) Commercial paper with a maturity date of less than nine months (270 days)

    5.) Stock dividends, stock splits, and securities issued in connection with corporate reorganizations

    6.) Insurance, endowment, and annuity contracts

i. Regulation A requires less demanding disclosures and registration for small issues of less than $1,500,000

j. Transactions that are exempt from registration requirement (Regulation D)

    1.) Private, noninvestment company sales of less than $500,000 worth of securities in a 12-month period to investors who will not resell the securities within two years

    2.) Private, noninvestment company sales of less than $5,000,000 worth of securities in a 12-month period to the following types of investors

        a.) Accredited investors

            • Anyone whose individual net worth, or joint net worth with spouse, is greater than $1,000,000 at the time of investment

            • Anyone whose individual income was greater than $200,000, or joint income with spouse was greater than $300,000, in each of the two most recent years who can expect to reach that same level of income in the current year

            • Any trust with total assets in excess of $5,000,000, not formed for the specific purpose of acquiring the securities offered, whose purchase of the securities is directed by a person who has such knowledge and experience in financial and business matters that he is capable of evaluating the merits and risks of the prospective investment

            • Any organization that was not formed for the purpose of acquiring the securities being sold, with total assets in excess of $5,000,000

            • Any entity in which all of the equity owners are accredited investors

        b.) Investors who are furnished with purchaser representatives who are knowledgeable and experienced regarding finance and business

        c.) Up to 35 unaccredited investors who have financial and business knowledge and experience and who are furnished with the same information as would be contained in a full registration statement prospectus

3.) Sales of any amount of securities to accredited investors or those furnished with independent purchaser representatives (private placement)

   k. Civil liability for failure to register and for misstatements and omissions in a registration statement

      1.) Imposed on the issuing corporation, its directors and anyone who signed or provided information that was incorporated in the registration statement, and underwriters

      2.) Liable to persons acquiring shares

3. Securities Exchange Act of 1934

   a. Although the Securities Act of 1933 was limited to new issues, the 1934 Securities Act extended the regulation to securities sold in the secondary markets; the Act provided the following provisions

      1.) Establishment of the SEC—the SEC's primary function is to regulate the securities markets

      2.) Disclosure requirements for secondary market—annual reports and other financial reports are required to be filed with the SEC prior to listing on the organized exchanges. These reports include the annual 10-K Report, which must be audited, and the quarterly 10-Q Report, which is not required to be audited

      3.) Registration of organized exchanges—all organized exchanges must register with the SEC and provide copies of their rules and bylaws

      4.) Credit regulation—Congress gave the Federal Reserve Board the power to set margin requirements for credit purchases of securities; securities dealers' indebtedness was also limited to 20 times their owners' equity capital by this Act

      5.) Proxy solicitation—specific rules governing solicitation of proxies were established

      6.) Exemptions—securities of federal, state, and local governments; securities that are not traded across state lines; and any other securities specified by the SEC are exempt from registering with the SEC. This includes Treasury bonds and municipal bonds.

      7.) Insider activities—a public report, called an insider report, must be filed with the SEC for every month in which a change in the holding of a firm's securities occurs for an officer, director, or 10% or more shareholder. The 1934 Act forbids insiders profiting from securities held less than 6 months and requires these profits be returned to the organization. In addition, short sales are not permitted by individuals considered to be insiders.

      8.) Price manipulation—the Securities Exchange Act of 1934 forbids such price manipulation schemes as wash sales, pools, circulation of manipulative information, and false and misleading statements about securities

   b. Liability under the Securities Exchange Act of 1934

      1.) Insider trading

         a.) Liability is imposed on directors and others (tippees) who, because of their positions, have access to information not available to the public that may affect the future market value of the corporation's securities

         b.) Liability is imposed when misleading or deceptive omissions or misrepresentations of material facts are given in connection with the purchase or sale of securities

    c.) SEC, purchaser, or seller of securities who has been damaged may bring action

    d.) An outsider who comes into possession of nonpublic market information does not have a duty to make a Rule 10b-5 disclosure

2.) Rule 10b-5 applies when the facilities of a stock exchange, the US mail, or an instrumentality of interstate commerce are used

3.) Insider reporting and trading—officers, directors, and large shareholders are required to file reports with the SEC and may be liable to the corporation for gains made in trading in securities

4.) The Insider Trading Sanctions Act of 1984 authorizes the SEC to bring a civil suit against a person who, while in possession of material nonpublic information, violates or aids in the violation of the 1934 Act or SEC rules

5.) Proxy statements (Sec. 14(a))—full disclosure is required of those soliciting proxies from shareholders

6.) A financial planner may be held liable to a person who purchased or sold securities when the following can be established

    a.) The statement or omission was material

    b.) The financial planner intended to deceive others

    c.) As a result of his reasonable reliance on the misrepresentation, the purchaser or seller incurred a loss

4. Investment Company Act of 1940 requires registration with the SEC and restricts activities of investment companies (including mutual funds)

5. State regulation of securities (blue-sky laws)—state securities laws also regulate the offering and sale of securities in intrastate commerce; these are usually covered within a Series 63 registration requirement

    a. Antifraud provisions similar to federal laws

    b. Regulation of brokers and dealers in securities

    c. Registration and disclosure are required before securities can be offered for sale

    d. Some state statutes impose standards of fairness

    e. Some state statutes are more restrictive than the federal statute and SEC rules

C. NASD

> **Note:** The following excerpts from "An Explanation of the NASD Regulations and Qualification Requirements—February 1998" have been reprinted with the permission of NASD

EXHIBIT 10: QUALIFICATIONS/REGISTRATION REQUIREMENT CHART FOR REGISTERED REPRESENTATIVES		
Securities Transaction/Activity	**Qualification**	**Registration Requirement**
Mutual funds (closed-end funds on the initial offering only); variable annuities; variable life insurance; unit investment trusts (initial offering only)	Investment Company Products/Variable Contracts Limited Representative	Series 6
Corporate securities (stocks and bonds); rights; warrants; mutual funds; money market funds; unit investment trusts; REITs; asset-backed securities; mortgage-backed securities; options; options on mortgage-backed securities; municipal securities; government securities; repos, and certificates of accrual on government securities; direct participation programs; securities traders; mergers and acquisitions; venture capital; corporate financing	General Securities Representative	Series 7
Direct participation programs (real estate; oil and gas; equipment leasing; and other limited partnerships)	Direct Participation Programs Limited Representative	Series 22
Municipal securities	Municipal Securities Representative	Series 52
Equity traders	Equity Traders Limited Representative	Series 55
Corporate securities (stocks and bonds); rights; warrants; closed-end funds; unit investment trusts; money market funds; REITs; repos and certificates of accrual on corporate securities; securities traders; mergers and acquisitions; venture capital; corporate financing	Corporate Securities Limited Representative	Series 62
Accept unsolicited securities orders (all securities except municipal securities and direct participation programs) only from the firm's clients	Assistant Representative —Order Processing	Series 11
Government securities; government agency securities; mortgage-backed securities	Government Securities Representative	Series 72
Both the Series 65 and Series 66 exams were developed by the North American Securities Administrators Association (NASAA) and administered by NASD Regulation. Unlike NASD exams, such as the Series 6 and 7, you do not need to be sponsored by a broker-dealer.	Investment Advisor Representative	Series 65/66

XXII. INVESTMENT ADVISERS' REGULATION AND REGISTRATION

A. INTRODUCTION

The Securities and Exchange Commission (SEC) regulates investment advisers and their activities under the Investment Advisers Act of 1940. Unless exempt under specific provisions of the act, a person covered by the act must register with the SEC as an investment adviser.

B. REGULATION

1. Definition—an investment adviser is a person who does any of the following

    a. Provides advice or issues reports or analyses regarding securities

    b. Is in the business of providing such services

    c. Provides such services for compensation

        1.) Compensation is the receipt of any economic benefit that includes commissions on the sale of products

        2.) Certain organizations and individuals are excluded

            a.) Banks and bank holding companies (except as amended by the Gramm-Leach-Bliley Act of 1999)

            b.) Lawyers, accountants, engineers, or teachers, if their performance of advisory services is solely incidental to their professions

            c.) Brokers or dealers, if their performance of advisory services is solely incidental to the conduct of their business as brokers or dealers and they do not receive any special compensation for their advisory services

            d.) Publishers of bona fide newspapers, newsmagazines, or business or financial publications of general and regular circulation

            e.) Those persons whose advice is related only to securities that are direct obligations of or guaranteed by the United States

            f.) Incidental practice exception is not available to individuals who hold themselves out to the public as providing financial planning, pension consulting, or other financial advisory services

2. Exceptions—the act provides limited exemptions. Investment advisers who, during the course of the preceding 12 months, had fewer than 15 clients and do not hold themselves out generally to the public as investment advisers and those whose only clients are insurance companies are exempt.

3. Disclosure—the act generally requires investment advisers entering into an advisory contract with a client to deliver a written disclosure statement on their background and business practices; Form ADV Part II must be given to a client under Rule 204-3, which is known as the brochure rule

    a. In accordance with the Investment Adviser Brochure Rule, an investment adviser shall furnish each advisory client and prospective client with a written disclosure statement, which may be a copy of Part II of Form ADV, or written documents containing at least the information then so required by Part II of Form ADV, or such other information as the administrator may require

b. Disclosure should be delivered not less than 48 hours before entering into any investment advisory contract with the client or prospective client, or at the time of entering into any contract, if the advisory client has a right to terminate the contract without penalty within five business days after entering into the contract

c. If an investment adviser renders substantially different types of investment advisory services to different advisory clients, any information required by Part II of Form ADV may be omitted from the statement furnished to an advisory client or prospective advisory client if the information is applicable only to a type of investment advisory service or fee that is not rendered or charged, or proposed to be rendered or charged, to that client or prospective client

4. Inspections—the 1940 Advisor's Act and the SEC's rules require that advisers maintain and preserve specified books and records and are made available for inspection

5. Restriction on the use of the term *investment counsel*—a registered investment adviser may not use the term *investment counsel* unless its principal business is acting as an investment adviser and a substantial portion of its business is providing investment supervisory services

6. Antifraud provisions

a. Section 206 of the Act, Section 17 of the Securities Act of 1933, Section 10(b) of the Securities Exchange Act of 1934, and Rule 10b-5 prohibit misstatements or misleading omissions of material facts, fraudulent acts, and practices in connection with the purchase or sale of securities or the conduct of an investment advisory business

b. An investment adviser owes his clients undivided loyalty and may not engage in activity that conflicts with a client's interest

7. Registration—Form ADV is kept current by filing periodic amendments; Form ADV-W is used to withdraw as an investment adviser

8. Filing requirements

a. Forms—ADV and ADV-W can be obtained from the SEC's Office of Consumer Affairs and Information Services in Washington DC or from the Commission office in your area (**www.sec.gov/about/forms/secform.htm**)

b. Copies—all advisers' filings must be submitted in triplicate and typewritten. Copies can be filed, but each must be signed manually.

c. Fees—must include a registration fee of $150, by check or money order payable to the Securities and Exchange Commission, with your initial application of Form ADV. No part of this fee can be refunded.

d. Name and signatures—full names are required. Each copy of an execution page must contain an original manual signature.

9. Prohibition on commission registration

a. In the fall of 1996, Congress amended the Advisers Act to reallocate regulatory responsibility for investment advisers between the SEC and state authorities. Congress did this by prohibiting certain advisers from registering with the SEC. As a result, for the most part, larger advisers will be regulated by the SEC, and smaller advisers will be regulated by state securities authorities.

b. Only certain types of advisers are permitted to register with the SEC (and, therefore, must register with the SEC, unless exempt under a specific rule). The following advisers are permitted to register with the SEC.

    1.) Advisers with assets under management of $25 million or more (the $25 million threshold has been increased to $30 million); however, advisers with assets under management between $25 million and $30 million may still register with the SEC

    2.) Advisers to registered investment companies

    3.) Advisers who have their principal office and place of business in a state that has not enacted an investment adviser statute or that have their principal office and place of business outside the United States

10. Advisers are required to report their eligibility for SEC registration on Schedule I to Form ADV upon initial registration. Schedule I must be filed every year to establish and report their continuing eligibility for SEC registrations.

C. REFORM OF PREVIOUS ACTS

1. The Glass-Steagall Act (1933) prohibited commercial banks from acting as investment bankers, established the Federal Deposit Insurance Corporation (FDIC), and prohibited commercial banks from paying interest on demand deposits. This was one of the first of many securities regulation laws that has affected the investment markets. However, the Gramm-Leach-Bliley Act, passed by Congress in November 1999, eliminates many of the restrictions against affiliations among banks, securities firms, and insurance companies.

    a. The act repeals the affiliation sections of the Glass-Steagall Act that prohibit a bank holding company and a securities firm that underwrites and deals in ineligible securities from owning and controlling each other

    b. It also amends the Bank Holding Company Act (1956) to permit cross-ownership and control among bank holding companies, securities firms and insurance companies, provided that such cross-ownership and control is effected through a financial holding company that engages in activities that conform to the act

    c. A bank must register as an investment adviser if it provides investment advice to a registered investment company, provided that if the bank provides such advice through a separately identified department or division, that department or division shall be deemed to be the investment adviser

D. INVESTMENT ADVISER REGISTRATION DEPOSITORY

1. The Investment Adviser Registration Depository (IARD) is an electronic filing system for Investment Advisers sponsored by the Securities and Exchange Commission (SEC) and North American Securities Administrators Association (NASAA), with NASD Regulation, Inc., serving as the developer and operator of the system

2. The IARD system collects and maintains the registration and disclosure information for Investment Advisers and their associated persons. The new IARD system supports electronic filing of the revised Forms ADV and ADV-W, centralized fee and form processing, regulatory review, the annual registration renewal process, and public disclosure of investment adviser information.

3. IARD provides regulators with the ability to monitor and process investment adviser information via a single, centralized system (www.iard.com)

XXIII. CFP BOARD'S STANDARDS OF PROFESSIONAL CONDUCT

> **Note:** This content was taken directly from the CFP Board's *Standards of Professional Conduct*, revised December 2007.

CODE OF ETHICS AND PROFESSIONAL RESPONSIBILITY

Part I—PRINCIPLES

Preamble and Applicability

The *Code of Ethics and Professional Responsibility* (*Code of Ethics*) has been adopted by Certified Financial Planner Board of Standards, Inc. (CFP Board) to provide principles and rules to all persons whom it has recognized and certified to use the CFP®, CERTIFIED FINANCIAL PLANNER™ and CFP®(with flame logo) (collectively "the marks"). CFP Board determines who is certified and thus authorized to use the marks. Implicit in the acceptance of this authorization is an obligation not only to comply with the mandates and requirements of all applicable laws and regulations but also to take responsibility to act in an ethical and professionally responsible manner in all professional services and activities. For purposes of this *Code of Ethics*, a person recognized and certified by CFP Board to use the marks is called a CFP Board designee. This *Code of Ethics* applies to CFP Board designees actively involved in the practice of personal financial planning, in other areas of financial services, in industry, in related professions, in government, in education or in any other professional activity in which the marks are used in the performance of professional responsibilities. This *Code of Ethics* also applies to candidates for the CFP certification who are registered as such with CFP Board. For purposes of this *Code of Ethics*, the term CFP Board designee shall be deemed to include current certificants, candidates and individuals who have been certified in the past and retain the right to reinstate their CFP certification without passing the current CFP® Certification Examination.

Composition and Scope

The *Code of Ethics* consists of two parts: Part I—Principles and Part II—Rules. The Principles are statements expressing in general terms the ethical and professional ideals that CFP Board designees are expected to display in their professional activities. As such, the Principles are aspirational in character but are intended to provide a source of guidance for CFP Board designees. The comments following each Principle further explain the meaning of the Principle. The Rules in Part II provide practical guidelines derived from the tenets embodied in the Principles. As such, the Rules describe the standards of ethical and professionally responsible conduct expected of CFP Board designees in particular situations. This *Code of Ethics* does not undertake to define standards of professional conduct of CFP Board designees for purposes of civil liability.

Due to the nature of a CFP Board designee's particular field of endeavor, certain Rules may not be applicable to that CFP Board designee's activities. For example, a CFP Board designee who is engaged solely in the sale of securities as a registered representative is not subject to the written disclosure requirements of Rule 402 (applicable to CFP Board designees engaged in personal financial planning) although he or she may have disclosure responsibilities under Rule 401. A CFP Board designee is obligated to determine what responsibilities he or she has in each professional relationship including, for example, duties that arise in particular circumstances from a position of trust or confidence that a CFP Board designee may have. The CFP Board designee is obligated to meet those responsibilities. The *Code of Ethics* is structured so that the presentation of the Rules parallels the presentation of the Principles. For example, the Rules which relate to Principle 1—Integrity are numbered in the 100 to 199 series, while those Rules relating to Principle 2—Objectivity are numbered in the 200 to 299 series.

Compliance

CFP Board requires adherence to this *Code of Ethics* by all CFP Board designees. Compliance with the *Code of Ethics*, individually and by the profession as a whole, depends on each CFP Board designee's knowledge of and voluntary compliance with the Principles and applicable Rules, on the influence of fellow professionals and public opinion, and on disciplinary proceedings, when necessary, involving CFP Board designees who fail to comply with the applicable provisions of the *Code of Ethics*.

Terminology In This *Code of Ethics*

"Client" denotes a person, persons, or entity who engages a practitioner and for whom professional services are rendered. For purposes of this definition, a practitioner is engaged when an individual, based upon the relevant facts and circumstances, reasonably relies upon information or service provided by that practitioner. Where the services of the practitioner are provided to an entity (corporation, trust, partnership, estate, etc.), the client is the entity acting through its legally authorized representative.

"CFP Board designee" denotes current certificants, candidates for certification, and individuals that have any entitlement, direct or indirect, to the CFP certification marks.

"Commission" denotes the compensation received by an agent or broker when the same is calculated as a percentage on the amount of his or her sales or purchase transactions.

"Compensation" is any economic benefit a CFP Board designee or related party receives from performing his or her professional activities.

"Conflict(s) of interest" exists when a CFP Board designee's financial, business, property and/or personal interests, relationships or circumstances, reasonably may impair his/her ability to offer objective advice, recommendations or services.

"Fee-only" denotes a method of compensation in which compensation is received solely from a client with neither the personal financial planning practitioner nor any related party receiving compensation which is contingent upon the purchase or sale of any financial product. A "related party" for this purpose shall mean an individual or entity from whom any direct or indirect economic benefit is derived by the personal financial planning practitioner as a result of implementing a recommendation made by the personal financial planning practitioner.

A **"financial planning engagement"** exists when a client, based on the relevant facts and circumstances, reasonably relies upon information or services provided by a CFP Board designee using the financial planning process.

"Personal financial planning" or **"financial planning"** denotes the process of determining whether and how an individual can meet life goals through the proper management of financial resources.

"Personal financial planning process" or **"financial planning process"** denotes the process which typically includes, but is not limited to, these six elements: establishing and defining the client-planner relationship, gathering client data including goals, analyzing and evaluating the client's financial status, developing and presenting financial planning recommendations and/or alternatives, implementing the financial planning recommendations and monitoring the financial planning recommendations.

"Personal financial planning subject areas" or "financial planning subject areas" denotes the basic subject fields covered in the financial planning process which typically include, but are not limited to, financial statement preparation and analysis (including cash flow analysis/planning and budgeting), investment planning (including portfolio design, i.e., asset allocation, and portfolio management), income tax planning, education planning, risk management, retirement planning, and estate planning.

"Personal financial planning professional" or "financial planning professional" denotes a person who is capable and qualified to offer objective, integrated, and comprehensive financial advice to or for the benefit of individuals to help them achieve their financial objectives. A financial planning professional must have the ability to provide financial planning services to clients, using the financial planning process covering the basic financial planning subjects.

"Personal financial planning practitioner" or "financial planning practitioner" denotes a person who is capable and qualified to offer objective, integrated, and comprehensive financial advice to or for the benefit of clients to help them achieve their financial objectives and who engages in financial planning using the financial planning process in working with clients.

Part 1: Principles

Introduction

These *Code of Ethics'* Principles express the profession's recognition of its responsibilities to the public, to clients, to colleagues, and to employers. They apply to all CFP Board designees and provide guidance to them in the performance of their professional services.

Principle 1—Integrity

A CFP Board designee shall offer and provide professional services with integrity.

As discussed in "Composition and Scope", CFP Board designees may be placed by clients in positions of trust and confidence. The ultimate source of such public trust is the CFP Board designee's personal integrity. In deciding what is right and just, a CFP Board designee should rely on his or her integrity as the appropriate touchstone. Integrity demands honesty and candor which must not be subordinated to personal gain and advantage. Within the characteristic of integrity, allowance can be made for innocent error and legitimate difference of opinion; but integrity cannot co-exist with deceit or subordination of one's principles. Integrity requires a CFP Board designee to observe not only the letter but also the spirit of this *Code of Ethics*.

Principle 2—Objectivity

A CFP Board designee shall be objective in providing professional services to clients.

Objectivity requires intellectual honesty and impartiality. It is an essential quality for any professional. Regardless of the particular service rendered or the capacity in which a CFP Board designee functions, a CFP Board designee should protect the integrity of his or her work, maintain objectivity, and avoid subordination of his or her judgment that would be in violation of this *Code of Ethics*.

Principle 3—Competence

A CFP Board designee shall provide services to clients competently and maintain the necessary knowledge and skill to continue to do so in those areas in which the designee is engaged.

One is competent only when he or she has attained and maintained an adequate level of knowledge and skill, and applies that knowledge effectively in providing services to clients. Competence also includes the wisdom to recognize the limitations of that knowledge and when consultation or client referral is appropriate. A CFP Board designee, by virtue of having earned the CFP certification, is deemed to be qualified to practice financial planning. However, in addition to assimilating the common body of knowledge required and acquiring the necessary experience for certification, a CFP Board designee shall make a continuing commitment to learning and professional improvement.

Principle 4—Fairness

A CFP Board designee shall perform professional services in a manner that is fair and reasonable to clients, principals, partners, and employers and shall disclose conflict(s) of interest in providing such services.

Fairness requires impartiality, intellectual honesty, and disclosure of conflict(s) of interest. It involves a subordination of one's own feelings, prejudices, and desires so as to achieve a proper balance of conflicting interests. Fairness is treating others in the same fashion that you would want to be treated and is an essential trait of any professional.

Principle 5—Confidentiality

A CFP Board designee shall not disclose any confidential client information without the specific consent of the client unless in response to proper legal process, to defend against charges of wrongdoing by the CFP Board designee or in connection with a civil dispute between the CFP Board designee and client.

A client, by seeking the services of a CFP Board designee, may be interested in creating a relationship of personal trust and confidence with the CFP Board designee. This type of relationship can only be built upon the understanding that information supplied to the CFP Board designee or other information will be confidential. In order to provide the contemplated services effectively and to protect the client's privacy, the CFP Board designee shall safeguard the confidentiality of such information.

Principle 6—Professionalism

A CFP Board designee's conduct in all matters shall reflect credit upon the profession.

Because of the importance of the professional services rendered by CFP Board designees, there are attendant responsibilities to behave with dignity and courtesy to all those who use those services, fellow professionals, and those in related professions. A CFP Board designee also has an obligation to cooperate with fellow CFP Board designees to enhance and maintain the profession's public image and to work jointly with other CFP Board designees to improve the quality of services. It is only through the combined efforts of all CFP Board designees, in cooperation with other professionals, that this vision can be realized.

Principle 7—Diligence

A CFP Board designee shall act diligently in providing professional services.

Diligence is the provision of services in a reasonably prompt and thorough manner. Diligence also includes proper planning for and supervision of the rendering of professional services.

Part II—RULES

Introduction

As stated in **Part I—Principles,** the Principles apply to all CFP Board designees. However, due to the nature of a CFP Board designee's particular field of endeavor, certain Rules may not be applicable to that CFP Board designee's activities. The universe of activities by CFP Board designees is indeed diverse and a particular CFP Board designee may be performing all, some or none of the typical services provided by financial planning professionals. As a result, in considering the Rules in Part II, a CFP Board designee must first recognize what specific services he or she is rendering and then determine whether or not a specific Rule is applicable to those services. To assist the CFP Board designee in making these determinations, this *Code of Ethics* includes a series of definitions of terminology used throughout the *Code of Ethics*. Based upon these definitions, a CFP Board designee should be able to determine which services he or she provides and, therefore, which Rules are applicable to those services.

Rules that Relate to the Principle of Integrity

Rule 101

A CFP Board designee shall not solicit clients through false or misleading communications or advertisements:

a.   Misleading Advertising: A CFP Board designee shall not make a false or misleading communication about the size, scope or areas of competence of the CFP Board designee's practice or of any organization with which the CFP Board designee is associated; and

b.   Promotional Activities: In promotional activities, a CFP Board designee shall not make materially false or misleading communications to the public or create unjustified expectations regarding matters relating to financial planning or the professional activities and competence of the CFP Board designee. The term "promotional activities" includes, but is not limited to, speeches, interviews, books and/or printed publications, seminars, radio and television shows, and video cassettes; and

c.   Representation of Authority: A CFP Board designee shall not give the impression that a CFP Board designee is representing the views of the CFP Board or any other group unless the CFP Board designee has been authorized to do so. Personal opinions shall be clearly identified as such.

Rule 102

In the course of professional activities, a CFP Board designee shall not engage in conduct involving dishonesty, fraud, deceit or misrepresentation, or knowingly make a false or misleading statement to a client, employer, employee, professional colleague, governmental or other regulatory body or official, or any other person or entity.

Rule 103

A CFP Board designee has the following responsibilities regarding funds and/or other property of clients:

a.   In exercising custody of or discretionary authority over client funds or other property, a CFP Board designee shall act only in accordance with the authority set forth in the governing legal instrument (e.g., special power of attorney, trust, letters testamentary, etc.); and

b.   A CFP Board designee shall identify and keep complete records of all funds or other property of a client in the custody of or under the discretionary authority of the CFP Board designee; and

c.   Upon receiving funds or other property of a client, a CFP Board designee shall promptly or as otherwise permitted by law or provided by agreement with the client, deliver to the client or third party any funds or other property which the client or third party is entitled to receive and, upon request by the client, render a full accounting regarding such funds or other property; and

d. A CFP Board designee shall not commingle client funds or other property with a CFP Board designee's personal funds and/or other property or the funds and/or other property of a CFP Board designee's firm. Commingling one or more clients' funds or other property together is permitted, subject to compliance with applicable legal requirements and provided accurate records are maintained for each client's funds or other property; and

e. A CFP Board designee who takes custody of all or any part of a client's assets for investment purposes shall do so with the care required of a fiduciary.

Rules that Relate to the Principle of Objectivity

Rule 201

A CFP Board designee shall exercise reasonable and prudent professional judgment in providing professional services.

Rule 202

A financial planning practitioner shall act in the interest of the client.

Rules that Relate to the Principle of Competence

Rule 301

A CFP Board designee shall keep informed of developments in the field of financial planning and participate in continuing education throughout the CFP Board designee's professional career in order to improve professional competence in all areas in which the CFP Board designee is engaged. As a distinct part of this requirement, a CFP Board designee shall satisfy all minimum continuing education requirements established for CFP Board designees by the CFP Board. [**Note from the authors**: To gain more information on the continuing education requirements, visit the CFP Board Website at **www.CFP-Board.org** and select CFP Certificants, then Continuing Education Requirements.]

Rule 302

A CFP Board designee shall offer advice only in those areas in which the CFP Board designee has competence. In areas where the CFP Board designee is not professionally competent, the CFP Board designee shall seek the counsel of qualified individuals and/or refer clients to such parties.

Rules that Relate to the Principle of Fairness

Rule 401

In rendering professional services, a CFP Board designee shall disclose to the client:

a. Material information relevant to the professional relationship, including but not limited to conflict(s) of interest, the CFP Board designee's business affiliation, address, telephone number, credentials, qualifications, licenses, compensation structure and any agency relationships, and the scope of the CFP Board designee's authority in that capacity, and

b. The information required by all laws applicable to the relationship in a manner complying with such laws.

Rule 402

A CFP Board designee in a financial planning engagement shall make timely written disclosure of all material information relative to the professional relationship. In all circumstances and prior to the engagement, a CFP Board designee shall, in writing:

a. Disclose conflict(s) of interest and sources of compensation;

b. Inform the client or prospective client of his/her right to ask at any time for information about the compensation of the CFP Board designee.

As a guideline, a CFP Board designee who provides a client or prospective client with the following written disclosures, using Form ADV, a CFP Board Disclosure Form or an equivalent document, will be considered to be in compliance with this Rule:

- The basic philosophy of the CFP Board designee (or firm) in working with clients. This includes the philosophy, theory and/or principles of financial planning which will be utilized by the CFP Board designee; and

- Resumes of principals and employees of a firm who are expected to provide financial planning services to the client and a description of those services. Such disclosures shall include educational background, professional/employment history, professional designations and licenses held; and

- A statement that in reasonable detail discloses (as applicable) conflict(s) of interest and source(s) of, and any contingencies or other aspects material to, the CFP Board designee's compensation; and

- A statement describing material agency or employment relationships a CFP Board designee (or firm) has with third parties and the nature of compensation resulting from such relationships; and

- A statement informing the client or prospective client of his/her right to ask at any time for information about the compensation of the CFP Board designee.

Rule 403

Upon request by a client or prospective client, the CFP Board designee in a financial planning engagement shall communicate in reasonable detail the requested compensation information related to the financial planning engagement, including compensation derived from implementation. The disclosure may express compensation as an approximate dollar amount or percentage or as a range of dollar amounts or percentages. The disclosure shall be made at a time and to the extent that the requested compensation information can be reasonably ascertained. Any estimates shall be clearly identified as such and based on reasonable assumptions. If a CFP Board designee becomes aware that a compensation disclosure provided pursuant to this rule has become significantly inaccurate, he/she shall provide the client with corrected information in a timely manner.

Rule 404

The disclosures required of a CFP Board designee in a financial planning engagement described under Rule 402 shall be offered at least annually for current clients, and provided if requested.

Rule 405

A CFP Board designee's compensation shall be fair and reasonable.

Rule 406

A CFP Board designee who is an employee shall perform professional services with dedication to the lawful objectives of the employer and in accordance with this *Code of Ethics*.

Rule 407

A CFP Board designee shall:

a. Advise the CFP Board designee's employer of outside affiliations which reasonably may compromise service to an employer;

b. Provide timely notice to his or her employer and clients about change of CFP® certification status; and

c. Provide timely notice to clients, unless precluded by contractual obligations, about change of employment.

Rule 408

A CFP Board designee shall inform his/her employer, partners or co-owners of compensation or other benefit arrangements in connection with his or her services to clients, which are in addition to compensation from the employer, partners or co-owners for such services.

Rule 409

If a CFP Board designee enters into a personal business transaction with a client, separate from regular professional services provided to that client, the transaction shall be on terms which are fair and reasonable to the client and the CFP Board designee shall disclose, in writing, the risks of the transaction, conflicts(s) of interest of the CFP Board designee, and other relevant information, if any, necessary to make the transaction fair to the client.

Rules that Relate to the Principle of Confidentiality

Rule 501

A CFP Board designee shall not reveal—or use for his or her own benefit—without the client's consent, any personally identifiable information relating to the client relationship or the affairs of the client, except and to the extent disclosure or use is reasonably necessary:

a. To establish an advisory or brokerage account, to effect a transaction for the client, or as otherwise impliedly authorized in order to carry out the client engagement; or

b. To comply with legal requirements or legal process; or

c. To defend the CFP Board designee against charges of wrongdoing; or

d. In connection with a civil dispute between the CFP Board designee and the client.

For purposes of this rule, the proscribed use of client information is improper whether or not it actually causes harm to the client.

Rule 502

A CFP Board designee shall maintain the same standards of confidentiality to employers as to clients.

Rule 503

A CFP Board designee doing business as a partner or principal of a financial services firm owes to the CFP Board designee's partners or co-owners a responsibility to act in good faith. This includes, but is not limited to, adherence to reasonable expectations of confidentiality both while in business together and thereafter.

Rules that Relate to the Principle of Professionalism

Rule 601

A CFP Board designee shall use the marks in compliance with the rules and regulations of the CFP Board, as established and amended from time to time. [**Note from the authors:** To gain more information on the correct use of the CFP marks, see the CFP Board Website at **www.CFP-Board.org** and read the *Guide to Use of the CFP Certification Marks*.]

Rule 602

A CFP Board designee shall show respect for other financial planning professionals, and related occupational groups, by engaging in fair and honorable competitive practices. Collegiality among CFP Board designees shall not, however, impede enforcement of this *Code of Ethics*.

Rule 603

A CFP Board designee who has knowledge, which is not required to be kept confidential under this *Code of Ethics*, that another CFP Board designee has committed a violation of this *Code of Ethics* which raises substantial questions as to the designee's honesty, trustworthiness or fitness as a CFP Board designee in other respects, shall promptly inform CFP Board. This rule does not require disclosure of information or reporting based on knowledge gained as a consultant or expert witness in anticipation of or related to litigation or other dispute resolution mechanisms. For purposes of this rule, knowledge means no substantial doubt.

Rule 604

A CFP Board designee who has knowledge, which is not required under this *Code of Ethics* to be kept confidential, and which raises a substantial question of unprofessional, fraudulent or illegal conduct by a CFP Board designee or other financial professional, shall promptly inform the appropriate regulatory and/or professional disciplinary body. This rule does not require disclosure or reporting of information gained as a consultant or expert witness in anticipation of or related to litigation or other dispute resolution mechanisms. For purposes of this Rule, knowledge means no substantial doubt.

Rule 605

A CFP Board designee who has reason to suspect illegal conduct within the CFP Board designee's organization shall make timely disclosure of the available evidence to the CFP Board designee's immediate supervisor and/or partners or co-owners. If the CFP Board designee is convinced that illegal conduct exists within the CFP Board designee's organization, and that appropriate measures are not taken to remedy the situation, the CFP Board designee shall, where appropriate, alert the appropriate regulatory authorities including CFP Board in a timely manner.

Rule 606

In all professional activities a CFP Board designee shall perform services in accordance with:

a. Applicable laws, rules, and regulations of governmental agencies and other applicable authorities; and

b. Applicable rules, regulations, and other established policies of CFP Board.

Rule 607

A CFP Board designee shall not engage in any conduct which reflects adversely on his or her integrity or fitness as a CFP Board designee, upon the marks, or upon the profession.

Rule 608

The Investment Advisers Act of 1940 requires registration of investment advisers with the US Securities and Exchange Commission and similar state statutes may require registration with state securities agencies. CFP Board designees shall disclose to clients their firm's status as registered investment advisers. Under present standards of acceptable business conduct, it is proper to use registered investment adviser if the CFP Board designee is registered individually. If the CFP Board designee is registered through his or her firm, then the CFP Board designee is not a registered investment adviser but a person associated with an investment adviser. The firm is the registered investment adviser. Moreover, RIA or R.I.A. following a CFP Board designee's name in advertising, letterhead stationery, and business cards may be misleading and is not permitted either by this *Code of Ethics* or by SEC regulations.

Rule 609

A CFP Board designee shall not practice any other profession or offer to provide such services unless the CFP Board designee is qualified to practice in those fields and is licensed as required by state law.

Rule 610

A CFP Board designee shall return the client's original records in a timely manner after their return has been requested by a client.

Rule 611

A CFP Board designee shall not bring or threaten to bring a disciplinary proceeding under this *Code of Ethics*, or report or threaten to report information to CFP Board pursuant to Rules 603 and/or 604, or make or threaten to make use of this *Code of Ethics* for no substantial purpose other than to harass, maliciously injure, embarrass and/or unfairly burden another CFP Board designee.

Rule 612

A CFP Board designee shall comply with all applicable renewal requirements established by CFP Board including, but not limited to, payment of the biennial CFP Board designee fee as well as signing and returning the Terms and Conditions of Certification in connection with the certification renewal process.

Rules that Relate to the Principle of Diligence

Rule 701

A CFP Board designee shall provide services diligently.

Rule 702

A financial planning practitioner shall enter into an engagement only after securing sufficient information to satisfy the CFP Board designee that:

a. The relationship is warranted by the individual's needs and objectives; and

b. The CFP Board designee has the ability to either provide requisite competent services or to involve other professionals who can provide such services.

Rule 703

A financial planning practitioner shall make and/or implement only recommendations which are suitable for the client.

Rule 704

Consistent with the nature and scope of the engagement, a CFP Board designee shall make a reasonable investigation regarding the financial products recommended to clients. Such an investigation may be made by the CFP Board designee or by others provided the CFP Board designee acts reasonably in relying upon such investigation.

Rule 705

A CFP Board designee shall properly supervise subordinates with regard to their delivery of financial planning services, and shall not accept or condone conduct in violation of this *Code of Ethics*.

CFP BOARD'S *FINANCIAL PLANNING PRACTICE STANDARDS*

Statement of Purpose for *Financial Planning Practice Standards*

Financial Planning Practice Standards (*Practice Standards*) are developed and promulgated by Certified Financial Planner Board of Standards Inc. (CFP Board), for the ultimate benefit of consumers of financial planning services. These *Practice Standards* are intended to: (1) assure that the practice of financial planning by CERTIFIED FINANCIAL PLANNER™ professionals is based on established norms of practice; (2) advance professionalism in financial planning; and (3) enhance the value of the personal financial planning process.

Description of *Practice Standards*

A *Practice Standard* establishes the level of professional practice that is expected of CFP Board designees engaged in personal financial planning.

Practice Standards apply to CFP Board designees in performing the tasks of financial planning regardless of the person's title, job position, type of employment or method of compensation. Compliance with the *Practice Standards* is mandatory for CFP Board designees, but all financial planning professionals are encouraged to use the *Practice Standards* when performing financial planning tasks or activities addressed by a *Practice Standard*.

Conduct inconsistent with a *Practice Standard* in and of itself is neither intended to give rise to a cause of action nor to create any presumption that a legal duty has been breached. The *Practice Standards* are designed to provide CFP Board designees a framework the professional practice of financial planning. They are not designed to be a basis for legal liability.

Practice Standards are not intended to prescribe the services to be provided or step-by-step procedures for providing any particular service. Such procedures may be provided in practice aids developed by various financial planning organizations and other sources.

Practice Standard 100-1

Establishing and Defining the Relationship with the Client

Defining the Scope of the Engagement

The financial planning practitioner and the client shall mutually define the scope of the engagement before any financial planning service is provided.

Explanation of this *Practice Standard*

Prior to providing any financial planning service, a financial planning practitioner and the client shall mutually define the scope of the engagement. The process of "mutually-defining" is essential in determining what activities may be necessary to proceed with the client engagement.

This process is accomplished in financial planning engagements by:

- Identifying the service(s) to be provided;
- Disclosing the practitioner's material conflict(s) of interest;

- Disclosing the practitioner's compensation arrangement(s);
- Determining the client's and the practitioner's responsibilities;
- Establishing the duration of the engagement; and
- Providing any additional information necessary to define or limit the scope.

The scope of the engagement may include one or more financial planning subject areas. It is acceptable to mutually define engagements in which the scope is limited to specific activities. Mutually defining the scope of the engagement serves to establish realistic expectations for both the client and the practitioner. This *Practice Standard* does not require the scope of the engagement to be in writing. However, as noted in the "Relationship" section which follows, there may be certain disclosures that might be required to be in writing. As the relationship proceeds, the scope may change by mutual agreement. This *Practice Standard* shall not be considered alone, but in conjunction with all other *Practice Standards*.

Effective Date

Original version effective January 1, 1999. Updated version effective January 1, 2002.

Relationship of this *Practice Standard* to CFP Board's *Code of Ethics and Professional Responsibility*

This *Practice Standard* relates to CFP Board's *Code of Ethics and Professional Responsibility* (*Code of Ethics*) through the *Code of Ethics'* Principle 4—Fairness and Rule 402, and Principle 7—Diligence and Rule 702.

Principle 4 states "a CFP Board designee shall perform professional services in a manner that is fair and reasonable to clients ...." Although, as stated earlier, there is no requirement that the scope of the engagement be in writing, Rule 402 in the *Code of Ethics* requires a financial planning practitioner to make "timely written disclosure of all material information relative to the professional relationship. In all circumstances and prior to the engagement, a CFP Board designee shall, in writing: (a) Disclose conflict(s) of interest and sources of compensation; and (b) inform the client or prospective client of his/her right to ask at any time for information about the compensation of the CFP Board designee."

Principle 7 states "a CFP Board designee shall act diligently in providing professional services." Rule 702 requires that financial planning practitioners enter into an engagement only after obtaining sufficient information to satisfy that "the relationship is warranted by the individual's needs and objectives; and the CFP Board designee has the ability to either provide requisite competent services or to involve other professionals who can provide such services."

Practice Standard 200-1

Gathering Client Data

Determining a Client's Personal and Financial Goals, Needs and Priorities

The financial planning practitioner and the client shall mutually define the client's personal and financial goals, needs and priorities that are relevant to the scope of the engagement before any recommendation is made and/or implemented.

Explanation of this *Practice Standard*

Prior to making recommendations to a client, a financial planning practitioner (practitioner) and the client shall mutually define the client's personal and financial goals, needs and priorities. In order to arrive at such a definition, the practitioner will need to explore the client's values, attitudes, expectations and time horizons as they affect the client's goals, needs and priorities. The process of "mutually-defining" is essential in determining what activities may be necessary to proceed with the client engagement. Personal values and attitudes shape a client's goals and objectives and the priority placed on them. Accordingly, these goals and objectives must be consistent with the client's values and attitudes in order for the client to make the commitment necessary to accomplish them.

Goals and objectives provide focus, purpose, vision and direction for the financial planning process. It is important to determine clear and measurable objectives that are relevant to the scope of the engagement. The role of the practitioner is to facilitate the goal-setting process in order to clarify, with the client, goals and objectives, and, when appropriate, the practitioner must try to assist clients in recognizing the implications of unrealistic goals and objectives.

This *Practice Standard* addresses only the tasks of determining a client's personal and financial goals, needs and priorities; assessing a client's values, attitudes and expectations; and determining a client's time horizons. These areas are subjective and the practitioner's interpretation is limited by what the client reveals. This *Practice Standard* shall not be considered alone, but in conjunction with all other *Practice Standards*.

Effective Date

Original version effective January 1, 1999. Updated version effective January 1, 2002.

Relationship of this *Practice Standard* to the CFP Board's *Code of Ethics and Professional Responsibility*

This *Practice Standard* relates to the CFP Board's *Code of Ethics and Professional Responsibility* (*Code of Ethics*) through the *Code of Ethics'* Principle 7—Diligence, and Rules 701 through 703. Rule 701 states "a CFP Board designee shall provide services diligently." Rule 702 requires a financial planning practitioner to "enter into an engagement only after securing sufficient information to satisfy the CFP Board designee that ... the relationship is warranted by the individual's needs and objectives...." In addition, Rule 703 requires a financial planning practitioner to "make and/or implement only recommendations which are suitable for the client."

Practice Standard 200-2

Gathering Client Data

Information and Documents

Obtaining Quantitative Information and Documents

A financial planning practitioner shall obtain sufficient quantitative information and documents about a client relevant to the scope of the engagement before any recommendation is made and/or implemented.

Explanation of this *Practice Standard*

Prior to making recommendations to a client and depending upon the scope of the engagement, a financial planning practitioner (practitioner) shall determine what quantitative information and documents are sufficient and relevant.

A practitioner shall obtain sufficient and relevant quantitative information and documents pertaining to the client's financial resources, obligations and personal situation. This information may be obtained directly from the client or other sources such as interview(s), questionnaire(s), client records and documents.

A practitioner shall communicate to the client a reliance on the completeness and accuracy of the information provided and that incomplete or inaccurate information will impact conclusions and recommendations.

If a practitioner is unable to obtain sufficient and relevant quantitative information and documents to form a basis for recommendations, the practitioner shall either:

a. Restrict the scope of the engagement to those matters for which sufficient and relevant information is available; or

b. Terminate the engagement.

A practitioner shall communicate to the client any limitations on the scope of the engagement, as well as the fact that this limitation could affect the conclusions and recommendations. This *Practice Standard* shall not be considered alone, but in conjunction with all other *Practice Standards*.

Effective Date

Original version effective January 1, 1999. Updated version effective January 1, 2002.

Relationship of this *Practice Standard* to the CFP Board's *Code of Ethics and Professional Responsibility*

This *Practice Standard* relates to the CFP Board's *Code of Ethics and Professional Responsibility* (*Code of Ethics*) through the *Code of Ethics*' Principle 7—Diligence and Rules 701 through 703. Rule 701 states "a CFP Board designee shall provide services diligently." Rule 702 requires a financial planning practitioner to "enter into an engagement only after securing sufficient information to satisfy the CFP Board designee that.... the relationship is warranted by the individual's needs and objectives...." In addition, Rule 703 requires a financial planning practitioner to "make and/or implement only recommendations which are suitable for the client."

Practice Standard 300-1

Analyzing and Evaluating the Client's Financial Status

Analyzing and Evaluating the Client's Information

A financial planning practitioner shall analyze the information to gain an understanding of the client's financial situation and then evaluate to what extent the client's goals, needs and priorities can be met by the client's resources and current course of action.

Explanation of this *Practice Standard*

Prior to making recommendations to a client, it is necessary for the financial planning practitioner to assess the client's financial situation and to determine the likelihood of reaching the stated objectives by continuing present activities.

The practitioner will utilize client-specified, mutually agreed upon, and/or other reasonable assumptions. Both personal and economic assumptions must be considered in this step of the process. These assumptions may include, but are not limited to, the following:

• Personal assumptions, such as: retirement age(s), life expectancy(ies), income needs, risk factors, time horizon and special needs; and

• Economic assumptions, such as: inflation rates, tax rates and investment returns.

Analysis and evaluation are critical to the financial planning process. These activities form the foundation for determining strengths and weaknesses of the client's financial situation and current course of action. These activities may also identify other issues that should be addressed. As a result, it may be appropriate to amend the scope of the engagement and/or to obtain additional information.

Effective Date

Original version effective January 1, 2000. Updated version effective January 1, 2002.

Relationship of this *Practice Standard* to the CFP Board's *Code of Ethics and Professional Responsibility*

This *Practice Standard* relates to the CFP Board's *Code of Ethics and Professional Responsibility* (*Code of Ethics*) through the *Code of Ethics'* Principle 2—Objectivity and Rules 201 and 202; Principle 3—Competence and Rule 302, and Principle 7—Diligence and Rule 701. Principle 2 states "A CFP Board designee shall be objective in providing professional services to clients." Rule 201 states "A CFP Board designee shall exercise reasonable and prudent professional judgment in providing professional services." And Rule 202 states "A financial planning practitioner shall act in the interest of the client."

Principle 3 states "A CFP Board designee shall provide services to clients competently and maintain the necessary knowledge and skill to continue to do so in those areas in which the designee is engaged." Rule 302 states "A CFP Board designee shall offer advice only in those areas in which the CFP Board designee has competence. In areas where the CFP Board designee is not professionally competent, the CFP Board designee shall seek the counsel of qualified individuals and/or refer clients to such parties."

Under Principle 7, Rule 701 states "A CFP Board designee shall provide services diligently."

Practice Standard 400-1

Developing and Presenting the Financial Planning Recommendation(s)

Identifying and Evaluating Financial Planning Alternative(s)

A financial planning practitioner shall consider sufficient and relevant alternatives to the client's current course of action in an effort to reasonably meet the client's goals, needs and priorities.

Explanation of this *Practice Standard*

After analyzing the client's current situation (*Practice Standard* 300-1) and prior to developing and presenting the recommendation(s) (*Practice Standards* 400-2 and 400-3), the financial planning practitioner shall identify alternative actions. The practitioner shall evaluate the effectiveness of such actions in reasonably achieving the client's goals, needs and priorities.

This evaluation may involve, but is not limited to, considering multiple assumptions, conducting research or consulting with other professionals. This process may result in a single alternative, multiple alternatives or no alternative to the client's current course of action.

In considering alternative actions, the practitioner shall recognize and, as appropriate, take into account his or her legal and/or regulatory limitations and level of competency in properly addressing each of the client's financial planning issues.

More than one alternative may reasonably meet the client's goals, needs and priorities. Alternatives identified by the practitioner may differ from those of other practitioners or advisers, illustrating the subjective nature of exercising professional judgment.

This *Practice Standard* shall not be considered alone, but in conjunction with all other *Practice Standards*.

Effective Date

Original version effective January 1, 2001. Updated version effective January 1, 2002.

Relationship of this *Practice Standard* to the CFP Board's *Code of Ethics and Professional Responsibility*

This *Practice Standard* relates to the CFP Board's *Code of Ethics and Professional Responsibility* (*Code of Ethics*) through the *Code of Ethics'* Principle 2—Objectivity and Rules 201 and 202; Principle 3—Competence and Rule 302; Principle 6—Professionalism and Rule 609, and Principle 7—Diligence and Rules 701 and 703.

Principle 2 states "A CFP Board designee shall be objective in providing professional services to clients." Rule 201 states "A CFP Board designee shall exercise reasonable and prudent professional judgment in providing professional services." Rule 202 states "A financial planning practitioner shall act in the interest of the client."

Principle 3 states "A CFP Board designee shall provide services to clients competently and maintain the necessary knowledge and skill to continue to do so in those areas in which the designee is engaged." Rule 302 states "A CFP Board designee shall offer advice only in those areas in which the CFP Board designee has competence. In areas where the CFP Board designee is not professionally competent, the CFP Board designee shall seek the counsel of qualified individuals and/or refer clients to such parties."

Principle 6 states "A CFP Board designee's conduct in all matters shall reflect credit upon the profession." Rule 609 states "A CFP Board designee shall not practice any other profession or offer to provide such services unless the CFP Board designee is qualified ... and is licensed as required by state law."

Principle 7 states "A CFP Board designee shall act diligently in providing professional services." Rule 701 states "A CFP Board designee shall provide services diligently." Rule 703 states "A financial planning practitioner shall make and/or implement only recommendations which are suitable for the client."

Practice Standard 400-2

Developing and Presenting the Financial Planning Recommendation(s)

Developing the Financial Planning Recommendation(s)

A financial planning practitioner shall develop the recommendation(s) based on the selected alternative(s) and the current course of action in an effort to reasonably achieve the client's goals, needs and priorities.

Explanation of this *Practice Standard*

After identifying and evaluating the alternative(s) and the client's current course of action, the practitioner shall develop the recommendation(s) expected to reasonably achieve the client's goals, needs and priorities. A recommendation may be an independent action or a combination of actions which may need to be implemented collectively. The recommendation(s) shall be consistent with and will be directly affected by the following:

- Mutually defined scope of the engagement;
- Mutually defined client goals, needs and priorities;
- Quantitative data provided by the client;
- Personal and economic assumptions;

- Practitioner's analysis and evaluation of client's current situation; and
- Alternative(s) selected by the practitioner.

A recommendation may be to continue the current course of action. If a change is recommended, it may be specific and/or detailed or provide a general direction. In some instances, it may be necessary for the practitioner to recommend that the client modify a goal.

The recommendations developed by the practitioner may differ from those of other practitioners or advisers yet each may reasonably achieve the client's goals, needs and priorities.

This *Practice Standard* shall not be considered alone, but in conjunction with all other *Practice Standards*.

Effective Date

Original version effective January 1, 2001. Updated version effective January 1, 2002.

Relationship of this *Practice Standard* to the CFP Board's *Code of Ethics and Professional Responsibility*

This *Practice Standard* relates to the CFP Board's *Code of Ethics and Professional Responsibility* (*Code of Ethics*) through the *Code of Ethics'* Principle 2—Objectivity and Rules 201 and 202; Principle 3—Competence and Rule 302; Principle 6—Professionalism and Rule 609; and Principle 7—Diligence and Rules 701, 703 and 704.

Principle 2 states "A CFP Board designee shall be objective in providing professional services to clients." Rule 201 states "A CFP Board designee shall exercise reasonable and prudent professional judgment in providing professional services." Rule 202 states "A financial planning practitioner shall act in the interest of the client."

Principle 3 states "A CFP Board designee shall provide services to clients competently and maintain the necessary knowledge and skill to continue to do so in those areas in which the designee is engaged." Rule 302 states "A CFP Board designee shall offer advice only in those areas in which the CFP Board designee has competence. In areas where the CFP Board designee is not professionally competent, the CFP Board designee shall seek the counsel of qualified individuals and/or refer clients to such parties."

Principle 6 states "A CFP Board designee's conduct in all matters shall reflect credit upon the profession." Rule 609 states "A CFP Board designee shall not practice any other profession or offer to provide such services unless the CFP Board designee is qualified ... and is licensed as required by state law."

Principle 7 states "A CFP Board designee shall act diligently in providing professional services." Rule 701 states "A CFP Board designee shall provide services diligently." Rule 703 states "A financial planning practitioner shall make and/or implement only recommendations which are suitable for the client." Rule 704 states "... a CFP Board designee shall make a reasonable investigation regarding the financial products recommended to clients. Such an investigation may be made by the CFP Board designee or by others provided the CFP Board designee acts reasonably in relying upon such investigation."

Practice Standard 400-3

Developing and Presenting the Financial Planning Recommendation(s)

Presenting the Financial Planning Recommendation(s)

A financial planning practitioner shall communicate the recommendation(s) in a manner and to an extent reasonably necessary to assist the client in making an informed decision.

Explanation of this *Practice Standard*

When presenting a recommendation, the practitioner shall make a reasonable effort to assist the client in understanding the client's current situation, the recommendation itself, and its impact on the ability to achieve the client's goals, needs and priorities. In doing so, the practitioner shall avoid presenting the practitioner's opinion as fact.

The practitioner shall communicate the factors critical to the client's understanding of the recommendations. These factors may include but are not limited to material:

- Personal and economic assumptions;
- Interdependence of recommendations;
- Advantages and disadvantages;
- Risks; and/or
- Time sensitivity.

The practitioner should indicate that even though the recommendations may achieve the client's goals, needs and priorities, changes in personal and economic conditions could alter the intended outcome. Changes may include, but are not limited to: legislative, family status, career, investment performance and/or health.

If there are conflicts of interest that have not been previously disclosed, such conflicts and how they may impact the recommendations should be addressed at this time.

Presenting recommendations provides the practitioner an opportunity to further assess whether the recommendations meet client expectations, whether the client is willing to act on the recommendations, and whether modifications are necessary.

This *Practice Standard* shall not be considered alone, but in conjunction with all other *Practice Standards.*

Effective Date

Original version effective January 1, 2001. Updated version effective January 1, 2002.

Relationship of this *Practice Standard* to the CFP Board's *Code of Ethics and Professional Responsibility*

This *Practice Standard* relates to the CFP Board's *Code of Ethics and Professional Responsibility* (*Code of Ethics*) through the *Code of Ethics'* Principle 1—Integrity and Rule 102; Principle 2—Objectivity and Rule 201; and Principle 6—Professionalism and Rule 607.

Principle 1 states "A CFP Board designee shall offer and provide professional services with integrity." Rule 102 states "... a CFP Board designee shall not ... knowingly make a false or misleading statement to a client ...."

Principle 2 states "A CFP Board designee shall be objective in providing professional services to clients." Rule 201 states "A CFP Board designee shall exercise reasonable and prudent professional judgment in providing professional services."

Principle 6 states "A CFP Board designee's conduct in all matters shall reflect credit upon the profession." Rule 607 states "A CFP Board designee shall not engage in any conduct which reflects adversely on his or her integrity or fitness as a CFP Board designee ...."

Practice Standard 500-1

Implementing the Financial Planning Recommendation(s).

Agreeing on Implementation Responsibilities

A financial planning practitioner and the client shall mutually agree on the implementation responsibilities consistent with the scope of the engagement.

Explanation of this *Practice Standard*

The client is responsible for accepting or rejecting recommendations and for retaining and/or delegating implementation responsibilities. The financial planning practitioner and the client shall mutually agree on the services, if any, to be provided by the practitioner. The scope of the engagement, as originally defined, may need to be modified. The practitioner's responsibilities may include, but are not limited to, the following:

- Identifying activities necessary for implementation;
- Determining division of activities between the practitioner and the client;
- Referring to other professionals;
- Coordinating with other professionals;
- Sharing of information as authorized; and
- Selecting and securing products and/or services.

If there are conflicts of interest, sources of compensation or material relationships with other professionals or advisers that have not been previously disclosed, such conflicts, sources or relationships shall be disclosed at this time.

When referring the client to other professionals or advisers, the financial planning practitioner shall indicate the basis on which the practitioner believes the other professional or adviser may be qualified.

If the practitioner is engaged by the client to provide only implementation activities, the scope of the engagement shall be mutually defined, orally or in writing, in accordance with *Practice Standard* 100-1. This scope may include such matters as the extent to which the practitioner will rely on information, analysis or recommendations provided by others.

This *Practice Standard* shall not be considered alone, but in conjunction with all other *Practice Standards*.

Effective Date

January 1, 2002.

Relationship of this *Practice Standard* to the CFP Board's *Code of Ethics and Professional Responsibility*

This *Practice Standard* relates to the CFP Board's *Code of Ethics and Professional Responsibility* (*Code of Ethics*) through the *Code of Ethics*' Principle 3—Competence and Rule 302; Principle 4—

Fairness and Rule 402; Principle 6—Professionalism and Rules 606 and 609; and Principle 7—Diligence and Rule 701.

Principle 3 states "A CFP Board designee shall provide services to clients competently and maintain the necessary knowledge and skill to continue to do so in those areas in which the designee is engaged." Rule 302 states "A CFP Board designee shall offer advice only in those areas in which the CFP Board designee has competence. In areas where the CFP Board designee is not professionally competent, the CFP Board designee shall seek the counsel of qualified individuals and/or refer clients to such parties."

Principle 4 states "A CFP Board designee shall perform professional services in a manner that is fair and reasonable to clients … and shall disclose conflict(s) of interest in providing such services." Rule 402 states "A CFP Board designee in a financial planning engagement shall make timely written disclosure of all material information relative to the professional relationship. In all circumstances and prior to the engagement, a CFP Board designee shall, in writing: (a) Disclose conflicts(s) of interest and sources of compensation; and (b) Inform the client or prospective client of his/her right to ask at any time for information about the compensation of the CFP Board designee."

Principle 6 states "A CFP Board designee's conduct in all matters shall reflect credit upon the profession." Rule 606 states "… A CFP Board designee shall perform services in accordance with: (a) Applicable laws, rules, and regulations of governmental agencies and other applicable authorities …." Rule 609 states "A CFP Board designee shall not practice any other profession or offer to provide such services unless the CFP Board designee is qualified … and is licensed as required by state law."

Under Principle 7, Rule 701 states "A CFP Board designee shall provide services diligently."

Practice Standard 500-2

Implementing the Financial Planning Recommendation(s)

Selecting Products and Services for Implementation

A financial planning practitioner shall select appropriate products and services that are consistent with the client's goals, needs and priorities.

Explanation of this *Practice Standard*

The financial planning practitioner shall investigate products or services that reasonably address the client's needs. The products or services selected to implement the recommendation(s) must be suitable to the client's financial situation and consistent with the client's goals, needs and priorities.

The financial planning practitioner uses professional judgment in selecting the products and services that are in the client's interest. Professional judgment incorporates both qualitative and quantitative information.

Products and services selected by the practitioner may differ from those selected by other practitioners or advisers. More than one product or service may exist that can reasonably meet the client's goals, needs and priorities.

The practitioner shall make all disclosures required by applicable regulations.

This *Practice Standard* shall not be considered alone, but in conjunction with all other *Practice Standards*.

Effective Date

January 1, 2002.

Relationship of this *Practice Standard* to the CFP Board's *Code of Ethics and Professional Responsibility*

This *Practice Standard* relates to the CFP Board's *Code of Ethics and Professional Responsibility* (*Code of Ethics*) through the *Code of Ethics'* Principle 2—Objectivity and Rule 202; Principle 4—Fairness and Rules 402 and 409; Principle 6—Professionalism and Rule 606; and Principle 7—Diligence and Rules 701, 703 and 704.

Principle 2 states "A CFP Board designee shall be objective in providing professional services to clients." Rule 202 states "A financial planning practitioner shall act in the interest of the client."

Principle 4 states "A CFP Board designee shall perform professional services in a manner that is fair and reasonable to clients ... and shall disclose conflict(s) of interest in providing such services." Rule 402 states "A CFP Board designee in a financial planning engagement shall make timely written disclosure of all material information relative to the professional relationship. In all circumstances and prior to the engagement, a CFP Board designee shall, in writing: (a) Disclose conflicts(s) of interest and sources of compensation; and (b) Inform the client or prospective client of his/her right to ask at any time for information about the compensation of the CFP Board designee." Rule 409 states "If a CFP Board designee enters into a personal business transaction with a client, separate from regular professional services provided to that client ... the CFP Board designee shall disclose, in writing, the risks of the transaction, conflict(s) of interest of the CFP Board designee, and other relevant information ... necessary to make the transaction fair to the client."

Principle 6 states "A CFP Board designee's conduct in all matters shall reflect credit upon the profession." Rule 606 states "In all professional activities a CFP Board designee shall perform services in accordance with: (a) Applicable laws, rules, and regulations of governmental agencies and other applicable authorities; and (b) Applicable rules, regulations, and other established policies of the CFP Board."

Principle 7 states "A CFP Board designee shall act diligently in providing professional services." Rule 701 states "A CFP Board designee shall provide services diligently." Rule 703 states "A financial planning practitioner shall make and/or implement only recommendations which are suitable for the client." Rule 704 states "... A CFP Board designee shall make a reasonable investigation regarding the financial products recommended to clients."

Practice Standard 600-1

Monitoring

Defining Monitoring Responsibilities

The financial planning practitioner and client shall mutually define monitoring responsibilities.

Explanation of this *Practice Standard*

The purpose of this *Practice Standard* is to clarify the role, if any, of the practitioner in the monitoring process. By clarifying this responsibility, the client's expectations are more likely to be in alignment with the level of monitoring services which the practitioner intends to provide.

If engaged for monitoring services, the practitioner shall identify which monitoring activities may be appropriate. The practitioner shall make a reasonable effort to define and communicate which monitoring activities the practitioner is able and willing to provide. By explaining what is to be monitored, the frequency of monitoring and the communication method, the client is more likely to understand the monitoring service to be provided by the practitioner.

The monitoring process may reveal the need to reinitiate steps of the financial planning process. The current scope of the engagement may need to be modified.

Relationship of this *Practice Standard* to the CFP Board's *Code of Ethics and Professional Responsibility*

This *Practice Standard* relates to the CFP Board's *Code of Ethics and Professional Responsibility* through the *Code of Ethic's* Principle 7—Diligence and Rule 702.

Principle 7 states "A CFP designee shall act diligently in providing professional services." Rule 702 requires that financial planning practitioners enter into an engagement only after obtaining sufficient information to satisfy that "the relationship is warranted by the individual's goals and objectives; and the CFP designee has the ability to either provide requisite competent services or to involve other professionals who can provide such services."

CFP BOARD'S DISCIPLINARY RULES AND PROCEDURES

Article 1: Introduction

Certified Financial Planner Board of Standards Inc. (CFP Board) has adopted a Code of Ethics and Professional Responsibility (Code of Ethics) and Financial Planning Practice Standards (Practice Standards) which establish the expected level of professional conduct and practice for CFP Board designees. The Code of Ethics and Practice Standards may be amended from time to time, with revisions submitted to the public for comment before final adoption by CFP Board. To promote and maintain the integrity of its CFP®, CFP® and Certified Financial Planner™ certification marks for the benefit of the clients and potential clients of CFP Board designees, CFP Board has the ability to enforce the provisions of the Code of Ethics and Practice Standards . Adherence to the Code of Ethics by CFP Board designees or to Practice Standards by CFP® practitioners is required, with the potential for CFP Board sanctions against those who violate the regulations proscribed in these documents. CFP Board will follow the disciplinary rules and procedures set forth below when enforcing the Code of Ethics and Practice Standards.

Article 2: Board of Professional Review

2.1 Function and Jurisdiction of the Board of Professional Review

CFP Board's Board of Professional Review (referred to herein as the "Board"), formed pursuant to and governed by the bylaws of CFP Board, is charged with the duty of investigating, reviewing and taking appropriate action with respect to alleged violations of the *Code of Ethics* and alleged noncompliance with the *Practice Standards* as promulgated by CFP Board's Board of Governors and shall have original jurisdiction over all such disciplinary matters and procedures.

2.2 Powers and Duties of the Board

The Board shall be authorized and empowered to:

a. Enlist the assistance of CFP certificants to assist with investigations, or serve temporarily on a Hearing Panel;

b. Periodically report to CFP Board's Board of Governors on the operation of the Board;

    c.   Adopt amendments to these *Disciplinary Rules and Procedures*, subject to review and approval of CFP Board's Board of Governors; and

    d.   Adopt such other rules or procedures as may be necessary or appropriate to govern the internal operations of the Board.

2.3 Hearing Panel

The Hearing Panel may consist of members of the Board who have been designated Hearing Panel members, enlisted CFP certificants and up to one individual who is not a CFP certificant. A Panel shall consist of at least three persons. At least one member of every Hearing Panel shall be a member of the Board and at least two members of every Hearing Panel shall be CFP certificants. One member of each Hearing Panel shall serve as Chair of that hearing. The Chair shall rule on all motions, objections and other matters presented in the course of the hearing and must be a voting member of the Board of Professional Review.

2.4 Disqualification

Board members shall refrain from participating in any proceeding in which they, a member of their immediate family or a member of their firm have any interest or where such participation otherwise would involve a conflict of interest or the appearance of impropriety.

2.5 Staff Counsel

CFP Board Staff Counsel may be either full- or part-time employees of CFP Board or may be non-employees who are attorneys. It will be the duty of CFP Board and CFP Board Staff Counsel to maintain an office in the Denver metropolitan area (or such other location as approved by CFP Board's Board of Governors) to serve as a central office for the filing of requests for the investigation of CFP Board designee conduct, for the coordination of such investigations, for the administration of all disciplinary enforcement proceedings carried out pursuant to these *Procedures*, for the prosecution of charges of wrongdoing against CFP Board designees pursuant to these *Procedures* and for the performance of such other duties as are designated by the Board or the Chief Executive Officer of CFP Board. CFP Board Staff Counsel shall be under the day-to-day supervision of the Chief Executive Officer of CFP Board, but shall have ultimate responsibility to the Board.

Article 3: Grounds for Discipline

Misconduct by a CFP Board designee, individually or in concert with others, including the following acts or omissions, shall constitute grounds for discipline, whether or not the act or omission occurred in the course of a client relationship:

    a.   Any act or omission which violates the provisions of the *Code of Ethics*;

    b.   Any act or omission which fails to comply with the *Practice Standards*;

    c.   Any act or omission which violates the criminal laws of any State or of the United States or of any province, territory or jurisdiction of any other country, provided however, that conviction thereof in a criminal proceeding shall not be a prerequisite to the institution of disciplinary proceedings, and provided further, that acquittal in a criminal proceeding shall not bar a disciplinary action;

    d.   Any act which is the proper basis for professional suspension, as defined herein, provided professional suspension shall not be a prerequisite to the institution of disciplinary proceedings, and provided further, that dismissal of charges in a professional suspension proceeding shall not necessarily bar a disciplinary action;

    e.   Any act or omission which violates these *Procedures* or which violates an order of discipline;

f.   Failure to respond to a request by the Board, without good cause shown, or obstruction of the Board, or any panel or board thereof, or CFP Board staff in the performance of its or their duties. Good cause includes, without limitation, an assertion that a response would violate a CFP Board designee's constitutional privilege against self-incrimination;

g.   Any false or misleading statement made to CFP Board.

The enumeration of the foregoing acts and omissions constituting grounds for discipline is not exclusive and other acts or omissions amounting to unprofessional conduct may constitute grounds for discipline.

Article 4: Forms of Discipline

In cases where no grounds for discipline have been established, the Board may dismiss the matter as either without merit or with a cautionary letter. In all cases, the Board has the right to require CFP Board designees to complete additional continuing education or other remedial work. Such continuing education or remedial work may be ordered instead of, or in addition to, any discipline listed below. Where grounds for discipline have been established, any of the following forms of discipline may be imposed in these cases where grounds for discipline have been established.

4.1 Private Censure

The Board may order private censure of a CFP Board designee which shall be an unpublished written reproach mailed by the Board to a censured CFP Board designee.

4.2 Public Letter of Admonition

The Board may order that a Letter of Admonition be issued against a CFP Board designee, which shall be a publishable written reproach of the CFP Board designee's behavior. It shall be standard procedure to publish the Letter of Admonition in a press release or in such other form of publicity selected by the Board. In some cases when the Board determines that there are mitigating circumstances, it may decide to withhold public notification.

4.3 Suspension

The Board may order suspension for a specified period of time, not to exceed five (5) years, for those individuals it deems can be rehabilitated. In the event of a suspension, it shall be standard procedure to publish the fact of the suspension together with identification of the CFP Board designee in a press release, or in such other form of publicity as is selected by the Board. In some cases when the Board determines that there are extreme mitigating circumstances it may decide to withhold public notification. CFP Board designees receiving a suspension may qualify for reinstatement to use the marks as provided in Article 15.

4.4 Revocation

The Board may order permanent revocation of a CFP Board designee's right to use the marks. In the event of a permanent revocation it shall be standard procedure to publish the fact of the revocation together with identification of the CFP Board designee in a press release, or in such other form of publicity as is selected by the Board. In some cases when the Board determines that there are extreme mitigating circumstances it may decide to withhold public notification. Revocation shall be permanent.

4.5 Forms of Discipline Concerning Candidates

Under certain circumstances, the Board may take action in matters involving the conduct of candidates for CFP certification. Action that may be taken in these cases, where grounds have been established, correspond in character and degree to the four forms of discipline described in Articles 4.1 through 4.4 above, and are correspondingly as follows:

a. Subject to the candidate's meeting all other requirements of certification, if any, of the candidate with a private censure in the candidate's record in the form stated;

b. Subject to the candidate's meeting all other requirements of certification, if any, of the candidate with issuance of a Letter of Admonition, published as applicable, and in the candidate's record in the form stated;

c. Certification, if any, suspended for a specified period, not to exceed five (5) years;

d. Certification, if any, denied.

In the event of either a suspension or a denial of certification, the fact of such suspension or denial shall be publishable at the discretion of the Board. A candidate for the CFP certification who has been the subject of an order to suspend certification may seek to reapply for certification according to the same procedures in 15.2. Such candidates, in addition, shall meet the requirements of original certification.

Article 5: Interim Suspension Status

Interim suspension is the temporary suspension by the Board of a CFP Board designee's right to use the marks for a definite or indefinite period of time, while proceedings conducted pursuant to these *Procedures* are pending against the CFP Board designee. Imposition of an interim suspension shall not preclude the imposition of any other form of discipline entered by the Board in final resolution of the disciplinary proceeding.

5.1 Issuance of a Show Cause Order

Although a CFP Board designee's right to use the marks shall not ordinarily be suspended during the pendency of such proceedings, when it appears that a CFP Board designee has been convicted of a serious crime as defined in Article 12.5, or has been subject of a professional suspension as defined in Article 12.6, or has converted property or funds, has engaged in conduct which poses an immediate threat to the public, or has engaged in conduct the gravity of which impinges upon the stature and reputation of the marks, CFP Board Staff Counsel may issue an Order to Show Cause why the CFP Board designee's right to use the marks should not be suspended during the pendency of the proceedings.

5.2 Service

CFP Board shall serve the Order to Show Cause upon the CFP Board designee either by personal service or by certified mail, return receipt requested, mailed to the last known address of the CFP Board designee, as provided in article 17.2.

5.3 Response

All responses to Orders to Show Cause shall be in writing and shall be submitted within twenty (20) calendar days from the date of service of the Order to Show Cause upon the CFP Board designee. The CFP Board designee shall, in the response, either request or waive the right to participate in the Show Cause Hearing.

5.4 Failure to Respond to the Order to Show Cause

If the CFP Board designee fails to file a Response within the period provided in Article 5.3, that CFP Board designee shall be deemed to have waived the right to respond and the allegations set forth in the Order to Show Cause shall be deemed admitted and an interim suspension will automatically be issued.

5.5 Show Cause Hearing

Upon receiving the CFP Board designee's Response as provided in Article 5.3, a hearing shall be scheduled before no less than a quorum of the Board. If so requested, the CFP Board designee shall have the opportunity to participate at such hearing presenting arguments and evidence on his/her behalf. All evidence presented must be submitted to the CFP Board staff not less than twenty (20) days prior to the scheduled hearing. Any evidence not so submitted may only be admitted by motion at the hearing.

5.6 Interim Suspension

An interim suspension will be issued when the Board determines that the CFP Board designee has failed to provide evidence which establishes, by a preponderance of the evidence, that the CFP Board designee does not pose an immediate threat to the public and that the gravity of the nature of the CFP Board designee's conduct does not impinge upon the stature and reputation of the marks. The fact that a convicted or suspended CFP Board designee is seeking appellate review of the conviction or suspension shall not limit the power of the Board to impose an interim suspension.

5.7 Automatic Reinstatement Upon Reversal of Conviction or Suspension

A CFP Board designee subject to a suspension under this Article shall have the suspension vacated immediately upon filing with the Board a certificate demonstrating that the underlying criminal conviction or professional suspension has been reversed; provided, however, the reinstatement upon such reversal shall have no effect on any proceeding conducted pursuant to these *procedures* then pending against a CFP Board designee.

5.8 Publication

It shall be standard procedure to publish the fact of an interim suspension together with identification of the CFP Board designee in a press release.

Article 6: Investigation

6.1 Commencement

Proceedings involving potential ethics violations shall be commenced upon a written request for investigation made by any person which shall be directed to the Board or commenced at the behest of CFP Board Staff Counsel. Proceedings involving *Practice Standards* nonconformance shall be commenced upon a written request for investigation made by any person(s) who have a contractual relationship with the CFP Board designee whose practices are being called into question or by a CFP® certificant, or at the behest of CFP Board Staff Counsel. In either situation, the Board may, in making a determination of whether to proceed, make such inquiry regarding the underlying facts as they deem appropriate.

6.2 Procedures for Investigation

Upon receipt of a request for investigation containing allegations which, if true, could give rise to a violation of the *Code of Ethics*, or upon the acquisition by CFP Board Staff Counsel of information which, if true, could give rise to a violation of the *Code of Ethics*, the CFP Board designee in question shall be given written notice by CFP Board Staff Counsel that the CFP Board designee is under investigation and of the general nature of the allegations asserted against the CFP Board designee. The CFP Board designee shall have thirty (30) calendar days from the date of notice of the investigation to file a written response to the allegations with the Board.

a. *No Response.* At the expiration of the thirty (30) calendar-day period if no response has been received, the matter shall be referred to a Hearing Panel.

b. *Response.* Upon receipt of a response, CFP Board Staff Counsel shall compile all documents and materials and commence probable cause determination procedures as soon thereafter as is reasonably practicable.

6.3 Probable Cause Determination Procedures

CFP Board Staff Counsel shall determine if there is probable cause to believe grounds for discipline exist and shall either: (1) dismiss the allegations as not warranting further investigation at his time; (2) dismiss the allegations with a letter of caution recommending remedial action and/ or entering other appropriate orders; or (3) begin preparation and processing of a Complaint against the CFP Board designee in accordance with Article 7. For matters that are dismissed, CFP Board Staff Counsel may reserve the right to reopen the investigation in the future if appropriate.

6.4 Disposition

CFP Board Staff Counsel shall conduct CFP Board's investigation as expeditiously as reasonably practicable.

Article 7: Complaint—Answer—Default

7.1 Complaint

An original Complaint shall be prepared by CFP Board staff and forwarded to the CFP Board designee. Copies of the Complaint shall be included with the materials provided to the Hearing Panel in advance of the hearing. The Complaint shall reasonably set forth the grounds for discipline with which the CFP Board designee is charged and the conduct or omission which gave rise to those charges.

7.2 Service of the Complaint

CFP Board staff shall promptly serve the Complaint upon the CFP Board designee either by personal service or by certified mail, return receipt requested, mailed to the last known address of the CFP Board designee or as provided in Article 17.2.

7.3 Answer

All Answers to Complaints shall be in writing. The Answer shall be submitted within twenty (20) calendar days from the date of service of the Complaint upon the CFP Board designee. The CFP Board designee shall file an original of such Answer with CFP Board. A copy of the Answer shall be included with the materials provided to the Hearing Panel in advance of the hearing. In the Answer, the CFP Board designee shall respond to every material allegation contained in the Complaint. In addition, the CFP Board designee shall set forth in the Answer any defenses or mitigating circumstances..

7.4 Default and Orders of Revocation and Denial

If the CFP Board designee fails to file an Answer within the period provided by Article 7.4, such CFP Board designee shall be deemed to be in default, and the allegations set forth in the Complaint shall be deemed admitted. In such circumstance, CFP Board Staff Counsel shall serve upon the CFP Board designee, consistent with Article 7.3, an Order of Revocation or, in cases involving a candidate for certification, an Order of Denial. Such orders shall state clearly and with reasonable particularity the grounds for the revocation or denial of the CFP Board designee's right to use the marks. These Orders are subject to the CFP Board designee's right of appeal as outlined in Article 11.

7.5 Request for Appearance

Upon the filing for an Answer, the CFP Board designee may request an appearance at the hearing before the Hearing Panel, at which the CFP Board designee may present arguments, witnesses and evidence on his behalf.

Article 8: Discovery and Evidence

8.1 Discovery

Discovery of a disciplinary case may be obtained only after a Complaint has been issued against a CFP Board designee. The CFP Board designee may obtain copies of all documents in the CFP Board designee's disciplinary file which are not privileged and which are relevant to the subject matter in the pending action before the Hearing Panel. Requests for copies of CFP Board documents must be made to CFP Board Staff Counsel in writing. Release of information contained in a CFP Board designee's disciplinary file is premised on the understanding that materials will be used only for purposes directly connected to the pending CFP Board action.

8.2 Documents

Documents submitted by CFP Board designees to the Board for consideration in resolution of the issues raised during an investigation shall be limited to 100 pages. No evidence may be accepted less than thirty (30) days prior to the scheduled hearing, except by motion at the hearing.

Should a CFP Board designee deem it necessary to exceed the 100 page limit, the CFP Board designee shall be required to submit a written memorandum that outlines clearly and with reasonable particularity how each and every document submitted by the CFP Board designee or on his or her behalf relates to the allegations contained in the CFP Board Complaint. After reviewing such outline, the Board shall determine which documents will be permitted.

8.3 Witnesses

Witnesses, if any, shall be identified to the Board no later than thirty (30) days prior to the scheduled hearing. When witnesses are identified, the CFP Board designee shall also state the nature and extent of the witnesses' testimony.

8.4 Administrative Dismissal

If, upon receipt of a CFP Board designee's Answer to the Complaint, new information becomes available that may warrant a dismissal of the case prior to review by a Hearing Panel, the Director of the professional review department and the Chair of the Board of Professional Review shall review all relevant materials and make such determination at that time.

Article 9: Hearings

9.1 Notice

Not less than thirty (30) calendar days before the date set for the hearing of a Complaint, notice of such hearing shall be given as provided in Article 17.2 to the CFP Board designee or to the CFP Board designee's counsel. The notice shall designate the date and place of the hearing and shall also advise the CFP Board designee that the CFP Board designee is entitled to be represented by counsel at the hearing, to cross-examine witnesses and to present evidence on behalf of the CFP Board designee.

9.2 Designation of a Hearing Panel

All hearings on Complaints seeking disciplinary action against a CFP Board designee shall be conducted by the Hearing Panel.

9.3 Procedure and Proof

Hearings shall be conducted in conformity with such rules of procedure and evidence as established by the Hearing Panel. It shall not be necessary that rules of procedure and evidence applicable in a court of law are followed in any hearing, but the Hearing Panel may be guided by such rules to the extent it believes it is appropriate. Proof of misconduct shall be established by a preponderance of the evidence. A CFP Board designee may not be required to testify or to produce records over the objection of the CFP Board designee if to do so would be in violation of the CFP Board designee's constitutional privilege against self-incrimination in a court of law. In the course of the proceedings, the Chair of the Hearing Panel shall have the power to require the administration of oath and affirmations. A complete record shall be made of all testimony taken at hearings before the Hearing Panel.

Article 10: Report, Findings of Fact and Recommendation

10.1 Hearing Panel

At the conclusion of the hearing, the Hearing Panel shall record its findings of fact and recommendations and submit the findings and recommendations to the Board for its consideration. In making its recommendation, the Hearing Panel may take into consideration the CFP Board designee's prior disciplinary record, if any.

10.2 Report of the Hearing Panel

The Hearing Panel shall report its findings and recommendations to the Board. In this report, the Hearing Panel shall: (1) determine that the Complaint is not proved or that the facts as established do not warrant the imposition of discipline and recommend the Complaint be dismissed, either as without merit or with caution; or (2) refer the matter to the Board with the recommendation that discipline by the Board is appropriate. The recommendation of the Hearing Panel shall state specifically the form of discipline the Hearing Panel deems appropriate. The Hearing Panel may also recommend that the Board enter other appropriate orders.

10.3 Power of the Board

The Board reserves the authority to review any determination made by the Hearing Panel in the course of a disciplinary or *Practice Standards* proceeding and to enter any order with respect thereto including an order directing that further proceedings be conducted as provided by these *Procedures.* The Board shall review the report of the Hearing Panel and may either approve the report or modify it. The Board must accept the Hearing Panel's findings of fact, unless, on the basis of its own review of the record, it determines that such findings are clearly erroneous. The Board may modify the Hearing Panel's recommendation without reviewing the record and must state the reasons for the modification.

Article 11: Appeals

All appeals from orders of the Board shall be submitted to CFP Board's Board of Appeals in accordance with the Rules and Procedures of the Board of Appeals. If an order of the Board is not appealed within thirty (30) calendar days after notice of the order is sent to the CFP Board designee, such order shall become final.

Article 12: Conviction of a Crime or Professional Suspension

12.1 Proof of Conviction or Professional Suspension

Except as otherwise provided in these *Procedures,* a certificate from the clerk of any court of criminal jurisdiction indicating that a CFP Board designee has been convicted of a crime in that court or a letter or other writing from a governmental or industry self-regulatory authority to the effect that a CFP Board designee has been the subject of an order of professional suspension (as hereinafter defined) by such authority, shall conclusively establish the existence of such conviction or such professional suspension for purposes of disciplinary proceedings and shall be conclusive proof of the commission of that crime or of the basis for such suspension, by the CFP Board designee.

12.2 Duty to Report Criminal Conviction or Professional Suspension

Every CFP Board designee, upon being convicted of a crime, except misdemeanor traffic offenses or traffic ordinance violations unless such offense involves the use of alcohol or drugs, or upon being the subject of professional suspension, shall notify the CFP Board in writing of such conviction or suspension within ten (10) calendar days after the date on which the CFP Board designee is notified of the conviction or suspension.

12.3 Commencement of Disciplinary Proceedings Upon Notice of Conviction or Professional Suspension

Upon receiving notice that a CFP Board designee has been convicted of a crime other than a serious crime (as defined herein), CFP Board Staff Counsel shall commence an investigation. If the conviction is for a serious crime or if a CFP Board designee is the subject of a professional suspension, CFP Board shall obtain the record of conviction or proof of suspension and file a Complaint against the CFP Board designee as provided in Article 7. If the CFP Board designee's criminal conviction or professional suspension is either proved or admitted as provided herein, the CFP Board designee shall have the right to be heard by the Hearing Panel only on matters of rebuttal of any evidence presented by Staff Counsel other than proof of the conviction or suspension.

12.4 Conviction of Serious Crime or Professional Suspension—Immediate Suspension

Upon receiving notification of a CFP Board designee's criminal conviction or professional suspension, CFP Board Staff Counsel may, at its discretion, issue a notice to the convicted or suspended CFP Board designee directing that the CFP Board designee show cause why the CFP Board designee's right to use the marks should not be immediately suspended pursuant to Article 5.

12.5 Serious Crime Defined

The term serious crime as used in these rules shall include: (1) any felony; (2) any lesser crime, a necessary element of which as determined by its statutory or common law definition involves misrepresentation, fraud, extortion, misappropriation or theft; and/or (3) an attempt or conspiracy to commit such crime, or solicitation of another to commit such crime.

12.6 Definition of a Professional Suspension

A professional suspension as used herein shall include the suspension or bar as a disciplinary measure by any governmental or industry self-regulatory authority of a license as a registered securities representative, broker/dealer, insurance or real estate salesperson or broker, insurance broker, attorney, accountant, investment adviser or financial planner.

Article 13: Settlement Procedure

A CFP Board designee or CFP Board Staff Counsel may propose an Offer of Settlement in lieu of a disciplinary hearing pursuant to these *Procedures*. Submitting an Offer of Settlement shall stay all proceedings conducted pursuant to these *Procedures*.

13.1 Offer of Settlement

Offers of Settlement may be made where the nature of the proceeding, and the interests of the public and CFP Board permit. The Offer of Settlement shall be in writing and must be submitted to the CFP Board staff at least 30 days prior to the CFP Board designee's scheduled disciplinary hearing. A Hearing Panel will consider the Offer and take one of the actions described in Articles 13.2 and 13.3. The Hearing Panel will consider only one Offer of Settlement during the course of a disciplinary proceeding. The Offer must be made in conformity with the provisions of this Article and should not be made frivolously or propose an action inconsistent with the seriousness of the violations alleged in the proceedings. CFP Board Staff Counsel may negotiate a proposed Offer of Settlement with the CFP Board designee and endorse the Offer of Settlement to the Hearing Panel. Only the Board shall have final decision making authority to accept or reject an Offer of Settlement.

Every Offer of Settlement shall contain and describe in reasonable detail:

a. The act or practice which the member or person associated with a member is alleged to have engaged in or omitted;

b. The principle, rule, regulation or statutory provision which such act, practice or omission to act is alleged to have been violated;

c. A statement that the CFP Board designee consents to findings of fact and violations consistent with the statements contained in the offer required by paragraphs 13.1(a) and 13.1(b);

d. Proposed Board action to be taken and a statement that the CFP Board designee consents to the proposed Board action; and

e. A waiver of all rights of appeal to CFP Board's Board of Appeals and the courts or to otherwise challenge or contest the validity of the Order issued if the Offer of Settlement is accepted.

13.2 Acceptance of Offer

If an Offer of Settlement is accepted by a Hearing Panel, the decision of the Hearing Panel shall be reviewed by the Board. The Board's decision to affirm the decision of the Hearing Panel to accept the Offer of Settlement shall conclude the proceeding as of the date the Offer of Settlement is accepted. If the Offer of Settlement includes a penalty of revocation or suspension, the revocation or suspension shall become effective immediately upon acceptance by the Hearing Panel and affirmance by the Board.

13.3 Rejection of Offer; Counter Offer

If the Offer of Settlement is rejected by a Hearing Panel, the Offer of Settlement shall be deemed void and the matters raised in the Complaint will be set for hearing at the next meeting of the Board. The CFP Board designee shall not be prejudiced by the prior Offer of Settlement, and it shall not be given consideration in the determination of the issues involved in the pending or any other proceeding.

If the Hearing Panel deems it appropriate, it may make a Counter Settlement Offer to the CFP Board designee modifying the proposed finding(s) of fact, violation(s) and/or discipline. If the Counter Settlement Offer is rejected by the CFP Board designee, the Offer of Settlement and Counter Settlement Offer shall be deemed void and the matters raised in the Complaint will be set for hearing at the next meeting of the Board. The CFP Board designee shall not be prejudiced by the prior Offer of Settlement or the Counter Settlement Offer, and neither shall be given consideration in the determination of the issued involved in the pending or any other proceeding.

13.4 Publication

In the event proceedings pursuant to Article 13 result in a permanent revocation, or suspension, or otherwise result in a termination of the right to use the marks, it shall be standard procedure to publish such fact together with identification of the CFP Board designee in a press release, or in such other form of publicity as is selected by the Board.

Article 14: Required Action After Revocation or Suspension

After the entry of an order of revocation or suspension is final, the CFP Board designee shall promptly terminate any use of the marks and in particular shall not use them in any advertising, announcement, letterhead or business card.

Article 15: Reinstatement After Discipline

15.1 Reinstatement After Revocation

Revocation shall be permanent, and there shall be no opportunity for reinstatement.

15.2 Reinstatement After Suspension

Unless otherwise provided by the Board in its order of suspension, a CFP Board designee who has been suspended for a period of one (l) year or less shall be automatically reinstated upon the expiration of the period of suspension, provided the CFP Board designee files with CFP Board within thirty (30) calendar days of the expiration of the period of suspension an affidavit stating that the suspended CFP Board designee has fully complied with the order of suspension and with all applicable provisions of these *Procedures*, unless such condition is waived by the Board in its discretion. A CFP Board designee who has been suspended for a period longer than one (l) year must petition the Board for a reinstatement hearing within six months of the end of his/her suspension, or failure to do so will result in administrative relinquishment. Before any reinstatement hearing will be scheduled, the CFP Board designee must meet all administrative requirements for recertification, pay the reinstatement hearing costs and provide evidence, if necessary, that all prior hearing costs have been paid. At the reinstatement hearing, the CFP Board designee must prove by clear and convincing evidence that the CFP Board designee has been rehabilitated, has complied with all applicable disciplinary orders and provisions of these *Procedures*, and that the CFP Board designee is fit to use the marks.

15.3 Investigation

Immediately upon receipt of a petition for reinstatement, CFP Board Staff Counsel will initiate an investigation. The petitioner shall cooperate in any such investigation, and CFP Board Staff Counsel shall submit a report of the investigation to the Board which shall report on the petitioner's past disciplinary record and any recommendation regarding reinstatement.

15.4 Successive Petitions

If an individual is denied reinstatement, he/she must wait two (2) years to again petition for reinstatement. The second petition must be received by CFP Board within six (6) months of the expiration of the two (2) year period, and failure to submit a second petition within this time period will result in the individual's right to use the marks being administratively relinquished. If the second petition is denied, the individual's right to use the marks shall be administratively relinquished.

15.5 Reinstatement Fee

Petitioners for reinstatement will be assessed the costs of the reinstatement proceeding.

Article 16: Confidentiality of Proceedings

16.1 Confidentiality

Except as otherwise provided in these *Procedures*, all proceedings conducted pursuant to these *Procedures* shall be confidential and the records of the Board, Hearing Panel, CFP Board Staff Counsel and CFP Board staff shall remain confidential and shall not be made public.

16.2 Exceptions to Confidentiality

The pendency, subject matter and status of proceedings conducted pursuant to these *Procedures* may be disclosed if (1) the proceeding is predicated on criminal conviction or professional suspension as defined herein; or (2) the CFP Board designee has waived confidentiality; or (3) such disclosure is required by legal process of a court of law or other governmental body or agency having appropriate jurisdiction; or (4) in proceedings involving a consumer, CFP Board staff contacts the consumer and/or the CFP Board designee's current and/or former employer to request documents relevant to the proceeding.

Article 17: General Provisions

17.1 Quorum

A majority of members of the Board shall be present in order to constitute a quorum of such Board, and the approval of a majority of the quorum shall be the action of such Board.

17.2 Notice and Service

Except as may otherwise be provided in these Procedures, notice shall be in writing and the giving of notice and/or service shall be sufficient when made either personally or by certified mail or overnight mail sent to the last known address of the CFP Board designee according to the records of CFP Board.

17.3 Costs

In all disciplinary cases wherein a hearing is convened, the Board will assess against the CFP Board designee the costs of the proceedings. In addition, a CFP Board designee who desires an appearance, whether telephonically or in person, or who submits an Offer of Settlement pursuant to Article 13, will be required to submit hearing costs not less than thirty (30) days prior to the date of the scheduled hearing. In the event that the hearing results in a dismissal without merit, the hearing costs shall be refunded to the CFP Board designee. Hearing costs will not be refunded if the hearing results in any action other than a dismissal without merit. A CFP Board designee who petitions from a suspension or revocation or who petitions for appeal shall bear the costs of such proceeding.

17.4 Electronic Signature

Some documents that require a handwritten signature may be submitted electronically through CFP Board's closed Web site. Any document received by CFP Board through this process shall constitute conclusive proof that: (1) the CFP Board designee whose name appears on the document submitted such document; and (2) the CFP Board designee intended to be bound by the terms and conditions contained therein. Accordingly, the document shall be as legally binding as any containing a handwritten signature.

CANDIDATE FITNESS STANDARDS

The Board of Professional Review recommended and the Board of Governors recently approved specific character and fitness standards for candidates for certification to ensure an individual's conduct does not reflect adversely on his or her fitness as a candidate for CFP® certification, or upon the profession or the CFP® certification marks. CFP Board determined that such standards would also benefit individuals who are interested in attaining CFP® certification, as many candidates have indicated that if they had known that their prior conduct would bar or delay their certification, they would not have sat for the CFP® Certification Examination. These standards will become effective on January 1, 2007.

The following conduct is unacceptable and will always bar an individual from becoming certified:

- Felony conviction for theft, embezzlement or other financially-based crimes.
- Felony conviction for tax fraud or other tax-related crimes.
- Revocation of a financial (e.g., registered securities representative, broker/dealer, insurance, accountant, investment advisor, financial planner) professional license, unless the revocation is administrative in nature, i.e., the result of the individual determining not to renew the license by not paying the required fees.
- Felony conviction for any degree of murder or rape.
- Felony conviction for any other violent crime within the last five years.
- Two or more personal or business bankruptcies.

The following conduct is presumed to be unacceptable and will bar an individual from becoming certified unless the individual petitions the Board of Professional Review for reconsideration:

- One personal or business bankruptcy within the last five years.
- More than one judgment lien.
- Revocation or suspension of a non-financial professional (e.g. real estate, attorney) license, unless the revocation is administrative in nature, i.e. the result of the individual determining not to renew the license by not paying the required fees.
- Suspension of a financial professional (e.g., registered securities representative, broker/dealer, insurance, accountant, investment advisor, financial planner) license, unless the suspension is administrative in nature, i.e. the result of the individual determining not to renew the license by not paying the required fees.
- Felony conviction for non-violent crimes (including perjury) within the last five years.
- Felony conviction for violent crimes other than murder or rape that occurred more than five years ago.

Other matters that very rarely result in the delay or denial of certification will continue to be reviewed by staff and the Board of Professional Review under the current procedures, after the candidate has successfully completed the education, examination and experience requirements for certification. These include customer complaints, arbitrations and other civil proceedings, felony convictions for non-violent crimes that occurred more than five years ago, misdemeanor convictions, and employer reviews and terminations. CFP Board will continue to require candidates for CFP® certification to disclose certain matters on the ethics portion of the Initial Certification Application.

Individuals who have a transgression that falls under the "presumption" list must petition the Board of Professional Review for reconsideration and a determination whether their conduct will bar certification. The basic process for these reviews will be:

1. The individual will submit a written petition for reconsideration to Professional Review staff and sign a form agreeing to CFP Board's jurisdiction to consider the matter.

2. Staff will review the request to ensure the transgression falls within the "presumption" list.

3. If the transgression does not fall within the "presumption" list, i.e., falls in the "always bar" list, staff will so notify the individual.

4. If the transgression falls within the "presumption" list, staff will request all relevant documentation from the individual. A fee will be charged all candidates submitting a reconsideration request.

5. All of the relevant information will be provided to the Board of Professional Review for a determination.

The Board of Professional Review may make one of the following decisions regarding a petition for reconsideration:

- Grant the petition after determining the conduct does not reflect adversely on the individual's fitness as a candidate for CFP® certification, or upon the profession or the CFP® certification marks, and certification should be permitted; or

- Deny the petition after determining the conduct does reflect adversely on the individual's fitness as a candidate for CFP® certification, or upon the profession or the CFP® certification marks, and certification should be barred.

The Board of Professional Review's decision regarding a petition for reconsideration is final and may not be appealed, unless the relevant professional revocation or suspension is vacated or the relevant felony conviction is overturned, at which time the individual may submit a new petition.

© **Certified Financial Planner Board of Standards Inc. (reprinted with permission)**

APPENDIX 1: FUTURE VALUE TABLE

Periods	Interest Rates (i)									
(n)	1%	2%	3%	4%	5%	6%	7%	8%	9%	10%
1	1.0100	1.0200	1.0300	1.0400	1.0500	1.0600	1.0700	1.0800	1.0900	1.1000
2	1.0201	1.0404	1.0609	1.0816	1.1025	1.1236	1.1449	1.1664	1.1881	1.2100
3	1.0303	1.0612	1.0927	1.1249	1.1576	1.1910	1.2250	1.2597	1.2950	1.3310
4	1.0406	1.0824	1.1255	1.1699	1.2155	1.2625	1.3108	1.3605	1.4116	1.4641
5	1.0510	1.1041	1.1593	1.2167	1.2763	1.3382	1.4026	1.4693	1.5386	1.6105
6	1.0615	1.1262	1.1941	1.2653	1.3401	1.4185	1.5007	1.5869	1.6771	1.7716
7	1.0721	1.1487	1.2299	1.3159	1.4071	1.5036	1.6058	1.7138	1.8280	1.9487
8	1.0829	1.1717	1.2668	1.3686	1.4775	1.5938	1.7182	1.8509	1.9926	2.1436
9	1.0937	1.1951	1.3048	1.4233	1.5513	1.6895	1.8385	1.9990	2.1719	2.3579
10	1.1046	1.2190	1.3439	1.4802	1.6289	1.7908	1.9672	2.1589	2.3674	2.5937

APPENDIX 2: FUTURE VALUE OF AN ORDINARY ANNUITY

$$FVOA_{i,n} = \frac{(1 + i)^n - 1}{i}$$

Periods	Interest Rates (i)									
(n)	1%	2%	3%	4%	5%	6%	7%	8%	9%	10%
1	1.0000	1.0000	1.0000	1.0000	1.0000	1.0000	1.0000	1.0000	1.0000	1.0000
2	2.0100	2.0200	2.0300	2.0400	2.0500	2.0600	2.0700	2.0800	2.0900	2.1000
3	3.0301	3.0604	3.0909	3.1216	3.1525	3.1836	3.2149	3.2464	3.2781	3.3100
4	4.0604	4.1216	4.1836	4.2465	4.3101	4.3746	4.4399	4.5061	4.5731	4.6410
5	5.1010	5.2040	5.3091	5.4163	5.5256	5.6371	5.7507	5.8666	5.9847	6.1051
6	6.1520	6.3081	6.4684	6.6330	6.8019	6.9753	7.1533	7.3359	7.5233	7.7156
7	7.2135	7.4343	7.6625	7.8983	8.1420	8.3938	8.6540	8.9228	9.2004	9.4872
8	8.2857	8.5830	8.8923	9.2142	9.5491	9.8975	10.2598	10.6366	11.0285	11.4359
9	9.3685	9.7546	10.1591	10.5828	11.0266	11.4913	11.9780	12.4876	13.0210	13.5795
10	10.4622	10.9497	11.4639	12.0061	12.5779	13.1808	13.8164	14.4866	15.1929	15.9374

FUNDAMENTALS SUPPLEMENT

Outline

Fundamentals Supplement

Note: The Fundamentals Supplement is included to provide support material to what is covered in the main text. The likelihood of the supplemental material being tested on the CFP® Exam is low; however, the possibility still exists. We recommend that you review the supplement although it is not imperative that you study the material in intimate detail.

I. FINANCIAL INSTITUTIONS

A. MUTUAL SAVINGS BANKS AND SIMILAR INSTITUTIONS

1. There are other financial institutions that offer various forms of checking and savings accounts

    a. Mutual savings banks

    b. Credit unions

2. Mutual savings banks

    a. A mutual savings bank (MSB) is quite similar to a savings and loan association (S&L). Historically, MSBs accepted deposits in order to make housing loans.

    b. Technically, the depositors of savings are the owners of the institution

    c. MSBs are state chartered and have either FDIC's BIF insurance or a state-approved insurance program, up to $100,000 per account

    d. MSBs are not permitted in all states; most are located in the Northeast

    e. Similar to S&Ls, MSBs compete for consumer loans and offer interest-bearing negotiable order of withdrawal (NOW) accounts

3. Credit unions

    a. Credit unions are not-for-profit cooperative ventures that are largely run by volunteers. They are developed to pool the deposits of members. These funds are used to invest or lend to members/owners.

    b. Members are usually joined by a common bond such as work, union, or fraternal association

    c. Regulations make it possible for people to remain members of a credit union after the common bond has been severed

    d. Credit unions with federal charters have their accounts insured up to $100,000 through the National Credit Union Share Insurance Fund (NCUSIF), which is administered by the National Credit Union Administration (NCUA) and provides the same safety as that for deposits insured by the FDIC

    e. Credit unions accept deposits and make loans for consumer products; they also make home loans

    f. Employment-related credit unions typically make use of payroll deductions for deposits and loan repayments, often offer free term life insurance up to certain limits, and usually offer free credit life insurance

B. MONEY MARKET MUTUAL FUNDS

1. A mutual fund is an investment company that raises money by selling shares to the public and investing the money in a diversified portfolio of securities; the investments are professionally managed, with securities purchased and sold at the discretion of the fund manager

2. Many mutual fund companies have created money market mutual funds (MMMFs) that serve as money market accounts; the accounts can be used for purposes of cash management

3. An MMMF is a mutual fund that pools the cash of many investors and specializes in earning a relatively safe and high return by buying securities that have short-term maturities (always less than one year)

4. The average maturity for the portfolio cannot exceed 120 days; this reduces price swings so that the money funds maintain a constant share value

5. Securities are bought and sold almost daily in money markets that yield payment of the highest daily rates available to small investors

6. Money deposited in mutual funds is not insured by the federal government; however, MMMFs are considered extremely safe because of the high quality of the securities

7. Accounts in money market mutual funds provide a convenient and safe place to keep money while awaiting alternative investment opportunities

C. STOCK BROKERAGE FIRMS

1. A stock brokerage firm is a licensed financial institution that specializes in selling and buying investment securities

2. Such firms usually receive a commission for the advice and assistance they provide; commissions are based on the buy/sell orders they execute

3. Stock brokerage firms usually offer money market fund accounts in which clients may place money while waiting to make investments in stocks and bonds

4. Money held in a money market mutual fund at a stock brokerage firm is not insured against loss by any government agency; however, most brokerage firms purchase private insurance against such losses

D. FINANCIAL SERVICES COMPANIES

1. Financial services companies are national or regional corporations that offer a number of financial services to consumers, including traditional checking, savings, lending, credit card accounts, and MMMFs, as well as advice on investments, insurance, real estate, and general financial planning

2. Financial services companies are also referred to as nonbank banks because they provide limited traditional banking services, either accepting deposits or making commercial loans, but not both

II. TIME VALUE OF MONEY

A. FUTURE VALUE OF A SINGLE SUM DEPOSIT—AN ALTERNATIVE METHOD

1. A dollar in hand today is worth more than a dollar to be received next year. If you had one dollar now, you could invest, earn interest, and end up next year with more than one dollar.

Example

Calculation 2:

Another way to look at this problem is with a timeline. On a timeline, Time 0 is today; Time 1 is 1 period from today, or the end of 1 period; Time 2 is 2 periods from today, or the end of 2 periods; and so on. Thus, the values on timelines represent end-of-period values. At Time 0 (today), when Connie opens her bank account, she has $100. The timeline below shows $100 at Year 0. She would like to know how much she would have at the end of the year (Year 1 on the timeline) if the account pays an interest rate of 10%. The interest rate of 10% is shown above the timeline to indicate how much her deposit will increase. The equation shows that the account will grow to $110 at the end of the year, so she could replace the first question mark with $110.

Year 0	10%	Year 1	10%	Year 2	10%	Year 3	10%	Year 4	10%	Year 5
$100		?		?		?		?		?

Now suppose Connie leaves her funds on deposit for 5 years. How much will she have at the end of the fifth year? The answer is $n = 5$; $i = 10$; $PV = \$100$; $FV = \$161.05$.

Year	Beginning Amount	Interest Factor	Ending Amount	Interest (Annual)
1	$100.00	1.10	$110.00	$10.00
2	110.00	1.10	121.00	11.00
3	121.00	1.10	133.10	12.10
4	133.10	1.10	146.41	13.31
5	146.41	1.10	161.05	14.64
			TOTAL	$61.05

B. PRESENT VALUE

1. This calculation is used to determine what a sum of money to be received in a future year is worth in today's dollars, on the basis of a specific discount rate

   a. Calculation 1

   The example above shows that an initial amount of $100 growing at 10% a year would be worth $161.05 at the end of 5 years. One should be indifferent to the choice between $100 today and $161.05 at the end of 5 years, assuming that the opportunity cost was 10% per year. The $100 is defined as the present value, or PV, of $161.05 due in 5 years when the opportunity cost is 10%. Therefore, if x is anything less than $100, one should prefer the promise of $161.05 in 5 years to x dollars today; if x were greater than $100, one should prefer x.

The concept of present values can also be illustrated using a timeline. The following timeline shows the future value amount of $161.05 at Year 5. A question mark appears at Year 0—this is the value of interest—and the interest rate of 10% appears above the timeline, indicating opportunity cost.

0	10%	1	10%	2	10%	3	10%	4	10%	5
?										$161.05

The present value of a sum due n years in the future is the amount that, if it were on hand today, would grow to equal the future sum. Since $100 would grow to $161.05 in 5 years at a 10% interest rate, $100 is the present value of $161.05 due 5 years in the future when the appropriate interest rate is 10%.

Finding present value, or discounting, is simply the reverse of compounding.

$FV_n = PV(1+i)^n$, can be transformed into a present value formula by solving for PV:

$$PV = \frac{FV_n}{(1+i)^n} = FV_n(1+i)^{-n} = FV_n\left(\frac{1}{1+i}\right)^n$$

Tables have been constructed for the last term in parentheses for various values of i and n; Exhibit 2 is an example. For our illustrative case, look down the 10% column in Exhibit 2 to the fifth row. The figure shown there, 0.6209, is the present value interest factor $(PV_{i,n})$ used to determine the present value of $161.05 payable in 5 years, discounted at 10%.

$PV = FV_5(PV_{10\%,\ 5\ years})$

$= (\$161.05)(0.6209)$

$= \$100$

EXHIBIT 1: PRESENT VALUE OF $1 DUE AT THE END OF n PERIODS.

$$PV_{k,n} = \frac{1}{(1+i)^n} = \left(\frac{1}{1+i}\right)^n$$

Periods	Interest Rates (i)									
(n)	1%	2%	3%	4%	5%	6%	7%	8%	9%	10%
1	.9901	.9804	.9709	.9615	.9524	.9434	.9646	.9259	.9174	.9091
2	.9803	.9612	.9426	.9246	.9070	.8900	.8734	.8573	.8417	.8264
3	.9706	.9423	.9151	.8890	.8638	.8396	.8163	.7938	.7722	.7513
4	.9610	.9238	.8885	.8548	.8227	.7921	.7629	.7350	.7084	.6830
5	.9515	.9057	.8626	.8219	.7835	.7473	.7130	.6806	.6499	.6209
6	.9420	.8880	.8375	.7903	.7462	.7050	.6663	.6302	.5963	.5645
7	.9327	.8706	.8131	.7599	.7107	.6651	.6227	.5835	.5470	.5132
8	.9235	.8535	.7894	.7307	.6768	.6274	.5820	.5403	.5019	.4665
9	.9143	.8368	.7664	.7026	.6446	.5919	.5439	.5002	.4604	.4241
10	.9053	.8203	.7441	.6756	.6139	.5584	.5083	.4632	.4224	.3855

C. PRESENT VALUE OF AN ANNUITY

Example

Tim, who was injured in an automobile accident, won a judgment that provides him $1,500 at the end of each 6-month period over the next 6 years. If the escrow account that holds Tim's settlement award earns an average annual rate of 11% compounded semiannually, the defendant would initially be required to pay Tim $12,927.78 to compensate for his injuries.

PMT_{OA} = $1,500

i = 5.5 (11 ÷ 2)

n = 12 (6 × 2)

PV_{OA} = $12,927.78

Example

Jane wants to withdraw $4,000 at the beginning of each year for the next 7 years. She expects to earn 10.5% compounded annually on her investment. The lump sum Jane should deposit today is $21,168.72.

PMT_{AD} = $4,000

i = 10.5

n = 7

PV_{AD} = $21,168.72

III. EDUCATIONAL FUNDING

A. GOVERNMENT GRANTS AND LOANS (FINANCIAL AID)

1. Determining financial need

    a. Financial need, also known as demonstrated financial need, refers to the difference between what it costs to attend a particular college and the amount that a student and the student's family can afford to pay toward those expenses. This need is determined through the use of standardized formulas. Although a student is usually eligible for all of the student's demonstrated financial need, colleges are not necessarily able to meet the full need.

    b. The amount of money that students and parents can be expected to contribute toward a college education is referred to as the Estimated Family Contribution (EFC)

    c. The EFC is composed of two parts

        1.) The parents' contribution

        2.) The student's contribution (UTMA/UGMA assets held within a 529 savings plan is <u>not</u> included when determining the EFC)

        Both of these are determined by using federal and/or alternate guidelines

    d. Federal guidelines, or federal methodology, are formulas that are used to determine the demonstrated financial need of a student; the federal methodology is used by the government and takes into consideration income, some assets, expenses, and family size

    e. The alternate methodology is called institutional methodology. It is used to determine a student's need for nonfederal financial aid. Although it is similar to the federal methodology, it assumes a minimum expected contribution from the student and takes home equity into consideration. Furthermore, it allows a more generous treatment of some expenses.

    f. The amount of aid for which students are eligible can be influenced by their dependency status. Students are either considered dependent on their parents for financial support or independent of financial support. For federal aid, dependency status is determined according to federal guidelines. Colleges may have different definitions of independence when it comes to distributing college funds.

2. Applying for financial aid

    a. To apply for federal financial aid, students and their parents must fill out the Free Application for Federal Student Aid (FAFSA); this form, which is distributed by the Department of Education, is used to determine a student's need according to the federal methodology.

    b. When a student reapplies for federal financial aid, a partially preprinted form called the Renewal FAFSA is used

    c. To be eligible, certain requirements must be met

        1.) Be a US citizen or eligible noncitizen

        2.) Be registered with Selective Service (if required)

        3.) Attend a college that participates in the following programs

            a.) Federal Pell Grants (Pell Grants)

b.) Federal Supplemental Educational Opportunity Grants (FSEOG)

c.) Federal Subsidized and Unsubsidized Stafford Loans

d.) Stafford/Ford Federal Direct Subsidized and Unsubsidized Loans

e.) Federal Perkins Loans

f.) Federal Work-Study (FWS)

4.) Be working toward a degree or certificate

5.) Be making satisfactory academic progress

6.) Not owe a refund on a federal grant or be in default on a federal educational loan

7.) Have financial need as determined in part by the Free Application for Federal Student Aid (except for some loan programs)

d. Additional financial aid information

1.) Federal student loans must be repaid

2.) Less-than-half-time students may be eligible for Federal Pell Grants and some other federal student aid programs

3.) Students who have received a bachelor's degree are not eligible for Federal Pell Grants or FSEOG but may be eligible for other federal student aid programs

4.) Students attending two schools during the same enrollment period must inform both Financial Aid Administrators (FAAs); students cannot receive Pell Grants at both schools

5.) Conviction of drug distribution or possession may make a student ineligible

e. The US Department of Education also has a toll-free number to answer questions about federal student aid programs: 1-800-4-FED-AID

B. OTHER SOURCES

1. Aid directly from the institution

   a. Each school has its own method of providing aid through loans, scholarships, discounts, and campus jobs

   b. The school's financial aid adviser should adequately explain to the student the school's available options and programs

   c. Some schools will allow a student to pay tuition on a monthly installment plan, which may provide more flexibility to the student and parents

   d. Other schools may offer discounts or scholarships for superior athletic or academic performance either before or after enrollment. The school has an incentive to entice superior athletes and academic students in order to increase their level of top students and to better compete with other schools, which, in turn, enhances the school's image.

2. Aid from Armed Forces

   a. The US Armed Forces have numerous programs and scholarships that may pay for tuition, fees, and books for those who enlist or enroll in the military

   b. The student may also receive monthly payments for other expenses

    c.   Information regarding the many programs available through the US Armed Forces can be obtained from the college attended or from the administrative office of the desired branch of military

3.   Other scholarships

    a.   There are many forms of scholarships that are awarded by groups that are separate and apart from the school and state and federal governments

    b.   Numerous civic organizations award scholarships on the basis of need, merit, and/or the student's or parents' affiliation with that civic organization

    c.   There are various types of scholarships available to students who have high grades and high standardized (entrance) test scores, including National Merit Scholarships

4.   Scholarships can also be provided through a particular church or religious organization

IV. CONTRACTS

A. NATURE AND TYPES OF CONTRACTS

1. Based on compliance with a statute requiring a special formality

    a. Formal contract—some formality is prescribed for their creation

        1.) Contract under seal or notarial act

        2.) Recognizances

        3.) Negotiable instruments and letters of credit

    b. Informal contract—simple contracts for which no special form or formality is required

2. Based on the stage of performance of the contractual promises

    a. Executed contract—contract that has been completely performed by all parties

    b. Executory contract—contract that has been partly performed or totally unperformed by all parties

3. Based on legal validity and enforceability

    a. Valid and enforceable contract—all elements of a contract are present

    b. Void contract—agreement has no legal effect (it was not really a contract)

    c. Voidable contract—one of the parties has the option of avoiding contractual obligations

    d. Unenforceable contract—contract that cannot be proven in the manner required by law, and/or fails to meet a procedural or formal requirement

B. AGREEMENT

1. Terms

    a. Material, essential terms include identification of the parties, the subject matter, the consideration or price to be paid, and the quantity (if appropriate)

    b. Incidental terms

2. The offer—the offeror shows assent when he communicates a proposal (the offer) to the offeree that sets forth with reasonable clarity, definiteness, and certainty the material terms under which he is presently, objectively agreeing and intending to be bound

    a. Objective intent manifested by offeror

        1.) The words and/or conduct used by the offeror must be such that a reasonable person would be warranted, under the circumstances, in believing that a real agreement was intended by the offeror

        2.) It is necessary to distinguish offers from the following

            a.) Expressions of opinions

            b.) Preliminary negotiations and invitations soliciting offers

            c.) Statements of intention

            d.) Advertisements, catalogues, circulars, and price lists

            e.) Offers that are made in jest or under emotional stress

            f.) Other nonoffer situations

- Requests for bids

- Requests of auctioneer for bids at auctions

- Social invitations

- Agreements to agree

- Sham transactions

b. Definiteness and clarity of material terms—all of the material, essential terms must be indicated in the offer with clarity, definiteness, and certainty or a method stated by which the terms will be made certain

   1.) The offeror may provide that one or more of the terms be more definite by reference to an outside standard or third person

   2.) Material terms

   a.) The subject matter of the contract

   b.) The price

   c.) The quantity

c. Communication of offer—the terms of the offer must be received by the offeree

   1.) Offeree must have knowledge of all the material terms of the offer

   2.) An offer may be made to a specific offeree to whom it is communicated

   3.) A public offer, such as an offer for a reward, is treated as communicated to those people who have knowledge of it

d. Termination of offer

   1.) By actions of the parties

   a.) Revocation by the offeror

   - Revocation must be communicated to offeree; it must, therefore, be received by the offeree before acceptance

   - An offer to a specific offeree is effectively terminated when the revocation of the offer is received by the offeree

   - A public offer is effectively terminated when revocation is given in the same manner and for the same period as had been used in order to make the offer

   - Irrevocable offers (common law option contract or statutory firm offer)

   - Offer to enter into a unilateral contract

      — Traditional view—offer to enter into a unilateral contract may be revoked even though the offeree has begun performance

      — Modern view applies doctrine of promissory estoppel; the offeror is barred (estopped) from revoking the offer when the offeree has changed position in justifiable reliance on the offer b.) Rejection by offeree

- Offeree demonstrates his intention not to accept the offer
- Rejection must be communicated to the offeror
- A counteroffer constitutes a rejection
- An inquiry by the offeree is distinguishable from a rejection

2.) Because of lapse of time

a.) If a duration is stated in the offer, the offer terminates after expiration of the stated period

b.) If a duration is not stated in the offer, the offer lapses after a reasonable period

3.) By operation of law

a.) Destruction of the subject matter

b.) Death or insanity of an offeror or offeree

c.) Supervening illegality

3. Acceptance—the offeree accepts the offer when he unequivocally manifests assent to the terms of the offer

a. Effective moment of acceptance

1.) If a unilateral contract is contemplated, acceptance is effective when the performance or forbearance is completed

2.) If a bilateral contract is contemplated, acceptance is effective when the offeree gives the requisite promise (usually, when the acceptance is sent so that it is out of the offeree's control, even if the acceptance is not received by the offeror)

3.) The offeror may include a condition in the offer that acceptance will not be effective until it is received by the offeror

4.) A contract is created at the moment that the acceptance is effective

C. CONSIDERATION

1. Adequacy of consideration

a. The consideration received by one party was grossly inadequate (equitable principle)

b. No consideration was given

1.) Past or moral consideration, love, and affection

2.) Performance of a preexisting duty that is imposed by law or owed because of an existing contract

3.) Performance of an illegal act

4.) Illusory promise—a promise that appears to be a promise but is not really an undertaking to do anything

2. Problem areas in business concerning consideration

a. Methods for dealing with uncertainty as to future market conditions

1.) Requirements contracts

      a.) Consideration is given if a buyer agrees to purchase and a seller agrees to sell all or up to a specified amount that the buyer needs or requires

      b.) Contract is illusory if a buyer agrees to purchase only the goods that he may wish, want, or desire

   2.) Output contracts

      a.) A seller agrees to sell and a buyer agrees to purchase all or up to a specified amount of the seller's output

      b.) A contract is illusory if its terms permit a seller to sell to other purchasers or if a seller's obligation to produce is based on the seller's wish, want, or desire

   3.) Exclusive dealings contract

      a.) One party has the sole or exclusive right to deal in or with the products or property of the other

      b.) Parties have obligations to use their best efforts to promote subsequent sale, supply sufficient quantity, and so forth

   4.) Option to cancel clauses

      a.) If the right to cancel is absolute and unconditional, the contract is illusory

      b.) If the right to cancel is conditioned on the happening of some event, the contract is enforceable

  b. Settlement of claims or debts

   1.) A promise to pay or actual payment of part of a mature, liquidated, undisputed debt is not consideration for creditor's release of debtor's obligation to pay the remaining balance

   2.) Parties may settle by entering into an accord (new agreement) and satisfaction (performance of new terms) if the following conditions are met

      a.) The obligation to pay or the amount of the debt is disputed

      b.) The obligation to pay is not yet due; the debt is not a mature one

      c.) The amount owed is not liquidated; the amount is not a definite, certain, or exact sum of money or a sum that is capable of being made definite by computation

      d.) Other or additional consideration is given

      e.) Creditor's promise to release debtor is in a signed writing

   3.) Release and/or covenant not to sue

      a.) A release is a relinquishment of a right or discharge of an obligation or claim that one has against another person; it must be supported by consideration

      b.) A covenant not to sue is a promise by one who has a right to bring an action that he will not sue in order to enforce such right of action; it must be supported by consideration

3. Promises enforceable without consideration

  a. New promise to pay debt barred by the statute of limitations

  b. New written promise or reaffirmation of promise to pay debt that will otherwise be barred by discharge in bankruptcy

  c. Doctrine of promissory estoppel or detrimental reliance—in those states where the doctrine has been adopted, the promisor will not be able to plead lack of consideration if the following conditions are met

   1.) A promise is made to induce a promisee to act in a particular way

   2.) The promisor can foresee that the promisee will justifiably rely upon the promise

   3.) The promisee substantially changes his position in the foreseeable manner and incurs damage because of reasonably relying upon the promise

   4.) It is grossly unfair not to enforce the promise

  d. Charitable subscriptions

D. CAPACITY

 1. Contractual capacity

  a. Minors

   1.) Statutes prescribe the age of majority; in most states, age 18 is the age of majority

   2.) Minors' rights to disaffirm

    a.) Minors may disaffirm contracts during minority and for a reasonable period after attaining the age of majority

    b.) Minors may not disaffirm if a contract has been approved by a court or, in some states because of statute, if the contract is for any of the following

     • Life or medical insurance

     • Educational loan

     • Medical care

     • Marriage

     • Enlistment in armed forces

     • Transportation by common carrier

    c.) Conveyances of real property cannot be disaffirmed until the minor reaches the age of majority

    d.) The contract is voidable by the minor but not by the adult; if the minor disaffirms, each party must make restitution by returning consideration received from the other party

    e.) Executory contracts

     • Minor may disaffirm contract—because the minor received nothing from the other party, there is no need to make restitution

     • Majority rule—continued silence after reaching majority is treated as disaffirmance of an executory contract

    f.) Executed contracts—minor may disaffirm contract

     • The adult with whom a minor has contracted must make restitution (return any consideration received from minor)

     • If personal property was sold by a minor to an adult, who resold it to an innocent good faith purchaser, the purchaser will not be required to return the property to the minor

FUNDAMENTALS SUPPLEMENT

- The minor must return consideration received from the adult. The majority rule is that the minor must make restitution only if the minor is able to do so. In some states:

    — by statute, a deduction is made for deterioration, depreciation, and damage; and

    — minor must pay reasonable value for any benefit conferred.

    3.) Ratification

        a.) A contract will be enforceable if the minor indicates an intention to be bound (ratification) after reaching the age of majority

        b.) Express written or oral ratification

        c.) Implied ratification by conduct indicating satisfaction with the contract (retaining consideration or accepting benefits)

  b. Intoxicated persons

    1.) Contracts made by one who is so intoxicated that his judgment is impaired and cannot comprehend the legal consequences of entering into a contract are voidable

    2.) Contracts may be disaffirmed while intoxicated or within a reasonable time after becoming sober

        a.) Restitution must be made

        b.) Intoxicated persons cannot disaffirm if a third person would be injured

        c.) Intoxicated persons must pay the reasonable value for necessaries that were furnished

  c. Mentally incompetent persons

    1.) One is considered mentally incompetent or insane if his judgment is impaired and that person cannot understand or comprehend the nature and effect of a particular transaction

    2.) If a person is declared judicially incompetent, his contracts are void

    3.) A contract that is made by a person who is mentally incompetent but has not been so adjudicated is voidable by the mentally incompetent person while he is mentally incompetent, or within a reasonable time after regaining sanity, or by his guardian or other representative

    4.) Contracts for necessaries may be disaffirmed, but the mentally incompetent party is liable for reasonable value of necessaries furnished

  d. Others who may be treated as lacking capacity

    1.) Convicts—in some states, those who have been convicted of major felonies do not have full capacity to make contracts

    2.) Aliens

        a.) Citizens of other countries who are legally in the United States generally have contractual capacity, and their contracts are valid

        b.) Enemy aliens and illegal aliens have limited contractual capacity

2. Genuineness of assent

a. Mistake

1.) A mistake is an error or unconscious ignorance or forgetfulness of a past or present fact that is material, very important, or essential to the contract

2.) Mistakes as to material facts should be distinguished from mistakes of judgment as to value or quality

3.) Unilateral mistake—in general, if only one party to a contract has made a mistake, the party cannot avoid the contract unless the other party was responsible for the mistake being made, knew of the mistake, or should have known of the mistake and failed to correct it

4.) Mutual or bilateral mistakes concerning material facts—in general, if both parties have made a mistake as to a material fact, the contract is voidable at the option of either party (i.e., existence, nature, or identity of subject matter)

b. Fraudulent misrepresentation

1.) Fraud in the execution—if a party has been led to believe that an act that he is performing is something other than executing a contract, his assent is not real, and any contract that appears to have been formed is void

2.) Fraud in the inducement—a contract is voidable if a party was damaged by being induced to enter the contract while reasonably relying on a false representation of a material fact

a.) Elements of fraud in the inducement

- A misrepresentation of material fact was made via representation, other words, or conduct

- A misrepresentation of law

- A misrepresentation was made by one who had knowledge that it was false or who acted with reckless disregard

- A misrepresentation was made with intent to deceive; the evidence that the representation was made to induce the deceived party to enter into the contract is the fact that the contract was actually formed

- Reliance on the representation; reliance must have been such that a reasonable person would have been justified in relying on the representation

- Injury to the deceived innocent party; the contract would not have been formed or would have been more valuable if the representation had been true

b.) Fraud because of silence or concealment

- There is no duty to inform a contracting party of facts

- Exceptions

— A seller must disclose latent defects that are not ordinarily discoverable but that cause an object to be dangerous

— A seller with superior knowledge may not conceal facts, knowing that the other party lacks that knowledge

— When a party has previously misstated a material fact and later realizes that he made a misstatement, that party is then required to make a correction

— When parties have a fiduciary or confidential relationship, the party with knowledge of relevant facts has an obligation to disclose them to the other party

— Statutes, such as the Truth in Lending Act, require disclosure of certain relevant facts

- Innocent misrepresentation—if a party unintentionally makes a representation without knowledge of its falsity, the other party, who relied on the representation and was damaged, may rescind the contract

c.) Undue influence

- When a party who is in a dominant position because of a confidential relationship secures an unfair advantage in a contract with a weaker, dominated party, the contract is voidable and may be disaffirmed by the dominated party

- There is a rebuttable presumption of undue influence in the following situations

— The parties are in a familial or fiduciary relationship based on trust and confidence

— The contract is extremely unfair to the dominated party

- A presumption may be rebutted by showing the following

— Full disclosure was made

— Consideration received was adequate

— Independent advice was received by the weaker party

d.) Duress

- If a party is coerced into entering a contract because of the wrongful use of force or a threat of force, the contract is voidable

- Assent may have been induced by fear of the following

— Bodily injury to a party or relative

— Criminal (but not civil) prosecution of a party or relative

— Harm to property or business under unusual circumstances

e.) Adhesion contract and unconscionability

- An adhesion contract arises when one party with overwhelming bargaining power takes such unfair advantage of the other party that the latter has no choice but to adhere to dictated terms or do without a particular good or service

- The resulting contract may be held to be unenforceable because of unconscionability

E. THE STATUTE OF FRAUDS

1. To be enforceable, some contractual promises must be evidenced by a writing that is signed by the parties against whom they are being enforced

2. Contracts that must be in writing

   a. Contracts for sales of interests in real property

   b. Contracts that cannot be performed within one year

   c. Collateral, or secondary, promises to answer for obligations of others

    d. Promises that are within the Statute of Frauds and that must be in a signed writing

       1.) The promise is made to the obligee (rather than the principal obligor) by one who is not presently liable for the debt or who does not have a present duty to perform

       2.) The liability of the guarantor is secondary, or collateral, to that of the principal obligor

       3.) If the main purpose or primary object of the secondary promisor is to protect his own interest or to obtain a material benefit, an oral promise will be enforced

       4.) Promises are made by executors or administrators to personally pay the debts of the decedents' estates

    e. Unilateral promises made in consideration of marriage and prenuptial agreements

    f. Contracts for the sale of goods and other personal property

       1.) Contract for the sale of goods for a price of $500 or more. Exceptions:

          a.) Partial performance—buyer pays for or receives and accepts goods

          b.) Goods (not ordinarily suitable for resale) to be specially manufactured for the buyer by the seller who has begun production of the goods

          c.) Sales between merchants when either party, within a reasonable period, sends a written confirmation to which the other party fails to object within 10 days

          d.) Admissions, in pleadings or in court, that the contract existed

       2.) Other code provisions

          a.) The Statute of Frauds is satisfied by payment or delivery and acceptance of securities

          b.) Security agreements

          c.) Contract for sale of miscellaneous personal property when price is more than $5,000

3. Sufficiency of writing—memorandum evidencing the contract need only contain basic, essential terms of the contract

4. Parol evidence rule

    a. If a written instrument is regarded by the parties as their complete integrated agreement, other oral or written evidence is inadmissible for purposes of changing, altering, or contradicting the effect of the writing

    b. Parol evidence is admitted to show the following

       1.) A modification of the writing

       2.) The contract was void or voidable

       3.) The meaning of ambiguous or vague language

       4.) The writing was incomplete

       5.) A prior course of dealings or a trade usage

       6.) Gross typographical or clerical errors

       7.) Another separate contract with a different subject matter

F. DISCHARGE AND PERFORMANCE

1. Conditions

    a. A condition is an operative event, the occurrence or nonoccurrence of which changes, limits, precludes, gives rise to, or terminates a contractual obligation

    b. Types of conditions

        1.) Condition precedent—a conditioning event must occur before performance by the promisor is required; until then, the promisee has no right to receive performance

        2.) Condition subsequent—the occurrence of the conditioning event extinguishes an existing contractual duty

        3.) Concurrent condition—the performance of each party is conditioned on the performance of the other party

    c. How conditions arise

        1.) Express—condition clearly stated by parties

        2.) Implied in fact—condition that is understood or implied

        3.) Implied in law (constructive)—imposed by court in order to achieve justice or fairness

2. Discharge by performance

    a. Full, complete performance in a manner prescribed by the contract discharges the performing party

    b. Tender of complete performance—an unconditional offer to perform by one who is ready, willing, and able to do so discharges the party if his tender is not accepted

    c. Time for performance

        1.) If time for performance is not stated, performance is to be rendered within a reasonable period

        2.) If parties stipulate that time is of the essence (vital), the time requirement must be followed

        3.) If time for performance is stipulated, but not vital, performance before or within a few days of the stated time satisfies contract

    d. Part performance

        1.) If partial performance is accepted, the performing party can recover the value of performance

        2.) If performance is substantial (i.e., minor, trivial deviation from contractual obligation) and deviation is not the result of bad faith, the performing party is discharged but is liable for his failure to render complete performance

        3.) Partial performance that is something less than substantial performance is a breach of contract; it results in the discharge of the party entitled to receive performance but not the discharge of the partially performing party

    e. Effect of contractual conditions on discharge by performance

        1.) Strict compliance with express conditions is necessary

        2.) Substantial performance of constructive conditions is necessary

3.) Express personal satisfaction condition—the promise of one party to pay may be conditioned on that party's satisfaction with the other party's performance

a.) If personal taste, preferences, aesthetics, fancy, or comfort are involved, payment is excused if dissatisfaction is honest and in good faith, even though a reasonable person would have been satisfied

b.) If satisfaction relates to operative fitness, merchantability, or mechanical utility, payment is excused when dissatisfaction is honest and a reasonable person would have been dissatisfied

3. Discharge by breach of contact

a. A breach of contract is the nonperformance of a contractual duty

b. A party who totally fails to perform is not discharged and is liable for damages for breach of contract; the other party is, however, discharged and need not hold himself ready to perform

c. If a party performs in part, but his performance does not amount to substantial part performance, there is a material breach of contract

1.) The partially performing party is not discharged and is liable for the material breach of contract

2.) The other party is discharged and need not hold himself ready to perform

d. If there is a minor, nonmaterial breach of contract, the breaching party is liable for damages if the breach is not cured; the nonbreaching party is not discharged and is required to perform

e. Anticipatory breach of contract

1.) If a party repudiates a contract before he is required to perform, the other party may sue immediately and does not have to remain ready to perform

2.) The doctrine of anticipatory breach does not apply to a promise to pay a stated sum of money, a unilateral contract, or a bilateral contract that is executory on one side only

f. Privity of contract

1.) The connection or relationship between two parties each having a legally recognized interest in the same subject matter

2.) When you are talking of a privity of contract, it is the relationship between the parties of a contract that allows them to sue each other but prevents a third party to sue on the basis of the contract

---

Example

Assume a city contracted with a water company to provide water to the city's fire hydrants. A person's house catches on fire and burns down because there is no water in the hydrant. The person could not sue the water company because the water company breached its contract with the city because it is not a party to the contract, but the city could sue the water company under the contract.

---

g. Surety

1.) A surety is a person who has pledged as part of the contract to pay back money or perform a certain action if the principal to a contract fails, similar to collateral or similar to a guarantor

4. Discharge by agreement of the parties

   a. Provision in original contract

   b. New, subsequent, valid, enforceable contract

      1.) Elements of contract, including consideration, must be present

      2.) Mutual rescission—parties agree to discharge and relieve each other of their obligations

         a.) If the original bilateral contract was executory, consideration is present because each party gives up existing rights

         b.) If the original contract was either a unilateral or a bilateral contract executed by one party, new consideration must be given to the party who performed in exchange for his promise to relieve the nonperforming party of his contractual duty to render the originally promised performance

   c. Release—a statement by one party that relieves the other party of a contractual duty. A release often includes a promise not to sue for breach of contract

   d. Accord and satisfaction

      1.) Accord—parties agree that a different (substitute) performance will be rendered by one party in satisfaction of his original obligation

      2.) Satisfaction—the substitute performance is actually rendered and accepted

      3.) Until substitute performance is rendered, the original contractual obligations are merely suspended

   e. Substituted agreement—parties agree to enter a new agreement with different terms as a substitute for an original contract that is expressly or impliedly discharged

   f. Novation—parties agree with a third person that the contractual duties of one of the original parties will be assumed by the third person. The third person is substituted for one of the original parties with the consent of the party entitled to receive the performance.

5. Discharge by operation of law

   a. Material alteration of a written contract without consent

   b. Running of the statute of limitations, which operates to bar access to judicial remedies

   c. Discharge (decree) in bankruptcy

   d. Impossibility—the occurrence of a supervening, unforeseen event makes it impossible to perform

      1.) Object of contract becomes illegal

      2.) Death or serious illness or incapacitation of a party who was to perform personal services

      3.) Destruction of specific subject matter of the contract

      4.) Economic frustration—an unforeseen event occurs that frustrates the purpose for which one of the parties entered the contract; therefore, the value of the expected performance he is to receive is destroyed

      5.) Commercial impracticability—an extreme change in conditions makes performance impracticable because it will be extremely difficult, burdensome, or costly to render

6.) Temporary impossibility—when performance is temporarily suspended because of unexpected occurrences and subsequent circumstances make performance very difficult, parties may be discharged

G. REMEDIES

1. Remedies at law—money damages

   a. Compensatory damages—awarded to a nonbreaching party to compensate for the actual harm or loss caused by the breach

   b. Consequential or special damages—speculative, unforeseeable, remote, indirect, or unexpected damages that do not ordinarily flow from a breach of contract are not recoverable unless contemplated by the nonperforming party since he was given notice thereof

   c. Punitive or exemplary damages—an unusual award by a court to punish for willful, wanton, or malicious (tortious) harm caused to a nonbreaching party

   d. Nominal damages—an inconsequential sum that establishes that the plaintiff had a cause of action but suffered no measurable pecuniary loss

   e. Mitigation of damages—a party who suffers damages has a duty to reduce actual damages if he is able to do so

   f. Liquidated damages—the parties may provide in their contract that a stated sum of money or property will be paid, or, if previously deposited, forfeited, if one of the parties fails to perform in accordance with the contract; such provisions will be enforced unless they are unreasonable and, therefore, are penalties

2. Equitable remedies

   a. Not available if any of the following applies

      1.) Remedy at law (usually money damages) is adequate, determinable, and available

      2.) Aggrieved party has shown bad faith, fraud, and so forth

      3.) Aggrieved party has unnecessarily delayed in bringing an action (laches)

      4.) A court will have to supervise execution of remedy

   b. Rescission and restitution

      1.) *Rescission* means cancellation or abrogation of a contract; it may be mutually agreed to by parties to a contract or awarded as a remedy by a court

      2.) Usually, restitution is also given by a court so that previously rendered consideration, or its value, is returned

   c. Specific performance—an order by a court to render a contractually promised performance

      1.) Specified performance will be granted when the following are true

         a.) Contract involves unique personal property or real property that is always considered to be unique

         b.) Performance that is to be rendered is clear and unambiguous

      2.) Specified performance will not be granted when performance to be rendered involves personal services

d. Injunction—an order enjoining or restraining a person from doing some act

e. Reformation—a court may correct an agreement so that it will conform to the intentions of the parties

f. Quasi contract—a court may require one who has received a benefit to pay for the benefit conferred to prevent unjust enrichment

V. AGENCY RELATIONSHIPS

A. AGENT'S DUTIES TO PRINCIPAL

1. Remedies available to principal for breach of duties by agent

   a. Principal's right to indemnification—if a principal is required to pay damages to an injured party for an agent's tortious conduct or, as a result of an agent's violation of the principal's instructions, incurs a loss, the principal may recover the resulting damages from the agent

   b. A principal may seek remedies on the basis of breach of contractual duties or in tort on the basis of a breach of the fiduciary duty

   c. Transactions by an agent that violate the agent's fiduciary duty to the principal are voidable by the principal

   d. A court will impose a constructive trust on property received by an agent who has used his agency position in conflict with those of his principal; the property (or the proceeds of its sale) is treated as held for the benefit of the principal

B. PRINCIPAL'S DUTIES TO AGENT

1. Remedies available to an agent for breach of duties by a principal

   a. Indemnification—a principal may be required to indemnify an agent for payments or liabilities incurred in executing his obligations and for losses caused by the failure of the principal to perform his duties

   b. An agent may obtain a lien against the principal's property

   c. An agent may sue for breach of contract or file a counterclaim if sued by the principal

   d. An agent may bring an action for an accounting

   e. An agent may withhold further performance

C. TERMINATION OF AGENCY RELATIONSHIP

1. Termination by act of the parties

   a. Lapse of time

      1.) An agency expires at the end of a specified time if one is stated

      2.) An agency terminates after the expiration of a reasonable period if no term has been specified

   b. Purpose accomplished—an agency is terminated when the objective for which it was created has been achieved

   c. Occurrence of specific event—an agency ends on the happening of a particular event if its formation had been so conditioned

   d. Mutual agreement—the parties may consent to the termination of an agency

   e. Termination by one party

      1.) A principal may revoke the authority of an agent, or an agent may renounce his appointment as an agent

      2.) Either party may have the power, but not necessarily the right, to terminate an agency

    a.) If an agency is an agency at will (not for a stated term or for a particular purpose), either party has the power and right to terminate the agency

    b.) If an agency is not an agency at will, a party may not have the power and right to terminate the agency and is, therefore, liable to the other party for the wrongful termination (breach of contract)

3.) An agency may be terminated for cause

4.) A principal has neither the power nor the right to terminate an agency coupled with an interest (which is also referred to as a power coupled with an interest or a power given as security)

    a.) The agency is said to be irrevocable

    b.) This is distinguished from situations in which an agent merely derives proceeds or profits from transactions

2. Termination by operation of law

  a. Death or insanity terminates an agency

    1.) Knowledge of the death or insanity is not required

    2.) An agency coupled with an interest is not automatically terminated

    3.) Statutory exceptions exist

  b. Bankruptcy of the principal terminates the agency

    1.) Insolvency does not terminate the relationship

    2.) Bankruptcy of the agent does not necessarily terminate the agency relationship

  c. Impossibility

    1.) Destruction of the subject matter of the agency

    2.) Outbreak of war

    3.) Change in law making further conduct of the agency illegal

  d. Unforeseen change in circumstances

VI. NEGOTIABLE INSTRUMENTS

A. REQUIREMENTS

For an instrument to be negotiable, it must have all of the following requirements on the face of the instrument

1. In writing

2. Signed by maker or drawer

3. Contain an unconditional promise or order to pay

4. State a fixed amount in money

5. Payable on demand or at a definite time

6. Payable to order or to bearer, unless it is a check

B. AMBIGUITIES

1. Words control over figures

2. Handwritten terms control over typewritten and printed terms

3. Typewritten terms control over printed terms

4. Omission of a date does not destroy negotiability, unless the date is necessary to determine when it is payable

5. Omission of the interest rate is allowed because the judicial interest rate (rate used on court judgment) is automatically used

6. Statement of consideration or where the instrument is drawn or payable is not required

7. The instrument may be postdated or antedated and remain negotiable (e.g., a bank may pay a postdated check before the date on the check unless the drawer notifies the bank to defer the payment)

8. The instrument may have a provision that by endorsing or cashing it, the payee acknowledges full satisfaction of debt, and the instrument remains negotiable

9. If an instrument is payable to the order of more than one person, either payee may negotiate or enforce it; if it is payable to him and her, all payees must negotiate or enforce it

---

Example

- If the instrument states, "Pay to the order of H. Fetzer *or* J. Becknell," then only one signature is required to negotiate or enforce it.

- If the instrument states "Pay to the order of H. Fetzer *and* J. Becknell," then both signatures are required to negotiate or enforce it.

---

10. If it is not clear whether the instrument is a draft or a note, the holder may treat it as either

C. NEGOTIATION

1. Two methods of transferring commercial paper

    a. Negotiation

    1.) One who receives a negotiable instrument by negotiation is called a holder

    2.) If the holder further qualifies as a holder in due course, he can obtain more rights than the transferor had

    3.) There are two methods of negotiation

    a.) Negotiating order paper requires both endorsement by the transferor and delivery of the instrument. Order paper includes negotiable instruments made payable to the order of A.

    b.) Negotiating bearer paper is accomplished by delivery alone; endorsement is not necessary

    - Subsequent parties may require endorsements for identification

    - The holder may endorse the bearer paper if he so chooses

    b. Assignment

    1.) An assignment occurs when a transfer does not meet all requirements of negotiation

    2.) The assignee can obtain only the same rights that the assignor had

2. Endorsements

    a. Blank endorsement—it converts order paper into bearer paper, and the bearer paper may be negotiated by mere delivery

    b. Special endorsement—indicates the specific person whom the endorsee wishes to negotiate the instrument

    1.) The words "pay to the order of" are not required on the back as an endorsement. The back of the instrument needs to be payable to the order or to the bearer on the front only.

    2.) If the instrument is not payable to order or to bearer on its face, it cannot be turned into a negotiable instrument by using these words in an endorsement on the back

    3.) The bearer paper may be converted into order paper by the use of a special endorsement. For example, a check made out to "cash" is delivered to Julie. Julie writes on the back "payable to Keri," and Julie signs the back. It was bearer paper until this special endorsement.

    4.) If last (or only) endorsement on the instrument is a blank endorsement, any holder may convert that bearer paper into order paper by writing "Pay to A" above that blank endorsement

    c. Restrictive endorsement—requires endorsees to comply with certain conditions (e.g., "for deposit only")

    d. Qualified endorsement—disclaims the liability normally imposed on the endorser. Normally, by signing the check, the endorser promises, automatically, to pay the holder or any subsequent endorser the amount of the instrument if it is later dishonored. Qualified endorsements, otherwise, have the same effects as other endorsements.

3. If the payee's name is misspelled, the payee may endorse it with the proper spelling, the misspelling, or both; the endorsee may require both

4. If an order instrument is transferred for value without being endorsed, the transferee may require endorsement from the transferor; upon obtaining the endorsement, the transferee will become a holder

5. Federal law recently standardized endorsements on checks. The endorser should turn the check over and sign in the top portion of the check next to the short edge. The purpose is to avoid interference with the bank's endorsements. The endorsements placed outside of this area do not destroy the negotiability but may delay the clearing process.

6. If a check has a statement that it is nonnegotiable (i.e., it is not governed by Article 3), the check is still negotiable. This is not true of other negotiable instruments, whereby such statements destroy negotiability.

D. LIABILITY OF PARTIES

1. Signatures by authorized agents—an agent may sign on behalf of another person (or principal), and that principal is liable, not the agent, if the signature indicates that the principal is liable

2. An accommodation party is liable on the instrument in the capacity in which he has signed, even if the taker knows of his accommodation status

   a. Notice of default need not be given to an accommodation party

   b. The accommodation party has the right of recourse against the accommodated party if the accommodation party is held liable

3. If there are multiple endorsers, each is liable in full to subsequent endorsers or holders

4. Once the primary party pays, all endorsers are discharged from liability. Cancellation of a prior party's endorsement discharges that party from liability. Intentional destruction of an instrument by a holder discharges prior parties to the instrument.

5. Persons whose signatures were forged on an instrument are not liable on that instrument. The forged signature operates as the signature of the forger. Therefore, if the signature of the maker or drawer is forged, the instrument can still be negotiated between the parties, and a holder can therefore acquire good title. However, a forged endorsement does not transfer title. Accordingly, persons receiving it after forgery cannot collect on it.

E. BANKS

1. Banks include savings and loan associations, credit unions, and trust companies

2. The relationship between bank and depositor is debtor-creditor

3. Checks

   a. Banks are not obligated to pay on a check presented more than six months after the date, but they may pay in good faith and charge the customer's account

   b. Even if a check creates an overdraft, a bank may charge the customer's account

   c. Banks are liable to the drawer for damages caused by wrongful dishonor of a check. Wrongful dishonor may occur if the bank, in error, believes that funds are insufficient when, actually, they are sufficient.

   d. Payment of bad checks, such as forged or altered checks

1.) A bank is liable to the drawer for payment on bad checks, unless the drawer's negligence contributed, since the bank is presumed to know the signatures of its drawers

2.) A bank cannot recover from a holder in due course to whom the bank paid on a bad check

3.) If the drawer fails to notify the bank of a forgery or an alteration within 30 days of the bank statement, the drawer is held liable on subsequent forgeries or alterations done in the same way by the same person

e. An oral stop payment order is good for 14 days; a written stop payment order is good for 6 months and is renewable

1.) The stop payment order must be given so as to give the bank reasonable opportunity to act on it

2.) A bank is liable to the drawer if the bank pays after an effective stop payment order only when the drawer can prove that the bank's failure to obey the order caused the drawer's loss. If the drawer has no valid defense to justify dishonoring instruments, the bank has no liability for failure to obey the stop payment order.

3.) If the drawer stops payment on the check, the drawer is still liable to the holder of the check unless the drawer has a valid defense

VII. CONSUMER PROTECTION

A. PUBLIC POLICY ISSUES

1. The potential benefits and costs of consumer protection-related judicial decisions, statutes, and regulations must be balanced

2. Existing and potential costs of compliance may include increases in prices for consumer goods and services and a decrease in competition due to costs of compliance

B. ADVERTISING

1. The Federal Trade Commission (FTC) administers a number of federal consumer protection statutes and is authorized to prevent unfair or deceptive acts or practices in commerce (deceptive advertising)

2. Procedures are followed when the FTC believes that a deceptive advertisement is being used

   a. The FTC conducts an investigation of a possible deceptive advertisement on its own initiative or following a consumer's or competitor's complaint

   b. A hearing may be conducted by an administrative law judge whose ruling may be appealed by the advertiser to the FTC

   c. If the FTC upholds the decision against the advertiser, its decision can be appealed to a US Court of Appeals

3. The FTC may issue a cease and desist order requiring that an unfair or deceptive advertisement be discontinued and may initiate a consumer redress action for rescission or reformation of contracts that were entered into by consumers with the advertiser as a result of the misleading advertisement

4. Counter-advertising—the FTC may require that an advertiser correct misinformation in an advertisement

5. Unfair or deceptive acts or practices

   a. Deceptive advertising refers to intentional misrepresentations of facts that are material or relevant factors included in a purchaser's decisions to buy the advertised products or services

   b. Statements made in an advertisement are deceptive if they are scientifically untrue or contain false product differentiation

   c. An advertisement is deceptive if a reasonable consumer would be misled; in general, puffing is not considered to be deceptive

6. Bait-and-switch advertising

   a. The advertisement relates to one item, which is offered for sale at a low price. When a consumer tries to purchase that item, a salesperson tries to get the consumer to buy a more expensive item.

   b. FTC guidelines are designed to prevent such practices as refusal to sell an advertised item, failure to have an adequate quantity of an advertised item available, failure to supply the advertised item within a reasonable time, and discouragement of employees from selling an advertised item

   c. A credit card issuer may not bill a cardholder for unauthorized charges if a credit card is improperly issued

C. STATE LAWS

1. Statutes, which vary from state to state, have codified, simplified, and otherwise expanded the protection afforded by the common law (e.g., lemon laws and right of redhibition)

2. State consumer protection legislation may be stricter than comparable federal law

FUNDAMENTALS

Questions

Fundamentals

THE FINANCIAL PLANNING PROCESS

1. Analyzing and evaluating client information is one stage of the personal financial planning process. Which of the following tasks are completed in this stage?

    1. Identifying alternative investment vehicles.
    2. Identifying financial strengths and weaknesses.
    3. Recommending specific tax strategies.
    4. Preparing preliminary financial statements.
        a. 2 and 4.
        b. 1 and 3.
        c. 1, 2, and 3.
        d. 2, 3, and 4.
        e. 1, 2, 3, and 4.

2. Arrange the following financial planning functions into the logical order in which these functions are performed by a professional financial planner. (**CFP® Certification Examination, released 11/94**)

    1. Interview clients, identify preliminary goals.
    2. Monitor financial plans.
    3. Prepare financial plan.
    4. Implement financial strategies, plans, and products.
    5. Collect, analyze, and evaluate client data.
        a. 1, 3, 5, 4, 2.
        b. 5, 1, 3, 2, 4.
        c. 1, 5, 4, 3, 2.
        d. 1, 5, 3, 4, 2.
        e. 1, 4, 5, 3, 2.

3. You speak to a person for the first time. Which of the following would be appropriate if you are in the first two stages (goal setting and data gathering) of the financial planning process?

    1. Asking about the number of dependents.
    2. Asking about the age of the dependents or dates of birth.
    3. Determining which stocks to buy.
    4. Collecting personal financial statement information.
        a. 1 only.
        b. 1 and 2.
        c. 2 and 3.
        d. 1, 2 and 4.
        e. 1, 2, 3 and 4.

PERSONAL FINANCIAL STATEMENTS

4. A client provides the following information regarding his assets and liabilities as of December 31, 2007. Determine which of the items listed below should be presented on his Statement of Financial Condition as of December 31, 2007.

    1. Stock options granted September 30, 2007, exercisable one year from date of grant.

    2. A bonus receivable of $10,000. The client estimates the bonus based on the prior year bonus and cannot determine the amount precisely because the board of directors meets February 15, 2008, to determine if and when a bonus will be paid.

    3. Huge Oil, Inc. stock in the amount of $15,000. The client owns 1,000 shares priced at $10 per share at December 31, 2007. Huge Oil, Inc. declared a $5 per share dividend on December 10, 2007, payable January 15, 2008, to stockholders of record as of December 31, 2007. The client participates in the company's dividend reinvestment plan.

    4. The client is a cosigner on a loan. The proceeds were used to purchase an automobile by his son. The principal balance on the loan is $4,500 and his son has made all payments to date on a timely basis.

    5. Consulting fees receivable related to services performed by the client's spouse. The engagement was completed and an invoice was mailed December 10, 2007, and the credit terms were net 30.

        a. 1, 3 and 4.

        b. 3 and 5.

        c. 4 and 5.

        d. 2, 3 and 5.

        e. 1, 2 and 4.

5. Determine the order of liquidity for the following assets for purposes of presentation on the Statement of Financial Condition.

    1. Cash surrender value of life insurance.

    2. Equity mutual fund.

    3. Jewelry.

    4. Personal residence.

        a. 1, 2, 3, 4.

        b. 2, 1, 4, 3.

        c. 2, 1, 3, 4.

        d. 1, 2, 4, 3.

        e. 3, 2, 1, 4.

6. What is the appropriate date to identify the Statement of Financial Condition of a calendar-year client for the year 2007?

        a. At December 31, 2007.

        b. For the period beginning January 1, 2008.

        c. For the period ending December 31, 2007.

        d. For the period January 1 to December 31, 2007.

        e. At January 1, 2008.

7. What is the appropriate date to identify the Statement of Cash Flows of a calendar-year client for the year 2007?

    a. At December 31, 2007.

    b. For the period prior to January 1, 2008.

    c. For the period ending December 31, 2007.

    d. For the period beginning January 1, 2007.

    e. At January 1, 2008.

8. The estimated value of a real estate asset in a financial statement prepared by a Certified Financial Planner licensee should be based upon the: (CFP® Certification Examination, released 11/94)

    a. Basis of the asset, after taking into account all straight-line and accelerated depreciation.

    b. Client's estimate of current value.

    c. Current replacement value of the asset.

    d. Value that a well-informed buyer is willing to accept from a well-informed seller where neither is compelled to buy or sell.

    e. Current insured value.

9. Six months ago, a client purchased a new bedroom suite for $6,500. For purposes of preparing accurate financial statements, this purchase would appear as a(an): (CFP® Certification Examination, released 11/94)

    1. Use asset on the client's net worth statement.

    2. Investment asset on the client's net worth statement.

    3. Variable outflow on the client's historic cash flow statement.

    4. Fixed outflow on the client's cash flow statement.

        a. 1, 2, and 3.

        b. 1 and 3.

        c. 2 and 4.

        d. 4 only.

        e. 1, 2, 3, and 4.

ANALYSIS OF FINANCIAL STATEMENTS AND IDENTIFICATION OF STRENGTHS AND WEAKNESSES

10. Which of the following items would affect net worth?

    1. Repayment of a loan using funds from a savings account.

    2. Purchase of an automobile that is 75% financed with a 25% down payment.

    3. The S&P 500 increases, and the client has an S&P Indexed Mutual Fund.

    4. Interest rates increase, and the client has a substantial bond portfolio.

      a. 2 and 3.

      b. 3 and 4.

      c. 1, 3, and 4.

      d. 1, 2, and 4.

11. The Powells have a net worth of $200,000 before any of the following transactions:

    1. Paid off credit cards of $10,000 using a savings account.

    2. Transferred $4,000 from checking to their IRAs.

    3. Purchased $2,000 of furniture with credit.

What is the net worth of the Powells after these transactions?

      a. $184,000.

      b. $186,000.

      c. $190,000.

      d. $200,000.

12. Mr. and Mrs. Claiborne, both age 30, have provided you the following information:

Balance Sheet Information			
Cash	$4,000	Credit Cards	$25,000
IRA	25,000	Student Loans	20,000
Investments	40,000	Residence Mortgage	200,000
Personal Residence	240,000		

Statement of Cash Flows	
Annual Income	$48,000
Annual Expenditures:	
Housing Payments (P&I)	$21,062
Housing Payments (T&I)	4,000
Credit Card Repayments	10,000
Student Loans	5,000
All Other Expenses	4,000

How much is Mr. and Mrs. Claiborne's net worth?

 a. $64,000.
 b. $103,938.
 c. $107,938.
 d. $148,000.

13. Given the information in problem 12 above, which of the following is a correct statement regarding Mr. and Mrs. Claiborne?

 a. Their net worth is low for their age.
 b. They have an insufficient emergency fund if the IRA and the investment account are excluded from the calculation.
 c. They could qualify to refinance their home for the balance of the mortgage if interest rates fell from 10% to 8%.
 d. Their debt-to-asset ratio is good.

14. This year Anita sold her bond portfolio to pay off her home mortgage and invested the remainder in an IRA. Her stock portfolio increased in value by $450. All of Anita's income and expenses remained the same as in the previous year and her investments provided no income. Which is true of Anita's current financial situation as compared to last year?

      a.   Her emergency fund ratio has improved.

      b.   Her debt management ratios are unchanged.

      c.   Her savings ratio has increased.

      d.   Her current ratio has improved.

BUDGETING
---

15. Which of the following is correct regarding budgeting?

    a. The budget should be adjusted yearly to reflect actual expenditures.

    b. Inflation should not be considered when budgeting.

    c. If clients are close to retirement age, budgeting is not useful.

    d. Budgeting requires planning for the unexpected.

16. Which of the following statements is correct regarding budgeting?

    a. When preparing a budget, historical bank statements should be reviewed instead of historical credit card statements.

    b. When preparing a budget, insurance and utilities expenditures should be categorized as discretionary expenditures.

    c. If the client is sufficiently close to retirement, budgeting may be used to determine the Wage Replacement Ratio for capital needs analysis for retirement.

    d. If the client has a history of making large dollar purchases impulsively, the planner should not encourage investments in assets where withdrawal is difficult.

INTERNAL ANALYSIS

17. Which phase of the life cycle is typically begins when a client is in their late 30s or early 40s, and is characterized by an increase in cash flow, assets, and net worth, with some decrease in the proportional use of debt?

   a. Conservation/Protection Phase.

   b. Asset Accumulation Phase.

   c. Distribution/Gifting Phase.

   d. Pre-career Phase.

18. Which of the following statements regarding a client's risk tolerance is correct?

   a. Most devices used to measure risk provide accurate and reliable information.

   b. A client's willingness to accept risk is typically lower when the decision involved will affect other people.

   c. It is possible to categorize the client as a risk taker or risk averter by observing their behavior in a single situation.

   d. Monetary risk tolerance and physical risk tolerance are always highly correlated.

PERSONAL-USE ASSETS AND LIABILITIES

19. Frankie's house payments, including principal and interest, are $496.00 at the end of each month. She has a 15-year mortgage note with an 8.75% interest rate compounded monthly. What was the amount of Frankie's original mortgage note? (Round answer to the nearest hundred dollars).

    a. $55,600.
    b. $59,600.
    c. $49,600.
    d. $45,600.

20. A young couple would like to purchase a new home using one of the following mortgages:

    1: 10.5% interest with 5 discount points to be paid at time of closing.

    2: 11.5% interest with 2 discount points to be paid at time of closing.

    Assuming the couple could qualify for both mortgages, which of the following aspects should be considered in deciding between these two mortgages? (CFP® Certification Examination, released 11/94)

    1. Gross income.
    2. Estimated length of ownership.
    3. Real estate tax liability.
    4. Cash currently available.
        a. 1 and 2.
        b. 2 only.
        c. 2 and 4.
        d. 4 only.
        e. 1, 2, 3, and 4.

ECONOMIC ENVIROMENT—BASIC CONCEPTS

21. Which of the following costs best describes the cost of foregone income that results from making an economic decision to use funds to purchase a piece of equipment?

    a. Marginal cost.

    b. Opportunity cost.

    c. Variable cost.

    d. Fixed cost.

    e. Cost of capital.

22. The inverse relationship between the price of a product and the number of units sold would describe which of the following?

    a. The law of demand.

    b. Price controls.

    c. Supply side economics.

    d. The law of supply.

    e. Market price.

23. If the demand for a product is inelastic, it means that:

    a. An increase in the price would lead to an increase in the total amount spent on purchases of the product.

    b. An increase in the price would lead to a decrease in the total amount spent on purchases of the product.

    c. An increase in the price would have no effect on the total amount spent on purchases of the product.

    d. The demand and supply are in equilibrium.

    e. The price of the product cannot be increased or decreased.

24. If the Federal Reserve wanted to lower interest rates, it would consider which of the following?

    1. Purchase government securities.

    2. Increase the reserve requirement of member banks.

    3. Increase the discount rate.

    4. Decrease the reserve requirement of member banks.

    a. 1 and 2.

    b. 2 and 3.

    c. 1 only.

    d. 1 and 4.

    e. 3 and 4.

25. The average number of times a dollar is used per year is also known as:

    a. Inflation.

    b. Price elasticity.

    c. Devaluation.

    d. Velocity of money.

    e. GDP.

26. A common measure of inflation is the Consumer Price Index (CPI). The index begins with a base of 100 at 1967. If the index as of December 1992 was 125.6 and the index as of December 1993 was 133.5, what was the CPI rate of inflation for 1993 rounded to the nearest one-tenth of a percent?

    a. 10.6%.

    b. 7.9%.

    c. 5.9%.

    d. 6.0%.

    e. 6.3%.

27. If the US dollar equivalent of a Mexican Peso is 0.30656 and the US dollar equivalent of a Peruvian Inti is 0.4717, what is the value of a Mexican Peso in Peruvian Inti?

    a. MN 00.6499.

    b. MN 01.5387.

    c. MN 64.9900.

    d. MN 00.0154.

    e. MN 00.1446.

28. In a random sample, the value that occurs most frequently is known as:

    a. Mean.

    b. Median.

    c. Mode.

    d. Standard deviation.

    e. Beta.

29. The quantity demanded for an economic product varies inversely with its price is the definition of which of the following:

    a. The law of competition.

    b. The law of supply and demand.

    c. The law of demand.

    d. Laissez-faire.

    e. None of the above.

30. Supply for a product includes which of the following:

    1. Amount of a product available at any one time.
    2. Various amounts of a product that producers are willing to supply at all possible prices in the market.
    3. Total production in one year's time by a single firm.
    4. Amount that is supplied at equilibrium price.
        a. 1 only.
        b. 2 only.
        c. 3 and 4.
        d. 1, 2, 3, and 4.

31. The adjustment process in a competitive market moves toward:

    a. Equilibrium.
    b. Shortage.
    c. Surplus.
    d. Capitalism.

32. Which of the following describes pure competition?

    1. Buyers and sellers deal in a variety of products.
    2. Buyers and sellers act together.
    3. A large number of buyers and sellers exist.
    4. Buyers and sellers have little knowledge of the items for sale.
        a. 1 only.
        b. 3 only.
        c. 1 and 3.
        d. 1 and 4.
        e. 1, 2, 3, and 4.

33. A decrease, or shift to the left, in the supply curve occurs when:

    a. Some firms leave the industry.
    b. Government reduces regulations on production.
    c. The cost of inputs goes down.
    d. Taxes go down.
    e. Competition increases.

34. Which of the following occurs when the price of a product decreases and consumers buy more of the product?

    a. The product is a complementary product.
    b. There has been an increase in supply.
    c. A change in demand has taken place.
    d. A change in quantity demanded has taken place.

35. Consumer demand for sugar at 80 cents per pound results in $1,000 in company revenue, and a drop in price to 50 cents per pound results in $1,250 in revenue. Which of the following may be concluded about demand?

    a. Is unit elastic.

    b. Is inelastic.

    c. Would overtake supply.

    d. Is elastic.

36. What question can be asked to help determine the elasticity of demand for an item?

    a. Should production be decreased?

    b. Can the purchase be made by cash only?

    c. Could something else be substituted and work just as well?

    d. Is there enough of the product available?

37. Which of the following describes the law of downward-sloping demand?

    a. Consumer demand has not changed significantly.

    b. Consumer demand had dropped drastically.

    c. Consumers demand more at lower prices.

    d. Consumer demand has increased significantly.

38. An increase in the price of product A causes a decrease in the demand for product B. What are the two products?

    a. Complement products.

    b. Substitute products.

    c. Unrelated products.

    d. Demand-elastic products.

39. Which of the following explains the principle of diminishing marginal utility?

    a. The shape of the demand curve.

    b. A change in demand.

    c. The nature of inelastic demand.

    d. The substitution effect.

40. The Law of demand states that:

    a. Consumers select alternative ways of spending income.

    b. The relative change in price is caused by changes in demand.

    c. The relationship between changing prices and total receipts is a direct one.

    d. The demand for an economic product varies inversely with its price.

41. Which of the following are reasons for a change in consumer demand?

   1. Changes in consumer tastes: advertising, news reports, trends, and seasons can all affect consumer tastes.

   2. Changes in consumer demand may result from changes in consumer income: as income rises, consumers tend to buy more; if income declines, consumers buy less.

   3. Prices of related products: sometimes substitutes can be used in place of other products.

      a. 1 only.
      b. 2 only.
      c. 3 only.
      d. 1 and 2.
      e. 1, 2, and 3.

42. The relationship between a demand schedule and a demand curve is best described as:

   a. The two present the same information in different ways.
   b. There is no relationship between the two.
   c. A demand curve is part of a demand schedule.
   d. A demand schedule is created from a demand curve.

43. Which of the following are determinants of demand elasticity?

   1. Whether the purchase of the product can be delayed.
   2. Whether there are adequate substitutes for the product.
   3. Whether the purchase of the product requires a large portion of income.
   4. Whether the product has utility.

      a. 1 only.
      b. 2 only.
      c. 2 and 3.
      d. 1 and 3.
      e. 1, 2, 3 and 4.

44. Which of the following might cause an increase in supply?

   1. A decrease in productivity.
   2. Fewer sellers in the marketplace.
   3. More efficient technology.
   4. A decrease in government subsidies.

      a. 1 only.
      b. 2 only.
      c. 3 only.
      d. 1 and 4.
      e. 2 and 3.

45. Which of the following describes supply if the quantity supplied does not change significantly with a change in price?

    a. Supply is unit elastic.

    b. Supply is elastic.

    c. Supply is inelastic.

    d. Supply is fixed.

    e. Supply is variable.

46. Which of the following describes why changes in supply occur?

    1. Changes in the cost of inputs.

    2. Changes in productivity.

    3. Changes in technology.

    4. Changes in taxes.

    a. 1 only.

    b. 3 only.

    c. 1 and 2.

    d. 2 and 3.

    e. 1, 2, 3, and 4.

47. Inflation causes people living on a fixed income to have:

    1. No financial problems.

    2. Reduced systematic risk.

    3. Declining purchasing power.

    4. Unlimited resources.

    a. 1 only.

    b. 2 only.

    c. 3 only.

    d. 1 and 4.

    e. 1, 2, 3, and 4.

48. Which of the following describes an increase in the general level of prices?

    a. A market economy.

    b. A depression.

    c. Inflation.

    d. Deflation.

49. Which of the following statements are true regarding inflation?

    1. The opposite of inflation is disinflation, which is a decline in general price level.

    2. Deflation denotes a decline in the rate of inflation.

    3. Deflation is often caused by a reduction in the supply of money.

       a. 1 only.
       b. 1 and 3.
       c. 2 and 3.
       d. 1, 2, and 3.
       e. 3 only.

50. Which economic goal does minimum wage support?

    a. Economic equity.
    b. Economic efficiency.
    c. Economic growth.
    d. Full employment.

51. Movement through the phases of the business cycle is initiated by shifts in aggregate demand, which create fluctuations in Gross Domestic Product (GDP). Which combination of the following statements would be the most significant contributor to the upward shift in aggregate demand shown in the graph? (CFP® Certification Examination, released 11/94)

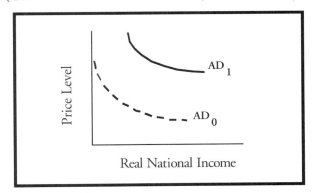

    1. Increase in demand for capital goods.
    2. Increase in interest rates.
    3. Increase in disposable income.
    4. Increase in savings.

       a. 1 and 3.
       b. 1, 2, and 3.
       c. 1, 3, and 4.
       d. 2 and 4.
       e. 3 and 4.

52. Under the Federal Fair Labor Standards Act, which of the following would be regulated?

    1. Minimum wage.
    2. Overtime.
    3. Number of hours in the work week.
        a. 1 only.
        b. 2 only.
        c. 3 only.
        d. 1, 2, and 3.

53. Which of the following provisions is basic to all workers compensation systems?

    a. The injured employee must prove the employer's negligence.
    b. The employer may invoke the traditional defense of contributory negligence.
    c. The employer may invoke the defense of assumption of the risk.
    d. The employer's liability may be ameliorated by a co-employee's negligence under the fellow-servant rule.
    e. The injured employee is allowed to recover on a strict liability theory.

54. If you have product with inelastic demand, which of the following is true?

    a. As the price increases, revenue decreases.
    b. As the price increases, revenue increases.
    c. There is no relationship between price and revenues.
    d. None of the above.

55. Which best describes increasing unemployment with businesses operating at their lowest capacity levels?

    a. Peak.
    b. Recession.
    c. Trough.
    d. Expansion.

56. When the economy experiences a decline in real GDP for two or more successive quarters, what stage of the economic cycle are we in?

    a. Trough.
    b. Recession.
    c. Peak.
    d. Recovery.

57. Which of the following statements concerning supply and/or demand is/are true? (CFP® **Certification Examination, released 12/96**)

    1. If demand increases and supply simultaneously decreases, equilibrium price will rise.

    2. There is an inverse relationship between price and quantity demanded.

    3. If demand decreases and supply simultaneously increases, equilibrium price will fall.

    4. If demand decreases and supply remains constant, equilibrium price will rise.

        a. 1, 2, and 3.

        b. 1 and 3.

        c. 2 and 4.

        d. 4 only.

        e. 1, 2, 3, and 4.

MONETARY AND FISCAL POLICY

58. Which of the following actions would best describe a fiscal policy economist?

 1. Increase in government spending.
 2. Decrease in the money supply.
 3. Decrease in income taxes.
 4. Increase in the inflation rate.
   a. 1, 2, 3, and 4.
   b. 1 and 3.
   c. 2 only.
   d. 2 and 4.
   e. 1 only.

59. Which of the following economic activities represent(s) examples of monetary policy?

 1. The discount rate is increased.
 2. Congress passes a tax cut.
 3. Bank reserve requirements are lowered by the Federal Reserve.
 4. The Federal Open Market Committee sells securities.
   a. 1 only.
   b. 1 and 3.
   c. 1, 3, and 4.
   d. 1, 2, and 3.
   e. 2, 3, and 4.

60. The purposes of the Federal Reserve include:

 1. Establishing the Prime Lending Rate (PLR).
 2. Influencing and monitoring the flow of capital in the United States.
 3. Establishing wage and price controls as economic circumstances dictate.
 4. Functioning as the federal government's agency to influence or control inflation.
   a. 1 only.
   b. 2 only.
   c. 2 and 4.
   d. 2, 3, and 4.
   e. 1, 2, 3, and 4.

61. The Federal Reserve can increase the money supply by doing which of the following?

   a. Reducing the required reserve ratio and/or the discount rate.
   b. Increasing the required reserve ratio and/or the discount rate.
   c. Selling securities to US citizens.
   d. Buying gold from the European Central Bank.

---

62. The Federal Reserve can decrease the money supply by doing all of the following except:

    a. Sell US Treasury securities on the open market.

    b. Sell US Treasury bonds to the general public.

    c. Raise the required reserve ratio.

    d. Raise the discount rate.

63. The primary function of the Federal Reserve System (central bank) is to:

    a. Implement fiscal policy.

    b. Carry out monetary policy.

    c. Issue bonds to the general public.

    d. Manage the revenues and expenditures of the federal government.

64. If the Federal Reserve wanted to reduce the supply of money as part of an anti-inflation policy, it might:

    a. Increase the reserve requirements.

    b. Buy US securities on the open market.

    c. Lower the discount rate.

    d. Buy US securities directly from the Treasury.

65. All of the following economic activities represent fiscal policy except:

    a. The government increases purchases of goods and services.

    b. The government cuts taxes.

    c. The government cuts the Federal Funds Rate.

    d. The government uses higher taxes to dampen consumption and private investment.

66. Which of the following monetary components would be included in the M-1 measure of the money supply?

    1. NOW accounts.

    2. Savings accounts.

    3. Checking accounts.

    4. Currency.

    5. Certificates of Deposit (CDs).

        a. 3 and 4.

        b. 1, 2, and 5.

        c. 1, 3, and 4.

        d. 4 only.

        e. All of the above.

67. Which of the following can the Fed do to reduce the money supply?

    1. Purchase Treasury securities.

    2. Decrease the reserve requirements for banks.

    3. Raise the discount rate.

        a. 1 only.

        b. 2 only.

        c. 3 only.

        d. 1 and 2.

        e. 2 and 3.

68. Which of the following can be done by the Fed to increase the money supply?

    1. Decrease the reserve requirements for banks from 8 percent to 6 percent.

    2. Increasing expenditures of the federal government, thereby circulating additional funds in the economy.

    3. Open-market transactions.

        a. 1 only.

        b. 2 only.

        c. 1 and 2.

        d. 1 and 3.

        e. 1, 2, and 3.

69. Which of the following actions taken by the Fed will lead to increased money supply?

        a. Lowering the prime rate.

        b. Lowering the discount rate.

        c. Selling treasury securities.

        d. Increasing reserve requirements.

70. Which of the following is/are methods that might be used to control the supply of money?

    1. Control of the Federal Reserve Discount Rate.

    2. Open-market operations.

    3. Fiscal policy.

        a. 1 only.

        b. 2 only.

        c. 1 and 3.

        d. 2 and 3.

        e. 1, 2, and 3.

71. Which of the following actions by the Federal Reserve Board would directly increase the money supply?

    a. Lower the discount rate.

    b. Buy securities.

    c. Sell securities.

    d. Increase the margin requirement.

72. The federal funds rate will tend to move upward under which of the following conditions? (**CFP®** **Certification Examination, released 8/2004**)

    a. The Federal Reserve is buying government securities.

    b. The Federal Reserve lowers the discount rate.

    c. A few banks have reserve deficiencies, and the rest have ample excess reserves.

    d. A few banks have excess reserves, and the rest have significant reserve deficiencies.

BUSINESS CYCLE THEORIES

73. The phases of a typical business cycle are as follows:

    a. Trough, Peak, Expansion, Recession.

    b. Peak, Recession, Expansion, Trough.

    c. Trough, Expansion, Peak, Recession.

    d. Recession, Peak, Expansion, Trough.

    e. Recession, Expansion, Trough, Peak.

74. In a typical business cycle, which one of the following phases would exhibit periods of increasing employment and increasing output?

    a. Intensity.

    b. Trough.

    c. Peak.

    d. Expansion.

    e. Recession.

FINANCIAL INSTITUTIONS

75. An investor wishing to invest $150,000 is concerned about the safety of his investment if he invests the funds through a national bank. Which of the following statements is/are correct?

    1. If the investor deposits the funds in a savings account, the FDIC guarantees the full amount of his investment.

    2. If the FDIC guaranteed the funds in a savings account, none of the investment the investor deposits is guaranteed if the amount exceeds $100,000.

    3. If the funds were invested in a mutual fund sold by the national bank, the FDIC affords the investor protection up to $100,000.

    4. If the investor deposits $75,000 into each of two savings accounts at the same bank in his name only, the full amount of his investment is afforded protection by the FDIC since neither account exceeds $100,000.

    a. 1 and 4.

    b. 4 only.

    c. 2 only.

    d. 3 only.

    e. None of the statements are correct.

76. John, age 55, is an unmarried retiree. He has the following liquid assets on deposit at Allworld bank, an FDIC-insured financial institution.

Account	Ownership	Balance
Certificate of Deposit	John	$125,000
Savings Account	Joint with son	$70,000
Rollover Traditional IRA	John	$150,000
Checking Account	John	$80,000

How much is currently insured by the FDIC?

    a. $100,000

    b. $155,000

    c. $270,000

    d. $320,000

TIME VALUE OF MONEY

77. Today Bob Jones purchased an investment grade gold coin for $50,000. He expects the coin to increase in value at a rate of 12% compounded annually for the next 5 years. How much will the coin be worth at the end of the fifth year if his expectations are correct?

    a. $89,792.82.
    b. $66,911.28.
    c. $88,117.08.
    d. $89,542.38.

78. A client invested $10,000 in an interest-bearing promissory note earning an 11% annual rate of interest compounded monthly. How much will the note be worth at the end of 7 years assuming all interest is reinvested at the 11% rate?

    a. $13,788.43.
    b. $20,762.60.
    c. $21,048.52.
    d. $21,522.04.

79. Bill Barnett purchased $60,000 worth of silver coins 8 years ago. The coins have appreciated 7.5% compounded annually over the last 8 years. How much are the coins worth today?

    a. $107,008.67.
    b. $102,829.46.
    c. $99,719.03.
    d. $99,542.95.

80. Sarah Attaya wants to give her daughter $25,000 in 8 years to start her own business. How much should she invest today at an annual interest rate of 8% compounded annually to have $25,000 in 8 years?

    a. $12,802.95.
    b. $13,506.72.
    c. $13,347.70.
    d. $13,210.34.

81. Cassie expects to receive $75,000 from a trust fund in 6 years. What is the current value of this fund if it is discounted at 9% compounded semiannually?

    a. $57,592.18.
    b. $44,720.05.
    c. $44,224.79.
    d. $42,794.31.

82. Bill McDowell expects to receive $75,000 in 5 years. His opportunity cost is 10% compounded monthly. What is this sum worth to Bill today?

    a. $45,584.14.

    b. $46,043.49.

    c. $46,569.10.

    d. $48,542.09.

83. Mary Sue wants to accumulate $57,000 in 8.5 years to purchase a boat. She expects an annual rate of return of 10.5% compounded quarterly. How much does Mary Sue need to invest today to meet her goal?

    a. $23,529.87.

    b. $23,619.30.

    c. $23,883.56.

    d. $24,364.33.

84. Joe purchased 10 shares of an aggressive growth mutual fund at $90 per share 7 years ago. Today he sold all 10 shares for $4,500. What was his average annual compound rate of return on this investment before tax?

    a.   17.46%.

    b.   19.58%.

    c.   21.73%.

    d.   25.85%.

85. John borrowed $800 from his father to purchase a mountain bike. John paid back $1,200 to his father at the end of 5 years. What was the average annual compound rate of interest on John's loan from his father?

    a.   11.5646%.

    b.   8.4472%.

    c.   7.7892%.

    d.   5.1990%.

86. Susan Jones purchased a zero-coupon bond 6.5 years ago for $525. If the bond matures today and the face value is $1,000, what is the average annual compound rate of return (calculated semiannually) that Susan realized on her investment?

    a.   11.3372%.

    b.   10.5713%.

    c.   10.400%.

    d.   10.163%.

87. Mike Kibley purchased an Oriental rug for $8,000. Today, he sold the rug for $15,000. Mike determined the average annual compound rate of return on the rug was 12%. Approximately how many years did Mike own the rug? (rounded to the nearest 0.0000)

    a. 6.8452.

    b. 5.5468.

    c. 4.5337.

    d. 5.8451.

    e. 6.0000.

88. Today, Raul put all of his cash into an account earning an annual interest rate of 9% compounded monthly. Assuming he makes no withdrawals or additions into this account, approximately how many years must Raul wait to double his money? (rounded to the nearest 0.00)

    a. 7.75.

    b. 8.25.

    c. 8.75.

    d. 7.25.

    e. 8.00.

89. Clarence Cushman has been investing $1,000 at the end of each year for the past 15 years. How much has accumulated assuming he has earned 10.5% compounded annually on his investment?

    a. $20,303.72.

    b. $23,349.28.

    c. $33,060.04.

    d. $36,531.34.

90. Christine Valico has been dollar cost averaging into a mutual fund by investing $2,000 at the end of every quarter for the past 7 years. She has been earning an average annual compound return of 11% compounded quarterly on this investment. How much is the fund worth today?

    a. $78,266.19.

    b. $81,170.29.

    c. $82,721.95.

    d. $84,996.80.

    e. $86,875.47.

91. Bill Russell has been investing $3,000 at the beginning of each year for the past 15 years. How much has accumulated assuming he has earned 8% compounded annually on his investment?

    a. $91,896.04.

    b. $87,972.85.

    c. $84,696.81.

    d. $81,456.34.

92. Chrissy Nables has been dollar cost averaging in a mutual fund by investing $2,000 at the beginning of every quarter for the past 7 years. She has been earning an average annual compound return of 11% compounded quarterly on this investment. How much is the fund worth today?

    a. $82,721.95.
    b. $93,902.42.
    c. $91,389.22.
    d. $84,996.80.

93. Stuart Wood expects to receive $5,000 at the end of each of the next 4 years. His opportunity cost is 14% compounded annually. What is this sum worth to Stuart today?

    a. $14,568.56.
    b. $16,608.16.
    c. $19,568.56.
    d. $17,165.41.

94. Tim, injured in an automobile accident, won a judgment that provides him $1,500 at the end of each 6-month period over the next 6 years. If the escrow account that holds Tim's settlement award earns an average annual rate of 11% compounded semiannually, how much was the defendant initially required to pay Tim to compensate him for his injuries?

    a. $6,345.81.
    b. $7,043.85.
    c. $12,927.78.
    d. $13,638.80.

95. Jane wants to withdraw $4,000 at the beginning of each year for the next 7 years. She expects to earn 10.5% compounded annually on her investment. What lump sum should Jane deposit today?

    a. $19,157.21.
    b. $18,667.20.
    c. $20,627.25.
    d. $21,168.72.

96. Connie wants to withdraw $1,200 at the beginning of each month for the next 5 years. She expects to earn 10% compounded monthly on her investments. What lump sum should Connie deposit today?

    a. $56,478.44.
    b. $56,949.10.
    c. $58,630.51.
    d. $59,119.10.

97. Gary received an inheritance of $200,000. He wants to withdraw equal periodic payments at the beginning of each month for the next 5 years. He expects to earn 12% annual interest, compounded monthly on his investments. How much can he receive each month?

    a. $4,404.84.

    b. $4,448.89.

    c. $49,537.45.

    d. $55,481.95.

98. Eugene wants to purchase a fishing camp in 5 years for $60,000. What periodic payment should he invest at the beginning of each quarter to attain the goal if he can earn 10.5% annual interest, compounded quarterly on investments?

    a. $2,319.42.

    b. $2,260.09.

    c. $8,805.91.

    d. $9,730.53.

99. Tina wants to purchase a home 6 years from now. She anticipates spending $150,000. To attain this goal, how much should Tina invest at the end of each 6-month period if she expects to earn a 12% annual compound rate of return, compounded semiannually, on her investments?

    a. $18,483.86.

    b. $16,503.44.

    c. $8,891.55.

    d. $8,388.26.

100. Janet purchased a car for $19,500. She is financing the auto at 11% annual interest rate, compounded monthly for 3 years. What payment is required at the end of each month to finance Janet's car?

    a. $606.71.

    b. $638.40.

    c. $632.61.

    d. $684.97.

101. Shane estimates his opportunity cost on investments to be 10.5% compounded annually. Which one of the following is the best investment opportunity for Shane?

    a. Receive $45,000 today.

    b. Receive $120,000 at the end of 10 years.

    c. Receive $5,500 at the beginning of each year for 15 years.

    d. Receive $5,500 at the end of each year for 19 years.

    e. Receive $5,750 at the end of each year for 17 years.

© 2007 Kaplan Financial

102. Richard estimates his opportunity cost on investments to be 9% compounded annually. Which one of the following is the best investment opportunity?

    a. Receive $100,000 today.

    b. Receive $310,000 at the end of 15 years.

    c. Receive $1,200 at the end of each month for 11 years compounded monthly.

    d. Receive $65,000 in 5 years and $125,000 5 years later.

    e. Receive $65,000 in 5 years and $200,000 10 years later.

103. Judy Martin estimates her opportunity cost on investments to be 12% compounded annually. Which one of the following is the best investment opportunity?

    a. Receive $50,000 today.

    b. Receive $250,000 at the end of 14 years.

    c. Receive $40,000 at the end of 4 years and $120,000 8 years later at the end of the 12th year.

    d. Receive $5,000 at the beginning of each 6-month period for 9 years compounded semiannually.

    e. Receive $60,000 at the end of 3 years.

104. Morris and JoAnn Simpson are ready to retire. They want to receive the equivalent of $25,000 in today's dollars at the beginning of each year for the next 20 years. They assume inflation will average 4% over the long run, and they can earn an 8% compound annual after-tax return on investments. What lump sum do Morris and JoAnn need to invest today to attain their goal?

    a. $265,089.98.

    b. $339,758.16.

    c. $353,348.49.

    d. $357,681.56.

105. Stuart needs an income stream equivalent to $50,000 in today's dollars at the beginning of each year for the next 12 years to maintain his standard of living. He assumes inflation will average 4.5% over the long run, and he can earn a 9% compound annual after-tax return on investments. What lump sum does Stuart need to invest today to fund his needs?

    a. $480,878.04.

    b. $455,929.00.

    c. $476,445.85.

    d. $461,025.81.

106. Clark Roberts wants to retire in 9 years. He needs an additional $300,000 (today's dollars) in 9 years to have sufficient funds to finance this objective. He assumes inflation will average 5.0% over the long run, and he can earn a 4.0% compound annual after-tax return on investments. What serial payment should Clark invest at the end of the first year to attain his objective?

    a. $34,623.42.

    b. $34,689.00.

    c. $36,354.60.

    d. $36,423.45.

107. Judy Danos wants to retire in 9 years. She needs an additional $300,000 (today's dollars) in 9 years to have sufficient funds to finance this objective. She assumes inflation will average 5.0% over the long run, and she can earn a 4.0% compound annual after-tax return on investments. What will be Judy's payment at the end of the second year?

    a. $38,244.62.

    b. $38,172.33.

    c. $36,354.60.

    d. $34,623.42.

108. John wants to start his own business in 6 years. He needs to accumulate $200,000 (today's dollars) in 6 years to sufficiently finance his business. He assumes inflation will average 4%, and he can earn a 9% compound annual after-tax return on investments. What serial payment should John invest at the end of the first year to attain his goal?

    a. $29,546.11.

    b. $30,727.95.

    c. $28,190.78.

    d. $29,318.41.

109. Sarah wants to start her own business in 6 years. She needs to accumulate $200,000 (today's dollars) in 6 years to sufficiently finance her business. She assumes inflation will average 4%, and she can earn a 9% compound annual after-tax return on investments. What will be Sarah's payment at the end of the second year?

    a. $28,190.78.

    b. $30,727.95.

    c. $30,491.00.

    d. $31,957.07.

110. Determine the future value of a periodic deposit of $6,100 made at the beginning of each year for 10 years to a mutual fund expected to earn 11.5% compounded annually during the projection period. Calculate the future value rounded to the nearest dollar.

    a. $104,493.

    b. $116,510.

    c. $113,040.

    d. $124,344.

    e. $39,229.

111. Determine the future value of a periodic deposit of $6,100 made at the beginning of each year for 10 years to a mutual fund expected to earn 11.5% compounded quarterly during the projection period. Calculate the future value rounded to the nearest dollar.

    a. $447,130.

    b. $116,510.

    c. $119,931.

    d. $107,076.

    e. $459,985.

112. A client is to receive $650 per month for 5 years beginning one year from today at the beginning of the month. What is the present value of all payments (rounded to the nearest dollar) assuming an annual discount rate of 9%?

    a. $33,070.

    b. $28,943.

    c. $30,339.

    d. $31,548.

    e. $28,728.

113. The rate that produces a net present value of a series of discounted cash flows equal to zero is called the:

    a. Return on investment (ROI).

    b. Internal rate of return (IRR).

    c. Average rate of return.

    d. Cost of capital.

    e. Inflation rate.

114. If the net present value of a series of discounted cash flows is greater than zero, one could interpret that:

    1. The discounted cash flows exceed the investment outlay.

    2. The rate of return is equal to the cost of capital.

    3. The return on investment is lower than the internal rate of return.

    4. The internal rate of return was the discount rate used.

        a. 1 only.

        b. 1 and 4.

        c. 1, 2, 3, and 4.

        d. 2 and 3.

        e. 2 only.

115. If the net present value of a series of discounted cash flows is equal to zero, one could interpret that:

    1. The discounted cash flows equal the investment outlay.

    2. The rate of return is lower than the cost of capital.

    3. The return on investment is lower than the internal rate of return.

    4. The internal rate of return was the discount rate used.

       a. 1 only.

       b. 1 and 4.

       c. 1, 2, 3, and 4.

       d. 2 and 3.

       e. 2 only.

116. If the net present value of a series of discounted cash flows is less than zero, one could interpret that:

    1. The discounted cash flows are lower than the investment outlay.

    2. The required rate of return is higher than the internal rate of return (IRR).

    3. The return on investment is higher than the internal rate of return.

    4. The internal rate of return was the discount rate used.

       a. 1 only.

       b. 1 and 4.

       c. 1, 2, 3, and 4.

       d. 2 and 3.

       e. 2 only.

117. What is the monthly payment made at the end of each month required to accumulate a balance of $150,000 in 10 years at an assumed interest rate of 11% compounded monthly and a beginning savings balance of $2,500?

       a. $684.97.

       b. $691.25.

       c. $656.81.

       d. $650.85.

       e. $712.14.

118. Joe wants to buy a business in 10 years. He estimates he will need $150,000 at that time. He currently has a zero-coupon bond with a market value of $1,157.98 that he will use as part of the required amount. The zero-coupon bond has a face value of $2,500 and will mature in 10 years. The bond has a semiannual effective interest rate of 3.923%. In addition to the bond, he wants to save a monthly amount to reach his goal. What is Joe's required monthly payment made at the beginning of each month in order to accumulate the $150,000, including the zero-coupon bond, at an assumed interest rate of 11%?

       a. $676.10.

       b. $673.56.

       c. $669.96.

       d. $679.73.

       e. $800.91.

119. A parent wishes to begin saving for a child's education. The child is born today, the first payment will be made today and the child will start college on his 18th birthday. The child will attend college for four years with the annual payment due at the beginning of the school year. The current cost of the college education is $25,000 per year. It is expected that the cost of a college education will increase at an average rate of 7% per year during the projection period and that the general rate of inflation will be 4%. The parent has the option of investing in the following: 1) A taxable mutual stock fund expected to earn 12.0% during the projection period and 2) A tax-free bond fund expected to earn 8.5% during the projection period. The parent's marginal tax bracket is 30.5% and the average tax bracket is 21%. Exclusive of risk, what do you recommend?

   a. The equity mutual fund because the after-tax rate of return (assuming the average tax bracket) is greater than the tax-free bond fund.

   b. The bond fund because the rate of return is greater than the after-tax rate of return for the equity mutual fund (assuming marginal tax bracket).

   c. Make the annual payment at the end of the year because the annual funding requirement is less than if made at the beginning of the year.

   d. Either investment is appropriate as long as the after-tax rate of return is greater than the underlying rate of inflation on an annual basis.

   e. Invest in the equity mutual fund because the pretax rate of return is greater than the rate of return of the bond fund.

120. Philip purchased a house for $185,000 with a down payment of 20%. If he finances the balance at 10% over 15 years, how much will his monthly payment be?

   a. $1,577.27.

   b. $1,590.42.

   c. $1,971.59.

   d. $1,988.02.

121. David Gregory recently purchased a house for $120,000. He put 20% down and financed the remaining amount over 15 years at 7.5%. How much interest will be paid over the life of the loan assuming he pays the loan as agreed? (Round to the nearest dollar.)

   a. $31,813.

   b. $64,187.

   c. $96,000.

   d. $160,187.

122. Brian, age 48, plans to retire at 65 and wants to be debt free at retirement. The balance sheet mortgage is $114,042 at the end of the 10th year of a 30-year loan. The monthly payment (cash outflow) from the cash flow statement (P&I only) was $953.89. What was the original balance of the loan if the interest rate was 8%?

   a. $119,572.

   b. $120,000.

   c. $125,000.

   d. $130,000.

   e. $140,428.

123. Using the information from the previous question, assume Brian can refinance at a 15-year rate for 6.5% or a 30-year rate for 7% and will incur closing costs of 3% of the mortgage amount to be financed in the new mortgage balance. What will be his new mortgage payment under the circumstances to achieve his objectives?

    a. $776.95.

    b. $781.49.

    c. $957.56.

    d. $980.57.

    e. $986.29.

124. Allen pays his mortgage as agreed. The mortgage is $120,000 for 15 years and has an interest rate of 7%. Allen makes payments monthly. What is the total amount of interest Allen will pay over the term of the mortgage? (Select closest answer.)

    a. $75,000.

    b. $80,000.

    c. $85,000.

    d. $90,000.

    e. $100,000.

125. A couple wants to accumulate a retirement fund of $300,000 in current dollars in 18 years. They expect inflation to be 4% per year during that period. If they set aside $20,000 at the end of each year and earn 6% on their investment, will they reach their goal? (**CFP® Certification Examination, released 8/2004**)

    a. Yes, they will accumulate $10,368 more than needed.

    b. Yes, they will accumulate $47,454 more than needed.

    c. No, they will accumulate $10,368 less than needed.

    d. No, they will accumulate $47,454 less than needed.

EDUCATIONAL FUNDING

126. Marleen and Billy Poor have two children ages 5 and 7. The Poors want to start saving for their children's education. Each child will spend 6 years at college and will begin at age 18. College currently costs $20,000 per year and is expected to increase at 6% per year. Assuming the Poors can earn an annual compound return of 12% and inflation is 4%, how much must the Poors deposit at the end of each year to pay for their children's educational requirements until the youngest is out of school? Assume that educational expenses are withdrawn at the beginning of each year and that the last deposit will be made at the beginning of the last year of the youngest child's college education.

    a. $11,984.

    b. $12,386.

    c. $14,186.

    d. $14,989.

    e. $15,230.

127. Sharon has a daughter, Debbie, who is 14 years old. College costs are currently $12,000 per year and are expected to increase 5% per year, including the 4 years Debbie is in college. Debbie will begin college at age 18. Pursuant to a divorce decree, Sharon is responsible for 1/3 of the total cost of Debbie's college tuition. Sharon wants to be able to have the total amount of tuition for which she is responsible by the time Debbie starts college but will pay the tuition at the beginning of each school year. She estimates she can put money in a fund that earns 9% after tax. What amount does Sharon have to deposit at the beginning of each month starting now to meet her goal?

    a. $317.56.

    b. $325.49.

    c. $341.80.

    d. $952.69.

    e. $959.84

128. Scott and Arleen Smith have two children ages 4 and 6. The Smiths want to start saving for their children's education. Each child will spend 5 years at college and will begin at age 18. College currently costs $30,000 per year and is expected to increase at 7% per year. Assuming the Smiths can earn an annual compound return of 12% and inflation is 4%, how much must the Smiths deposit at the end of each year to pay for their children's educational requirements until the youngest goes to school? Assume that educational expenses are withdrawn at the beginning of each year and that the last deposit will be made at the beginning of the first year of the youngest child.

    a. $19,894.

    b. $20,674.

    c. $22,272.

    d. $22,886.

    e. $23,615.

129. Which of the following statements is/are correct concerning Qualified Tuition Plans (QTPs)?

    1. Under Section 529 of the Internal Revenue Code, QTPs, which are created, sponsored, and maintained by individual states or institutions, have tax-exempt status.

    2. Under QTPs, individuals may purchase tuition credits on behalf of a designated beneficiary, which entitles the beneficiary to the waiver or payment of qualified higher education expenses of the beneficiary.

    3. Under QTPs, individuals may make contributions to an account that is established for the purpose of meeting the qualified higher education expenses of the designated beneficiary.

      a. 1 and 2 only.

      b. 1 and 3 only.

      c. 2 and 3 only.

      d. 1, 2, and 3.

130. All of the following are correct regarding Qualified Tuition Plans (QTPs), except:

      a. QTPs provide tax-deferred growth.

      b. The contributor/owner has full control of the account, but cannot change the beneficiary.

      c. The contributor can exclude the value of the QTP from his or her gross estate.

      d. Many states provide state tax deductions and/or tax exemptions for some contributions.

131. Kenneth and Liz, ages 50 and 39 respectively, want to invest $3,000 per year towards the future college expenses of their 8-year-old son, John (he will begin attending college in 10 years). Kenneth and Liz hope that John will get an athletic scholarship because he has proven to be a talented tennis player. Due to John's recent elbow injury, his parents have decided to plan for the unlikely event that he won't get a scholarship and because they have a modest income. They are concerned about qualifying for financial aid. Which of the following investment vehicles would best serve their needs?

      a. Section 529 Plan.

      b. Roth IRA for Liz.

      c. Coverdell Education Savings Account.

      d. Roth IRA for Kenneth.

      e. Savings account in John's name.

132. All of the following statements regarding Coverdell Education Savings Accounts are correct, except:

      a. A Coverdell Education Savings Account can be established to pay qualified educational expenses as long as the contributor does not have income in excess of $220,000 (married filing jointly) or $110,000 (if filing single).

      b. The proceeds of the Coverdell Education Savings Account must be distributed within 30 days of the beneficiary's 30th birthday.

      c. Only graduate and undergraduate level course expenses qualify for Coverdell Education Savings Account distributions.

      d. Withdrawals are tax free whether the student is enrolled full time, half time, or less than half time as long as the withdrawals do not exceed the student's qualified educational expenses.

133. Tom is an independent student (not living with his parents) who is attempting to educate himself on government assistance that is available for higher education expenses. Tom should know that all of the following are government-sponsored higher education (financial aid) grants, loans, and programs, except:

    a. Federal Pell Grant.

    b. Federal Supplemental Educational Opportunity Grant (SEOG).

    c. Federal Subsidized and Unsubsidized Stafford Loans.

    d. Federal Stanton Loans.

    e. Federal Work-Study.

134. Leroy and Tabitha Jones have three dependent children in college. Mike is a senior, Mary is a junior, and William is a freshman. The Joneses are filing their taxes and want to correctly use the HOPE scholarship credit and lifetime learning credit. Which of the following statements are correct? Assume the Joneses qualify for both credits.

    a. The Joneses can use the HOPE scholarship credit for the qualified educational expenses of both William and Mary and the lifetime learning credit for Mike.

    b. The Joneses can use the HOPE scholarship credit for qualified educational expenses for William, and use two lifetime learning credits for Mary and Mike.

    c. The Joneses can use the HOPE scholarship credit for the qualified education expenses of William and use one lifetime learning credit for Mary and Mike.

    d. The Joneses can only take one of the credits; whichever one will give them the greatest advantage.

    e. None of the above.

135. Which of the following is a characteristic of a Series EE savings bond?

    a. Series EE bonds are purchased at one-third of their face value.

    b. Series EE bonds have varying interest rates, but face value must be reached in 30 years.

    c. To attain tax-free status, Series EE bonds must be purchased in the name of the student/child.

    d. The bonds must be redeemed in the same year that the student's qualified higher educational expenses are paid in order to receive preferential tax treatment for educational use.

136. Jerry and Terry Martinez are concerned because they have not yet begun saving for their son, Paul's higher education expenses. Jerry and Terry are both 30 years old and Paul is 9 years old. Their combined income is $100,000, and they want to begin saving $5,000 per year in a tax efficient manner. Which of the following is the best investment choice for Jerry and Terry?

    a. UTMA account.

    b. Coverdell Education Savings Account.

    c. 529 Plan.

    d. Loans from the parents' Traditional IRAs.

    e. Annuity.

137. Tom and Samantha have an AGI of $150,000 and want to know what combination of available funds and tax benefits they can use to offset their daughter's higher education expenses. Which of the following choices is correct?

    a. HOPE scholarship credit and Series EE bonds.

    b. Lifetime learning credit, Coverdell Education Savings Account, and UTMA account distribution.

    c. Pell Grant, Coverdell Education Savings Account, and QTP account distribution.

    d. Coverdell Education Savings Account and 529 Plan.

138. Penelope has qualified education expenses of $10,000 for the spring semester of college but she wants an additional $2,000 for her spring break vacation. Penelope receives a $12,000 distribution from her 529 Plan. Which of the following statements is/are correct regarding tax treatment of the distribution?

    1. The entire $2,000 of the distribution will be included in Penelope's gross income.

    2. An additional 10% tax penalty will be applied to a distribution made for nonqualified expenses for the amount included in gross income.

    a. 1 only.

    b. 2 only.

    c. Both 1 and 2.

    d. Neither 1 nor 2.

139. Which of the following statements concerning educational tax credits and savings opportunities is correct? **(CFP® Certification Examination, released 8/2004)**

    a. The Lifetime Learning Credit is equal to 100% of qualified educational expenses up to a certain limit.

    b. The HOPE credit is available for the first 4 years of postsecondary education.

    c. A parent who claims a child as a dependent is entitled to take the HOPE credit for the educational expenses of the child.

    d. The contribution limit for Coverdell Education Savings Accounts is applied per year per donor.

CONTRACTS

140. Which of the following defenses could a surety assert successfully to limit the surety's liability to a creditor?

    a. A discharge in bankruptcy of the principal debtor.

    b. A personal defense the principal debtor has against the creditor.

    c. The incapacity of the surety.

    d. The incapacity of the principal debtor.

    e. The death of the principal debtor.

141. Bucky Corp. lent Forrest $50,000. At Bucky's request, Forrest entered into an agreement with Lanning and Snow for them to act as compensated cosureties on the loan in the amount of $100,000 each. Bucky Corp. released Snow without Lanning's or Forrest's consent, and Forrest later defaulted on the loan. Which of the following statements is correct?

    a. Lanning will be liable for 50% of the loan balance.

    b. Lanning will be liable for the entire loan balance.

    c. Bucky's release of Snow will have no effect on Forrest's and Lanning's liability to Bucky Corp.

    d. Forrest will be released to 50% of the loan balance.

    e. Snow will still be liable because Forrest and Lanning did not consent to the release.

142. Which of the following is/are required in a contract?

    1. In writing.

    2. Legal objective.

    3. Consideration.

    4. Legal capacity.

    a. 1 only.

    b. 2 only.

    c. 2 and 4.

    d. 1, 2, and 3.

    e. 2, 3, and 4.

143. Which of the following represents a distinction between a bilateral and a unilateral contract?

   1. Two promises are involved in a bilateral contract, but only one promise is involved in a unilateral contract.
   2. A formal written agreement is required for a bilateral contract, but not a unilateral contract.
   3. Rights are assignable in a bilateral contract, but are not in a unilateral contract.
   4. Specific performance is available for breach of a bilateral contract, but is not available for a unilateral contract.
        a. 1 only.
        b. 3 only.
        c. 1 and 2.
        d. 3 and 4.
        e. 1, 2, and 3.

144. Which of the following must exist for an offer to confer the power to form a contract by acceptance?

   1. Be communicated in writing only.
   2. Be sufficiently definite and certain.
   3. Manifest an intent to enter into a contract.
   4. Be communicated orally by the offeror to the offeree.
        a. 1 only.
        b. 2 only.
        c. 1 and 2.
        d. 2 and 3.
        e. 1, 2, 3, and 4.

AGENCY

---

145. Which of the following statements regarding the legal capacity of an agent is true?

    a. A minor cannot serve as an agent.

    b. An agent must have contractual capacity to create contracts binding on the principal.

    c. An agent is a party to a contract that he or she creates on behalf of the principal.

    d. Both natural persons and artificial persons, such as corporations, may act as agents.

146. Which of the following statements regarding agency is correct?

    a. An agency is a contractual relationship, and the principal must provide consideration for the contract to be effective.

    b. An agent may neither compete with his or her principal nor act for another principal unless full disclosure is made to the principal.

    c. A principal has no responsibility for the acts of its agent when the agent is acting within the scope of apparent authority.

    d. Implied authority is a type of apparent authority that is created as a result of the agent's conduct with third parties.

NEGOTIABLE INSTRUMENTS

147. Which of the following are correct regarding negotiable instruments?

    1. Must be written.
    2. Must be signed by the maker/drawer.
    3. Must contain an unconditional promise or order to pay.
        a. 1 only.
        b. 2 only.
        c. 3 only.
        d. 1 and 2.
        e. 1, 2, and 3.

148. Which of the following are correct regarding negotiable instruments?

    1. State a fixed amount in money.
    2. Payable to order/bearer.
    3. Payable on demand or at a definite time.
        a. 1 only.
        b. 2 only.
        c. 1 and 2.
        d. 2 and 3.
        e. 1, 2, and 3.

PROPERTY

149. Which of the following are characteristics of property ownership as community property?

 1. A joint interest held by husband and wife.
 2. Upon the death of a spouse both halves of community property are stepped to fair market value.
 3. Transfer of property requires consent of the other party.
 4. There is a right of survivorship for each spouse.
   a. 1 and 4.
   b. 3 and 4.
   c. 1, 2, and 3.
   d. 2, 3, and 4.
   e. 1, 2, 3, and 4.

150. What is one characteristic of tenancy by the entirety?

   a. Tenants have unequal rights in the property.
   b. Tenants have rights of survivorship in the property.
   c. Any tenant can exercise a general power of appointment over the property.
   d. Any tenant can bequeath interest in the property without consent of other tenants.
   e. None of the above.

151. Which of the following are characteristics of property ownership as tenants by the entirety?

 1. Joint interest held by husband and wife.
 2. If both spouses' names appear on the title, tenancy by the entirety is presumed.
 3. Transfer of property does not require consent of the other party.
 4. There is a right of survivorship for each spouse.
 5. Divorce does not affect tenancy by the entirety.
   a. 1, 3, and 5.
   b. 2, 3, and 4.
   c. 5 only.
   d. 1, 2, and 4.
   e. 3 and 5.

152. Which of the following property ownership arrangements may be entered into by spouses only?

    1. Tenancy in common.
    2. Joint tenancy with right of survivorship.
    3. Tenancy by the entirety.
    4. Community property.
        a. 3 only.
        b. 2 and 4.
        c. 3 and 4.
        d. 2, 3, and 4.
        e. 1, 2, 3, and 4.

153. If a child is under the age of 18, income earned in excess of $1,700 (for 2007) by the assets in a UTMA is:

    a. Taxed at the parents' income tax rate.
    b. Taxed at the child's tax rate.
    c. Not subject to income tax.
    d. Not subject to tax until the asset is withdrawn from the account.

154. If a child is 18 years of age or older, income earned by the assets in a UTMA is:

    a. Taxed at the parents' income tax rate.
    b. Taxed at the child's tax rate.
    c. Not subject to income tax.
    d. Not subject to tax until the asset is withdrawn from the account.

155. Mary and her sister Della purchased some land in Montana several years ago. They titled the property at Joint Tenants with Rights of Survivorship (JTWROS). At the time of purchase, Mary paid $120,000 and Della paid $60,000 toward the $180,000 purchase price. Della died when the fair market value of the land was $240,000. What is included in Della's gross estate?

    a. $60,000.
    b. $80,000.
    c. $120,000.
    d. $160,000.
    e. $240,000.

CONSUMER PROTECTION

156. A client had five credit cards in his wallet when the wallet was stolen. He reported the cards as missing the next morning, but the following transactions had already occurred:

   - Discover Card $350
   - MasterCard $100
   - VISA $425
   - Sears $25
   - Marshall Fields $685

How much is the client's expected liability for the fraudulent transactions on these cards? (**CFP®
Certification Examination, released 11/94**)

    a. $50.

    b. $225.

    c. $250.

    d. $1,235.

    e. $1,585.

157. Under the Federal Age Discrimination in Employment Act, which of the following practices would be prohibited?

    1. Compulsory retirement of employees below the age of 65.

    2. Termination of employees between the ages of 65 and 70 for cause.

    3. Termination of employees under the age of 65 for good cause.

        a. 1 only.

        b. 2 only.

        c. 3 only.

        d. 1 and 3.

        e. 2 and 3.

BANKRUPTCY AND REORGANIZATION

158. Landry Plumbing, Inc. filed bankruptcy under the reorganization provisions of Chapter 11 of the Federal Bankruptcy Code. A plan of reorganization was confirmed, and a final decree closing the proceedings was entered. Which of the following events usually occurs next?

    a. Landry Plumbing, Inc. will be liquidated.

    b. Landry Plumbing, Inc. will have negotiated with all creditors except as otherwise provided in the plan and applicable law.

    c. Discharged creditors of Landry Plumbing, Inc. will file suit to recover amounts due.

    d. A trustee will continue to operate the debtor's business.

    e. Landry Plumbing, Inc. will not be allowed to continue in the same business.

159. Andrew Martin, is an unsecured creditor of Golf Expo Co. for $6,000. Golf Expo Co. has a total of 10 creditors, all of whom are unsecured. Golf Expo Co. has not paid any of the creditors for three months. Under Chapter 11 of the Federal Bankruptcy Code, which of the following statements is correct?

    a. Golf may not be petitioned involuntarily into bankruptcy because there are less than 12 unsecured creditors.

    b. Golf may not be petitioned involuntarily into bankruptcy under the provisions of Chapter 11.

    c. Three unsecured creditors must join the involuntary petition in bankruptcy.

    d. Martin may file involuntary petition in bankruptcy against Golf.

    e. None of the above.

160. Which of the following claims will not be discharged in bankruptcy?

    a. A claim that arises from alimony or maintenance other than a lump-sum property settlement.

    b. A claim that arises out of the debtor's breach of a contract.

    c. A claim brought by a secured creditor that remains unsatisfied after the sale of the collateral.

    d. A claim brought by a judgment creditor whose judgment resulted from the debtor's negligent operation of a motor vehicle.

    e. All of the above.

161. Under the liquidation provisions of Chapter 7 of the Federal Bankruptcy Code, which of the following statements applies to a person who has voluntarily filed for and received a discharge in bankruptcy?

    1. The person will be discharged from all debts.

    2. The person can obtain another voluntary discharge in bankruptcy under Chapter 7 after three years have elapsed from the date of the prior filing.

    3. The person must surrender for distribution to the creditors amounts received as an inheritance, if the receipt occurs within 180 days after filing the bankruptcy petition.

    a. 1 only.

    b. 2 only.

    c. 3 only.

    d. 1 and 3.

    e. 2 and 3.

162. Which of the following items can be discharged in a Chapter 7 bankruptcy?

   1. Child support.

   2. Tort claim for negligence.

   3. Federal taxes (past two years).

   4. Consumer debt.

      a. 1 and 2.

      b. 2 and 3.

      c. 2 and 4.

      d. 1, 2, and 4.

      e. 2, 3, and 4.

163. Under the Bankruptcy laws, which of the following will not be discharged?

   1. Credit card debt used to pay college tuition (within the last five years).

   2. Taxes from four years ago in which the taxpayer purposely failed to report $10,000 of self-employment income.

   3. Alimony.

      a. 1 only.

      b. 2 only.

      c. 1 and 2.

      d. 2 and 3.

      e. 1, 2, and 3.

164. Under the Bankruptcy laws, which of the following will not be discharged?

   1. Federal taxes from two years ago.

   2. $4,000 debt from the embezzlement of funds from an insurance company.

   3. Child support.

      a. 1 only.

      b. 2 only.

      c. 1 and 2.

      d. 2 and 3.

      e. 1, 2, and 3.

TORTS

165. A tort is:

    a.   An offense against the state.

    b.   A breach of contract.

    c.   Based on socially unreasonable conduct.

    d.   Based on familiar obligations.

    e.   The civil equivalent of a crime.

166. Which of the following must the plaintiff establish with regard to intent necessary to establish a cause of action for fraud?

    a.   The defendant made a false representation of facts.

    b.   The plaintiff actually relied on the defendant's misrepresentation.

    c.   The defendant made a misrepresentation with a reckless disregard for the truth.

    d.   The plaintiff justifiably relied on the defendant's misrepresentation.

    e.   All of the above.

167. Which of the following is an essential element of the tort of battery?

    a.   The unauthorized use of a defendant's property.

    b.   A harmful or offensive bodily contact.

    c.   Actual physical danger.

    d.   The defendant need not have acted with intent.

    e.   The plaintiff must have been aware of the defendant's conduct.

168. Which of the following is a tort of negligence?

    a.   While playing golf, Jay swings a new golf club on the fairway and the head of the club flies off, and strikes another golfer standing 15 yards away.

    b.   Betty has a sudden chest pain while driving, which causes her to lose control of her car and hit an oncoming car.

    c.   Bubba throws a rock intending to hit a window and instead hits a pedestrian.

    d.   Stan takes medication that he knows makes him drowsy and then proceeds to drive. He later gets into an accident injuring the passenger in the other car.

    e.   Cherie locks Chris in a room to prevent him from leaving the building.

PROFESSIONAL LIABILITY—FINANCIAL PLANNERS

169. In which of the following common law actions, against a CFP® practitioner, would lack of privity be a viable defense?

    a. The plaintiff is the client's creditor who sues the CFP® practitioner for negligence.

    b. The plaintiff can prove the presence of gross negligence that amounts to a reckless disregard for the truth.

    c. The plaintiff is the CFP® practitioner's client.

    d. The plaintiff bases the action upon fraud.

    e. The plaintiff is the CFP® practitioner's employee.

170. At what point is a CFP® Certificant responsible for advice given to a client?

    a. Once the CFP® Certificant has been paid for the advice.

    b. Once an attorney reviews the advice and agrees.

    c. Once a 60-day contract has been signed by the client.

    d. Once the client is assumed to use the advice as fact.

REGULATORY REQUIREMENTS

171. Which of the following activities must be proven by a stock purchaser in order to prevail against a CFP® practitioner in a suit brought under the provisions of Section 10(b) and Rule 10b-5 of the Securities Exchange Act of 1934 (the 1934 Act)?

    1. Intentional conduct by the CFP® practitioner designed to deceive investors.

    2. Negligence by the CFP® practitioner.

    3. Strict liability by the CFP® practitioner.

        a. 1 only.

        b. 2 only.

        c. 3 only.

        d. 1 and 2.

        e. 1, 2, and 3.

172. Which of the following situations would require a company to be subject to the reporting provisions of the 1934 Act?

    1. Shares are listed on a national securities exchange.

    2. There is more than one class of stock.

    3. There are 100 shareholders.

        a. 1, 2, and 3.

        b. 1 only.

        c. 2 only.

        d. 3 only.

        e. None of the above.

173. Following registration, which of the following documents must a company, subject to the reporting provisions of the 1934 Act, file with the SEC?

    1. Quarterly reports (Form 10-Q).

    2. Annual report (Form 10-K).

    3. Proxy statements.

        a. 1 only.

        b. 2 only.

        c. 3 only.

        d. 1, 2, and 3.

        e. None of the above.

174. When certain transactions or events occur affecting a company subject to the reporting requirements of the 1934 Act, a report must be submitted to the SEC in conjunction with the transaction or event. Which of the following reports must also be submitted to the SEC?

    1. A report of proxy solicitations by current stockholders.

    2. A report by a party making a tender offer for a company's stock.

    3. A report by the heirs of a deceased shareholder.

        a. 1 only.

        b. 2 only.

        c. 3 only.

        d. 1 and 3.

        e. 2 and 3.

175. Which of the following securities would be regulated by the provisions of the Securities Act of 1933?

    a. Securities issued by not-for-profit, charitable organizations.

    b. Securities guaranteed by domestic governmental organizations.

    c. Securities issued by savings and loan associations.

    d. Securities issued by insurance companies.

    e. Securities issued by a domestic government.

176. Under the Securities Act of 1933, which of the following statements most accurately reflects how securities registration affects an investor?

    a. The investor is provided with information on the stockholders of the offering corporation.

    b. The investor is provided with information on the principal purposes for which the offering's proceeds will be used.

    c. The investor is guaranteed by the SEC that the facts contained in the registration statement are accurate.

    d. The investor is assured by the SEC against loss resulting from purchasing the security.

    e. All of the above.

177. Which combination of the following statements concerning federal law is correct? (**CFP® Certification Examination, released 11/94**)

   1. The Securities Act of 1933 provides for protection from misrepresentation, deceit, and other fraud in the sale of new securities.

   2. The Securities Investor Protection Act of 1970 is designed to protect individual investors from losses as a result of brokerage house failures.

   3. The Investment Advisers Act of 1940 requires that persons or firms advising others about securities investment must register with the Securities and Exchange Commission.

   4. The Investment Advisers Act of 1940 assures the investor safety of investment in companies engaged primarily in investing, reinvesting, and trading in securities.

     a. 1, 2, and 3.
     b. 1 and 3.
     c. 2 and 4.
     d. 2 and 3.
     e. 1, 2, 3, and 4.

178. Which of the following would require an individual to be registered as an investment adviser under the Investment Advisers Act of 1940?

   1. The individual provides advice about a specific security.

   2. The individual is in the business of providing advice about specific securities.

   3. The individual receives compensation for providing advice.

   4. The individual is a CFP® practitioner.

   5. The individual has fewer than 15 clients.

     a. 1, 2, 3, and 4.
     b. 3, 4, and 5.
     c. 4 only.
     d. All would require the individual to register.
     e. 1, 2, and 3.

INVESTMENT ADVISER REGULATION AND REGISTRATION

179. If an individual is required to be registered as an investment adviser, is NASD registration required?

   a. No, if he is licensed by the state to sell products.

   b. Yes, if the individual is a CFP® practitioner.

   c. Yes, if the individual sells products.

   d. No, if he agrees to be bound by the Code of Ethics.

   e. Further information is needed to answer the question.

180. You have acquired the Series 6 & 63 licenses and are insurance licensed. What can you sell?

   a. Mutual fund.

   b. Variable life insurance.

   c. Variable annuity.

   d. All of the above.

CFP BOARD'S STANDARDS OF PROFESSIONAL CONDUCT

---

181. Which of the following statements concerning the *Code of Ethics and Professional Responsibility* (*Code of Ethics*) is/are true?

    1. The *Code of Ethics* applies to CFP Board designees actively involved in the practice of personal financial planning, in other areas of financial services, in industry, in related professions, in government, in education or in any other professional activity in which the certification marks are used in the performance of professional responsibilities.

    2. The *Code of Ethics* does not apply to CFP® candidates who have not yet received certification or those individuals who have been certified in the past, but who have not reinstated their CFP® certification.

      a. 1 only.

      b. 2 only.

      c. Both 1 and 2.

      d. Neither 1 nor 2.

182. Which of the following statements concerning the Principles and Rules that make up the *Code of Ethics* is/are correct?

    1. The Principles are aspirational in character, but are intended to provide a source of guidance for CFP Board designees.

    2. The Rules describe the standards of ethical and professionally responsible conduct expected of CFP Board designees in particular situations.

      a. 1 only.

      b. 2 only.

      c. Both 1 and 2.

      d. Neither 1 nor 2.

183. All of the following statements concerning the Rules that relate to the Principle of Integrity in the *Code of Ethics* are correct except:

    a. A CFP Board designee shall not solicit clients through false or misleading communications, advertisements, or promotional activities, such as speeches, interviews, books and/or printed publications, seminars, radio and television shows, and video cassettes.

    b. A candidate for CFP® certification cannot offer personal views as the views of the CFP Board—only a CFP® certificant can do so.

    c. Commingling one or more clients' funds or other property together is permitted, subject to compliance with applicable legal requirements and provided accurate records are maintained for each client's funds or other property.

    d. A CFP Board designee who takes custody of all or any part of a client's assets for investment purposes shall do so with the care required of a fiduciary.

    e. In exercising custody over client funds or other property, a CFP Board designee shall act only in accordance with the authority set forth in the governing legal instrument.

---

184. Which of the following statements concerning the Rules that relate to the Principle of Competence in the *Code of Ethics* is/are correct?

    1. A CFP Board designee must not assist clients with areas in which he is not professionally competent, even if he has assistance of a qualified individual. Instead he must refer clients to such parties.

    2. A CFP Board designee shall keep informed of developments in the field of financial planning and participate in continuing education throughout the CFP Board designee's professional career.

       a. 1 only.

       b. 2 only.

       c. Both 1 and 2.

       d. Neither 1 nor 2.

185. All of the following Rules relate to the Principle of Fairness except:

       a. In rendering professional services, a CFP Board designee shall disclose to the client material information relevant to the professional relationship, as well as information required by all laws applicable to the relationship in a manner complying with such laws.

       b. A CFP Board designee in a financial planning engagement shall make timely written disclosure of all material information relative to the professional relationship including but limited to conflicts of interests and sources of compensation.

       c. A CFP Board designee shall disclose in writing, prior to establishing a financial planning engagement, relationships which reasonably may compromise the CFP Board designee's objectivity or independence.

       d. A CFP Board designee shall exercise reasonable and prudent professional judgment in providing professional services.

       e. A CFP Board designee shall disclose sources of compensation to ongoing clients at least annually.

186. Rachael, a CFP® certificant, recently took David on as a new financial planning client. After receiving an excessive number of questions from David regarding his plan, Rachael became desperate and changed her business phone number to an unlisted number. She notified David that he could not have her new phone number, and that he must communicate with her via e-mail or fax. Which Principle, if any, embodies Rules that require Rachel to provide David with her new number?

       a. Integrity.

       b. Objectivity.

       c. Fairness.

       d. Professionalism.

       e. None of the above.

187. Which of the following Rules concerning the Principle of Confidentiality is/are correct?

    1. A CFP Board designee shall not reveal, without the client's consent, any personally identifiable information relating to the client relationship except to the extent reasonably necessary.

    2. A CFP Board designee shall maintain the same standards of confidentiality to employers as to clients.

        a. 1 only.

        b. 2 only.

        c. Both 1 and 2.

        d. Neither 1 nor 2.

188. Which of the following uses of personal identifiable client information without the client's consent is not allowed under the Principle of Confidentiality?

        a. In connection with a civil dispute between the CFP Board designee and the client.

        b. Any use of client information that does not actually cause harm to the client.

        c. To defend the CFP Board designee against charges of wrongdoing.

        d. To establish an advisory or brokerage account, to effect a transaction for the client, or as otherwise impliedly authorized in order to carry out the client engagement.

        e. To comply with legal requirements or legal process.

189. Marie, a CFP® certificant, believes that there may be some illegal money laundering going on at the firm where she works. She has tried to investigate, but has been unable to ascertain if her assumptions are correct and has not yet notified anyone within her firm of her suspicions. Marie should make timely disclosure of the available evidence to any of the following except:

        a. CFP Board.

        b. Her direct supervisor.

        c. A partner in the firm.

        d. A co-owner of the firm.

190. Which of the following Rules relating to the Principle of Professionalism is not correct?

    a. A CFP Board designee who has knowledge (no substantial doubt), which is not required under the *Code of Ethics* to be kept confidential, and which raises a substantial question of unprofessional, fraudulent or illegal conduct by a CFP Board designee or other financial professional, shall promptly inform CFP Board, who will in turn notify the appropriate regulatory and/or professional disciplinary body.

    b. A CFP Board designee who has reason to suspect illegal conduct within the CFP Board designee's organization shall make timely disclosure of the available evidence to the CFP Board designee's immediate supervisor and/or partners or co-owners.

    c. If the CFP Board designee is convinced that illegal conduct exists within the CFP Board designee's organization, and that appropriate measures are not taken to remedy the situation, the CFP Board designee shall, where appropriate, alert the appropriate regulatory authorities including CFP Board in a timely manner.

    d. Under present standards of acceptable business conduct, it is proper to use the designation, Registered Investment Adviser, if the CFP Board designee is registered individually; however if the CFP Board designee is registered through his or her firm then the firm is the registered investment adviser, and the CFP Board designee is not permitted by the *Code of Ethics* and the SEC regulations to use RIA or R.I.A. after his or her name in advertising, letterhead stationery, or business cards.

    e. A CFP Board designee shall return the client's original records in a timely manner after their return has been requested by a client.

191. Which *Code of Ethics* Principle does the following Rule relate to?

"A financial planning practitioner shall enter into an engagement only after securing sufficient information to satisfy the CFP Board designee that: (a) the relationship is warranted by the individual's needs and objectives; and (b) the CFP Board designee has the ability to either provide requisite competent services or to involve other professionals who can provide such services."

    a. Professionalism.

    b. Competence.

    c. Fairness.

    d. Diligence.

    e. Confidentiality.

192. Which of the following statements concerning the *Disciplinary Rules and Procedures* is/are correct?

    1. Adherence to the *Code of Ethics* by CFP Board designees or to *Practice Standards* by CFP® practitioners is required, with the potential for CFP Board sanctions against those who violate the regulations proscribed in these documents.

    2. CFP Board will follow the disciplinary rules and procedures when enforcing the *Code of Ethics* and *Practice Standards*.

    a. 1 only.

    b. 2 only.

    c. Both 1 and 2.

    d. Neither 1 nor 2.

193. Which of the following statements concerning a CFP® practitioner's disclosure of confidential client data is generally correct?

    1. Disclosure may be made to any state agency without subpoena.

    2. Disclosure may be made to any party with consent of the client.

    3. Disclosure may be made to comply with an IRS audit request.

        a. 1 only.

        b. 2 only.

        c. 3 only.

        d. 1, 2, and 3.

        e. None of the above.

194. According to the regulations established by Certified Financial Planner Board of Standards Inc., which of the following are correct uses of the marks:

    1. Frank Smith, C.F.P.®.

    2. Frank Smith, CFP®.

    3. Frank Smith, CERTIFIED FINANCIAL PLANNER™.

    4. Frank Smith, CERTIFIED FINANCIAL PLANNER™.

    5. Frank Smith & Co., PA, CFP®'s.

        a. 1, 2, 3, and 4.

        b. 1, 2, and 4.

        c. 2, 3, and 4.

        d. 2, 3, 4, and 5.

        e. All are correct uses.

195. A CFP® certificant agrees to be bound by the Continuing Education (CE) Requirement established by the CFP Board. The CE Requirement for a regular continuing certificant (not a new certificant or a certificant who has been inactive) is as follows:

        a. 40 hours of CE every year.

        b. The number of CE hours required by other designations the certificant may hold.

        c. 30 hours of CE every year.

        d. 30 hours of CE every two years.

        e. 40 hours of CE every two years.

196. Which of the following Principles is/are not part of the *Code of Ethics and Professional Responsibility*?

1. Integrity.
2. Disclosure.
3. Objectivity.
4. Competence.
    a. 1 only.
    b. 2 only.
    c. 1 and 4.
    d. 1, 2, and 3.
    e. 1, 2, 3, and 4.

197. Which of the following Principles is/are not part of the *Code of Ethics and Professional Responsibility*?

1. Proper Training.
2. Fairness.
3. Confidentiality.
4. Professionalism.
    a. 1 only.
    b. 2 only.
    c. 1 and 4.
    d. 1, 2, and 3.
    e. 1, 2, 3, and 4.

198. Which of the following Principles is/are not part of the *Code of Ethics and Professional Responsibility*?

1. Independence.
2. Objectivity.
3. Competence.
4. Disclosure.
    a. 1 only.
    b. 2 only.
    c. 1 and 4.
    d. 1, 2, and 3.
    e. 1, 2, 3, and 4.

199. Which of the following Principles is/are not part of the *Code of Ethics and Professional Responsibility*?

    1. Independence.
    2. Diligence.
    3. Confidentiality.
    4. Fairness.
        a. 1 only.
        b. 2 only.
        c. 1 and 4.
        d. 1, 2, and 3.
        e. 1, 2, 3, and 4.

200. David Ramsey comes to you and wants you to invest $400,000 in such a way that will not attract the IRS. He refuses to allow you to do any financial planning and insists on paying you in cash. Which of the following would you do?

    a. Invest the money.
    b. Invest the money only after he signs a liability waiver.
    c. Refuse to help David.
    d. Inform the IRS.

201. Marion, a CFP® certificant, has a habit of commingling his client's money with his own. He keeps good records, however, and knows how much belongs to whom. One day he needs to pay off a drug debt and he uses some of the client's money to pay the debt. He did not have any other money in the account at the time except client money. Within three business days, he promptly repays the money with winnings from gambling. His client is unaware of the above and is not affected. Which of the following Principles has Marion violated?

    1. Integrity.
    2. Objectivity.
    3. Fairness.
    4. Professionalism.
        a. 1 and 4.
        b. 1, 2, and 4.
        c. 1, 2, and 3.
        d. 1, 2, 3, and 4.
        e. None of the above.

202. All of the following are forms of discipline that may be imposed by CFP Board's Board of Professional Review upon a CFP Board designee charged with misconduct except:

    a. Private censure.
    b. Public letter of admonition.
    c. Suspension – up to 10 years.
    d. Revocation of the right to use the certification marks.
    e. Additional continuing education requirements.

203. All of the following statements concerning the *Disciplinary Rules and Procedures* are correct except:

    a. Proceedings involving potential ethics violations shall be commenced upon a written request for investigation made by any person which shall be directed to the Board or commenced at the behest of CFP Board Staff Counsel.

    b. A Complaint, issued by the CFP Board Staff Counsel, shall set forth the grounds for discipline with which the CFP Board designee is charged and the conduct or omission which gave rise to those charges.

    c. A CFP Board designee may obtain copies of all documents in the CFP Board designee's disciplinary file, which are not privileged and which are relevant to the subject matter in the pending action before the Hearing Panel, through a written request to the CFP Board Staff Counsel.

    d. The notice of hearing shall advise the CFP Board designee that he or she is entitled to be represented by counsel at the hearing, to cross-examine witnesses and to present evidence on behalf of the CFP Board designee.

    e. If an order of the Board is not appealed within 30 business days after notice of the order is sent to the CFP Board designee, such order shall become final.

204. Which of the following statements concerning the Settlement Procedure in the *Disciplinary Rules and Procedures* is/are correct?

    1. A CFP Board designee against whom proceedings are pending (after a formal complaint and prior to final action by the Board) may tender an Offer of Settlement in exchange for a stipulated form of Board action.

    2. Submission of an Offer of Settlement does not suspend all proceedings conducted pursuant to these *Disciplinary Rules and Procedures*.

    a. 1 only.

    b. 2 only.

    c. Both 1 and 2.

    d. Neither 1 nor 2.

205. All of the following statements from the *Disciplinary Rules and Procedures* concerning Revocation, Suspension, and Reinstatement after Discipline are correct except:

    a. After the entry of an order of revocation is final, the CFP Board designee shall promptly terminate any use of the marks and in particular shall not use them in any advertising, announcement, letterhead, or business card.

    b. After the entry of an order of suspension is final, the CFP Board designee shall promptly terminate any use of the marks and in particular shall not use them in any advertising, announcement, letterhead, or business card.

    c. Revocation is permanent, and there shall be no opportunity for reinstatement unless specifically sanctioned by the CFP Board's Board of Professional Review.

    d. A CFP Board designee suspended for longer than one year must petition the Board for reinstatement, attend a hearing, and present clear and convincing evidence that the CFP Board designee has been rehabilitated.

206. Which of the following statements concerning the *Financial Planning Practice Standards* is not correct?

    a. The *Practice Standards* apply to CFP Board designees performing the tasks of personal financial planning regardless of the person's title, job position, type of employment, or method of compensation.

    b. *Practice Standards* should be considered by all personal financial planning professionals when performing the financial planning task or activity addressed by the Practice Standards, but are enforceable by CFP Board only against CFP Board designees.

    c. The *Practice Standards* were designed to be a basis for legal liability, thus, conduct inconsistent with the Practice Standards gives the presumption that a legal duty as been breached.

    d. The *Practice Standards* are designed to provide CFP Board designees a structure for identifying and implementing expectations regarding the professional practice of personal financial planning.

207. The *Practice Standard* that states, "The financial planning practitioner and the client shall mutually define the scope of the engagement before any financial planning service is provided," is *Practice Standard*:

    a. 100-1—Defining the Scope of the Engagement.
    b. 200-1—Determining a Client's Personal and Financial Goals, Needs and Priorities.
    c. 400-1—Identifying and Evaluating Financial Planning Alternative(s).
    d. 500-1—Agreeing on Implementation Responsibilities.
    e. 600-1—Defining Monitoring Responsibilities.

208. The *Practice Standard* that states, "The financial planning practitioner and the client shall mutually define the client's personal and financial goals, needs and priorities that are relevant to the scope of the engagement before any recommendation is made and/or implemented," is *Practice Standard*:

    a. 100-1—Defining the Scope of the Engagement.
    b. 200-1—Determining a Client's Personal and Financial Goals, Needs and Priorities.
    c. 300-1—Analyzing and Evaluating the Client's Information.
    d. 500-1—Agreeing on Implementation Responsibilities.
    e. 600-1—Defining Monitoring Responsibilities.

209. Arnie, a CFP® practitioner, has been hired by Marguerite to create her personal financial plan for her postretirement years. Marguerite plans to retire in 6 months at the age of 65. She has worked many places, but nowhere long enough to be covered by any company-sponsored retirement plan. While discussing Marguerite's retirement goals, Arnie learns that Marguerite's only plan to support herself in retirement is from crafting and selling lawn ornaments made from old Mardi Gras beads and used CDs. Arnie learns that Marguerite intends to set a high enough price for the ornaments to cover her living expenses from one month to the next. She has done no market research indicating the success of her product. Which *Practice Standard* states that Arnie must try to assist Marguerite to recognize the implications of this unrealistic plan?

    a.   100-1—Defining the Scope of the Engagement.

    b.   200-1—Determining a Client's Personal and Financial Goals, Needs and Priorities.

    c.   300-1—Analyzing and Evaluating the Client's Information.

    d.   500-1—Agreeing on Implementation Responsibilities.

    e.   No *Practice Standard* states that a CFP® practitioner must try to assist a client to recognize the implications of an unrealistic goal or objective.

210. The *Practice Standard* that states, "A financial planning practitioner shall obtain sufficient quantitative information and documents about a client relevant to the scope of the engagement before any recommendation is made and/or implemented," is *Practice Standard*:

    a.   200-2—Obtaining Quantitative Information and Documents.

    b.   300-1—Analyzing and Evaluating the Client's Information.

    c.   400-2—Developing the Financial Planning Recommendation(s).

    d.   500-1—Agreeing on Implementation Responsibilities.

    e.   600-1—Defining Monitoring Responsibilities.

211. The *Practice Standard* that states, "A financial planning practitioner shall analyze the information to gain an understanding of the client's financial situation and then evaluate to what extent the client's goals, needs and priorities can be met by the client's resources and current course of action," is *Practice Standard*:

    a.   200-2—Obtaining Quantitative Information and Documents.

    b.   300-1—Analyzing and Evaluating the Client's Information.

    c.   400-1—Identifying and Evaluating Financial Planning Alternative(s).

    d.   500-1—Agreeing on Implementation Responsibilities.

    e.   600-1—Defining Monitoring Responsibilities.

212. The *Practice Standard* that states, "A financial planning practitioner shall consider sufficient and relevant alternatives to the client's current course of action in an effort to reasonably achieve the client's goals, needs, and priorities," is *Practice Standard*:

    a.   200-1—Determining a Client's Personal and Financial Goals, Needs and Priorities.

    b.   300-1—Analyzing and Evaluating the Client's Information.

    c.   400-1—Identifying and Evaluating Financial Planning Alternative(s).

    d.   500-2—Selecting Products and Services for Implementation.

    e.   600-1—Defining Monitoring Responsibilities.

213. The *Practice Standard* that states, "A financial planning practitioner shall develop the recommendation(s) based on the selected alternative(s) and the current course of action in an effort to reasonably meet the client's goals, needs, and priorities," is *Practice Standard*:

    a. 200-1—Determining a Client's Personal and Financial Goals, Needs and Priorities.
    b. 300-1—Analyzing and Evaluating the Client's Information.
    c. 400-2—Developing the Financial Planning Recommendation(s).
    d. 500-2—Selecting Products and Services for Implementation.
    e. 600-1—Defining Monitoring Responsibilities.

214. The *Practice Standard* that states, "The financial planning practitioner shall communicate the recommendation(s) in a manner and to an extent reasonably necessary to assist the client in making an informed decision," is *Practice Standard*:

    a. 100-1—Defining the Scope of the Engagement.
    b. 200-1—Determining a Client's Personal and Financial Goals, Needs and Priorities.
    c. 300-1—Analyzing and Evaluating the Client's Information.
    d. 400-3—Presenting the Financial Planning Recommendation(s).
    e. 600-1—Defining Monitoring Responsibilities.

215. The *Practice Standard* that states, "The financial planning practitioner and the client shall mutually agree on the implementation responsibilities consistent with the scope of the engagement," is Practice Standard:

    a. 200-1—Determining a Client's Personal and Financial Goals, Needs and Priorities.
    b. 300-1—Analyzing and Evaluating the Client's Information.
    c. 400-1—Identifying and Evaluating Financial Planning Alternative(s).
    d. 500-1—Agreeing on Implementation Responsibilities.
    e. 600-1—Defining Monitoring Responsibilities.

216. The *Practice Standard* that states, "The financial planning practitioner shall select appropriate products and services that are consistent with the client's goals, needs, and priorities," is *Practice Standard*:

    a. 200-2—Obtaining Quantitative Information and Documents.
    b. 300-1—Analyzing and Evaluating the Client's Information.
    c. 400-2—Developing the Financial Planning Recommendation(s).
    d. 500-2—Selecting Products and Services for Implementation.
    e. 600-1—Defining Monitoring Responsibilities.

217. The *Practice Standard* that states, "The financial planning practitioner and client shall mutually define monitoring responsibilities," is *Practice Standard*:

    a. 200-1—Determining a Client's Personal and Financial Goals, Needs and Priorities.
    b. 300-1—Analyzing and Evaluating the Client's Information.
    c. 400-1—Identifying and Evaluating Financial Planning Alternative(s).
    d. 500-1—Agreeing on Implementation Responsibilities.
    e. 600-1—Defining Monitoring Responsibilities.

FUNDAMENTALS

Solutions

Fundamentals

1. a	26. e	51. a	76. d	101. a	126. d	151. d	176. b	201. d
2. d	27. a	52. d	77. c	102. c	127. a	152. c	177. a	202. c
3. d	28. c	53. e	78. d	103. d	128. d	153. a	178. e	203. e
4. b	29. c	54. b	79. a	104. d	129. d	154. b	179. c	204. a
5. c	30. b	55. c	80. b	105. a	130. b	155. b	180. d	205. c
6. a	31. a	56. b	81. c	106. c	131. d	156. b	181. a	206. c
7. c	32. b	57. a	82. a	107. b	132. c	157. a	182. c	207. a
8. d	33. a	58. b	83. b	108. b	133. d	158. b	183. b	208. b
9. b	34. d	59. c	84. d	109. d	134. c	159. d	184. b	209. b
10. b	35. d	60. c	85. b	110. b	135. d	160. a	185. d	210. a
11. d	36. c	61. a	86. d	111. c	136. c	161. c	186. c	211. b
12. a	37. c	62. b	87. b	112. b	137. d	162. c	187. c	212. c
13. b	38. a	63. b	88. a	113. b	138. b	163. d	188. b	213. c
14. d	39. a	64. a	89. c	114. a	139. c	164. e	189. a	214. d
15. d	40. d	65. c	90. c	115. b	140. c	165. c	190. a	215. d
16. c	41. e	66. c	91. b	116. a	141. a	166. c	191. d	216. d
17. a	42. a	67. c	92. d	117. c	142. e	167. b	192. c	217. e
18. b	43. e	68. d	93. a	118. b	143. a	168. d	193. b	
19. c	44. c	69. b	94. c	119. b	144. d	169. a	194. c	
20. c	45. c	70. e	95. d	120. b	145. d	170. d	195. d	
21. b	46. e	71. b	96. b	121. b	146. b	171. a	196. b	
22. a	47. c	72. d	97. a	122. d	147. e	172. b	197. a	
23. a	48. c	73. c	98. b	123. e	148. e	173. d	198. c	
24. d	49. e	74. d	99. c	124. a	149. c	174. e	199. a	
25. d	50. a	75. e	100. b	125. a	150. b	175. d	200. c	

THE FINANCIAL PLANNING PROCESS

Financial Planning Process

1. a

    Identifying financial strengths and weaknesses and preparing preliminary financial statements are completed in the third stage of the financial planning process. The other tasks would be done after the evaluating and analyzing stage. (Note: Preliminary financial statements need to be prepared during the third stage in order to evaluate the client's financial situation. Final and projected financial statements are prepared for the client during stage four.)

Financial Planning Functions (CFP® Certification Examination, released 11/94)

2. d

    This is simply a matter of which function as a planner comes in what order. Interview, collect, prepare, implement, and monitor.

Fundamentals—Process

3. d

    Everything (Statements 1, 2, and 4) except pick stocks, which is the implementation stage. The data gathering stage is the stage in which the planner compiles information about the client, their family, and their net worth, cash flow information. Determining the number of dependents, the age of the dependents, and collecting financial statement information are all appropriate actions during this stage.

PERSONAL FINANCIAL STATEMENTS

Financial Statement Presentation—Accrual vs. Cash

4. **b**

In order to determine whether the items should be included in the Statement of Financial Condition (balance sheet), the asset or liability should have the following characteristics:

- The asset or liability is a fixed and determinable amount.
- The receipt or payment is not contingent on the occurrence of a particular event.
- The receipt or payment does not require future performance of service.

Statement 1 is fixed and determinable but requires that one year pass before the options become exercisable.

Statement 2 is not fixed and determinable and requires that the board of directors meets and authorizes the bonus.

Statement 3 addresses the issue of constructive receipt of the dividend. Since the date of record was December 31, 2007, and the client held the shares as of that date, the client will receive the payment regardless of whether the client owns the stock after December 31, 2007. The amount should be shown on the Statement of Financial Condition.

Statement 4 requires that the client's son defaults on the loan and, therefore, should not be included in the Statement of Financial Condition.

Finally, Statement 5 should be included because the spouse is awaiting payment and no further service is required in order to receive the payment.

Since Statements 3 and 5 are the only two items that should be included in the Statement of Financial Condition, Option (b) is correct.

Financial Statement Presentation

5. **c**

The equity mutual fund is the most liquid asset presented. Following the mutual fund is the cash surrender value of the life insurance policy because redemption of those proceeds can be difficult and costly. Finally, the personal residence is not as liquid as the jewelry. Liquidity, in this sense, is the ability to convert to cash quickly, not the liquidity concept found in investments.

Financial Statement Presentation

6. **a**

The Statement of Financial Condition (balance sheet) is presented as of a date in time (a snapshot as of a particular date). Options (b), (c), and (d) identify a period of time and not a specific date. A period of time is appropriate for the Statement of Cash Flows. Option (e) could be a correct answer because it is a specific date but the question specified that the date was for a calendar-year client.

Financial Statement Presentation

7. c

Options (a) and (e) specify a point in time, which is appropriate for the Statement of Financial Condition (balance sheet). Option (b) is not correct because it does not specify an ending date. Option (d) is not descriptive about the ending date.

Note: The question addresses the year 2007. It is possible to prepare quarterly statements of cash flow. In the case of any period less than a full year, the beginning and ending period must be specified (i.e., For the Period Beginning April 1, 2007 and Ending June 30, 2007).

Asset Valuation (CFP® Certification Examination, released 11/94)

8. d

The question is what value should be used in preparation of a personal financial statement. The answer is fair market value (FMV), and Option (d) is the definition of FMV. The IRS defines fair market value as being the price that property will bring when offered for sale by a willing seller to a willing buyer, neither being obliged to sell or buy.

Client Data (CFP® Certification Examination, released 11/94)

9. b

1 is correct. On a client's net worth statement, assets are typically segregated based on use. Asset categories usually include "cash and cash equivalents," "investment assets," and "use assets." "Use assets" are assets that are used for personal reasons, such as a bedroom suite or furniture.

3 is correct. On the cash flow statement, the purchase of the bedroom suite would be reflected as a cash expenditure (outflow). The outflow would be variable, because it is not recurring in nature.

ANALYSIS OF FINANCIAL STATEMENTS AND IDENTIFICATION OF STRENGTHS AND WEAKNESSES

Analysis of Financial Statements

10. b

Statement 1 is incorrect. Payment of a liability would decrease the client's debt, and using the savings account would decrease the client's assets. Therefore, the net effect on net worth would be zero.

Statement 2 is incorrect. The addition of the automobile would increase the client's assets. However, the payment of the 25% down payment would decrease assets, and the 75% financed amount would increase the client's debt. therefore, the net effect on the worth would be zero.

Statement 3 would increase net worth, and Statement 4 would decrease net worth.

Analysis of Financial Statements

11. d

None of the transactions will change the net worth.

1. Payment of the credit cards will reduce debt by $10,000. However, use of the savings account (to pay off the debt) will reduce assets by $10,000. The net effect on net worth is zero.
2. The transfer from the checking account reduces assets by $4,000, and the transfer into the IRAs increases assets by $4,000. Therefore, the net effect on net worth is zero.
3. The addition of the furniture will increase the client's assets by $2,000. However, the use of credit will increase the client's debt by $2,000. Therefore, the net effect on net worth is zero.

Analysis of Financial Statements

12. a

Net worth is defined as assets minus liabilities. The statement of cash flows is irrelevant to this question.

Assets = $309,000 ($4,000 + $25,000 + $40,000 + $240,000)

Liabilities = $245,000 ($25,000 + $20,000 + $200,000)

Net Worth = $64,000 ($309,000 – $245,000)

Analysis of Financial Statements

13. b

They cannot meet either the 28% or 36% hurdle to refinance the home at 8%. Their income is too low and their indebtedness is too high. They do not have an adequate emergency fund even though they have the IRA and the investment account that they may choose to consider in an emergency fund analysis. It is inconclusive whether they have a low net worth for their age; it depends on their goals.

Analysis of Financial Statements

14. d

Because Anita's income, expenses and cash/cash equivalents are unchanged, her emergency fund ratio and savings ratio are unchanged. Because she has retired debt by cashing in a long-term investment asset, her debt management ratios and current ratio will improve.

BUDGETING

Budgeting

15. d

A budget should be adjusted monthly. Inflation is very important, as increases in costs affect the budget significantly. Individuals close to retirement age may often use budgeting to help determine the best wage replacement ratio for retirement, as they are generally closer to retirement and more able to make accurate predictions of expenses.

Budgeting

16. c

(a) is incorrect. Both bank and credit card statements should be analyzed to determine a client's spending and savings habits. (b) is incorrect. Insurance and utilities should be categorized as fixed expenses. (d) is incorrect. If the client has a history of making large dollar purchases impulsively, it would be wise to encourage investments in assets with early withdrawal penalties and/or those where withdrawal is difficult.

INTERNAL ANALYSIS

Internal Analysis

17. a

The conservation/protection phase of the life cycle is characterized by an increase in cash flow, assets, and net worth, with some decrease in the proportional use of debt. (b) is incorrect. The asset accumulation phase typically begins at age 20-25. The beginning of this phase is characterized by limited excess funds for investing, high degree of debt to net worth, and low net worth. (c) is incorrect. The distribution/gifting phase is the final phase of the life cycle. The first two phases of the life cycle make this phase possible. (d) is incorrect. The pre-career phase is not a phase of the lifecycle.

Internal Analysis

18. b

Studies have shown that when a client's decision will affect others, the client will typically display a lower risk tolerance than if the decision only affects the client. (a) is incorrect. Many of the risk measuring devices (questionnaires, etc.) are relatively new and unproven. (c) is incorrect. A planner must observe behavior in several situations. (d) is incorrect. A person's monetary risk (such as willingness to invest in risky securities) is often not correlated at all to their physical risk (willingness to climb mountains) tolerance.

PERSONAL-USE ASSETS AND LIABILITIES

Home Mortgage

19. c

PMT_{OA}	=	$496
n	=	180 (15 × 12)
i	=	0.729 (8.75 ÷ 12)
FV	=	$0
PV	=	($49,627) rounded to the nearest $100 = $49,600

Mortgages (CFP® Certification Examination, released 11/94)

20. c

Cash to pay points and length of ownership to reduce overall yield. Numbers 1 and 3 are irrelevant. The differential could be: (assume a $100,000, 30-year mortgage and add discount).

PMT_{OA}	$960.48/month		PMT_{OA}	$1,010.10/month
i	0.8750 (10.5 ÷ 12)		i	0.9583 (11.5 ÷ 12)
n	360 months		n	360 months
PV	$105,000		PV	$102,000

The indifference term is where amortization crosses over at about 43 months assuming payments were equalized at $1,010.10. If the young couple are interested in staying longer, use mortgage #1. Otherwise, use mortgage #2.

ECONOMIC ENVIRONMENT—BASIC CONCEPTS

Economic Environment

21. b

Economists refer to foregone income as a cost. The decision to use resources means that other forms of income are not realized, for example, the funds expended for a piece of machinery are not available to derive interest income. The foregone income costs are known as opportunity costs. Marginal costs are the cost to produce one more unit of product. Variable costs are costs that fluctuate with some cost driver (e.g., units produced). Fixed costs are costs that do not change as a result of producing additional units (i.e., rent). Cost of Capital is an internal measure of a company's borrowing costs from stockholders or outside creditors.

Supply / Demand

22. a

The law of demand states that as the price of a product decreases the demand for the product increases and vice versa. Option (b), Price Controls, is an attempt to adjust the balance between supply and demand. Option (c), Supply Side Economics, is a belief that offering incentives to produce can accomplish stated objectives. Option (d), the law of supply, states that there is a positive relationship between the price of a product and the amount producers are willing to produce (i.e., the higher the price, the more producers will produce). Option (e), Market Price, is the price at which a willing buyer and a willing seller achieve their objectives.

Supply / Demand

23. a

Option (b) is the description of a product whose demand is elastic. Option (c) describes the demand of a product that is perfectly elastic. Option (d) is a description of the equilibrium point in supply and demand. Option (e) is incorrect because price can be changed in a market economy.

Changes in Economic Activity

24. d

The Federal Reserve has the power to affect all of the controls listed. The manner in which it is done affects the objective of raising or lowering interest rates. If the Fed purchases securities on the open market, the money supply is increased and, therefore, interest rates are lowered. An increase in the reserve requirement causes the money supply to decrease because banks have to reduce their lendable reserves and this causes interest rates to rise. An increase in the discount rate causes banks to increase their interest rates to compensate for the spread between interest earned and interest paid. Finally, a decrease in the reserve requirement causes the money supply to increase because banks can increase their lendable reserves and this causes interest rates to fall. Therefore, since #1 and #4 lower interest rates, the correct answer is Option (d).

Economic Environment

25. d

The question is asking for the definition of the velocity of money and, therefore, all other answers are incorrect.

Inflation

26. e

This is determined by dividing the current year's index (133.5) by the prior year's index (125.6). The result is 1.063; that means the index of prices for 1993 is 1.063 times the index at the end of 1992, therefore, prices rose 6.3%. Options (a) and (d) are distracters. Option (b) is the difference between the two indexes and is incorrect. Option (c) calculates the percentage using the December 1993 index as the denominator and the difference as the numerator.

International Economics

27. a

This is calculated by dividing the US dollar equivalent of a Mexican Peso by the US dollar equivalent of a Peruvian Inti. If a Mexican Peso buys less of a US dollar than a Peruvian Inti, then a Mexican Peso would buy less than one full Peruvian Inti ($0.30656 \div 0.4717$). Option (b) divides the US dollar equivalent of the Peruvian Inti by the US dollar equivalent of the Mexican Peso. Option (c) is the same as (a), except it is multiplied by 100. Option (d) is the same as (b), except the answer is divided by 100. Option (e) multiplies the two US dollar equivalent amounts.

Statistical Series

28. c

Option (a), mean, is the mathematical average of all the values. Option (b), median, is the value where one half of the values are above the median and one half the values are below the median. The standard deviation, Option (d), relates to the deviation from the mean. Option (e), Beta, is the correlation of a particular security to the market.

Supply / Demand

29. c

This is the classic definition of the law of demand.

Supply / Demand

30. b

This is the classic definition of supply.

Adjustment Process

31. a

The adjustment process is the price process and moves to equilibrium.

Pure Competition

32. b

Pure competition occurs with large numbers of buyers and sellers.

Supply / Demand

33. a

The correct answer is (a) because less is produced at all price levels.

Supply / Demand

34. d

The law of demand states that "the quantity demanded for a product varies inversely with its price." When price decreases and consumers buy more of the product, there has been a change in the quantity demanded. A change in demand involves a shift of the entire demand curve.

Supply / Demand

35. d

Elasticity indicates a lower price will increase overall revenues.

Supply / Demand

36. c

If there is a substitute good, the product will be deemed elastic. A product is elastic when its quantity demanded responds greatly to price changes. If there is a substitute good that is less expensive, there will be a higher demand for the substitute product.

Supply / Demand

37. c

The option, consumers demand more at lower prices, describes a downward-sloping demand curve.

Supply / Demand

38. a

By definition, products are complements if an increase in the price of good A causes a decrease in the demand for its complementary good B. Therefore, the two products are examples of complements.

Supply / Demand

39. a

As the amount of goods consumed increases, the marginal utility of the good tends to decrease. From this concept, the law of downward sloping demand, the shape of the demand curve is formed. Therefore, Option (a) is correct.

Supply / Demand

40. d

The law of demand states that when the price of a good rises (at the same time all other things are constant) that less is demanded and vice versa. Therefore, Option (d) is correct.

Supply / Demand

41. e

All are reasons for changes in consumer demand.

Supply / Demand

42. a

The relationship between price and quantity purchased can be interpreted by a numerical table (demand schedule) or a graph where prices are measured on the vertical axis and quantity demanded on the horizontal axis (demand curve).

Supply / Demand

43. e

Elasticity of demand is an indicator of responsiveness of quantity demanded to changes in the market. Statements 1, 2, 3 and 4, all of which may affect the demand for a product, are determinants of demand elasticity.

Supply / Demand

44. c

A key element that affects supply is the cost of production. More efficient technology will decrease the cost of production.

Supply / Demand

45. c

Elasticity of supply indicates the amount of quantity supplied in response to a given rise in competition. If the amount supplied is fixed, or does not change significantly, then supply is inelastic.

Supply / Demand

46. e

All of the changes listed affect supply.

Inflation

47. c

Inflation generally means rising prices for goods and services. Someone on a fixed income in a time of rising prices will be forced to purchase less and, therefore, have declining purchasing power.

Economic Concepts

48. c

General definition of inflation.

Economic Concepts

49. e

The opposite of inflation is deflation, which is a decline in general price level. Disinflation denotes a decline in the rate of inflation.

Economic Concepts

50. a

Minimum wage is one example of government intervention to promote economic equity.

Economic Concepts (CFP® Certification Examination, released 11/94)

51. a

Shifts in aggregate demand are stimulated by increase in demand for capital goods #1 and increases in personal disposable income #3. Increase in interest rates #2 and savings #4 dampen aggregate demand.

Economics

52. d

All are regulated by the FLSA.

Workers Compensation

53. e

Strict liability is the basis for recovery according to most workers compensation statutes. The worker need only prove that an injury was suffered arising out of and occurring during the course and scope of employment.

Economics

54. b

If the demand is inelastic, price increases raise revenues.

Economics

55. c

A trough point in a business cycle occurs at the end of the contraction phase where businesses are operating at their lowest capacity levels.

Economics

56. b

A recession is characterized by a decline in real gross domestic product (GDP) for two or more successive quarters.

Other characteristics of a recession include: Decline in consumer purchases, expansion of inventory, decrease in labor demand, decline in capital investment and business profits.

Economics Supply and Demand (CFP® Certification Examination, released 12/96)

57. **a**

Statements 1, 2, and 3 are true. Statement 4 is false (the price would decrease).

1 is correct. An increase in demand typically causes prices to rise. A decrease in supply could also cause prices to rise, because fewer units of the product are available.

2 is correct. As price increases, the quantity demanded decreases, this is the law of demand.

3 is correct. If demand decreases, prices typically decline because fewer product are sold. If supply increases, prices typically decline because there are more products available for sale.

4 is incorrect. A decrease in demand typically causes a decline in price.

MONETARY AND FISCAL POLICY

Monetary and Fiscal Policy

58. b

Fiscal policy economists believe that the economy can be controlled through the use of government spending and income tax adjustments. Option (c) is the answer to describe economists who believe that economic activity is controlled through the use of the money supply. Option (a) is incorrect since that answer describes all the choices that include both fiscal policy as well as monetary policy economists. Option (d) is incorrect because inflation is determined by market factors. Option (e) partially describes a fiscal policy economist.

Monetary and Fiscal Policy

59. c

Tax legislation is fiscal not monetary policy.

The federal reserve bank controls monetary policy using the following methods:

1. Increasing/decreasing reserve requirements for member banks.

2. Increasing/decreasing discount rates.

3. Purchasing/selling government securities.

The federal government control fiscal policy using the following methods.

1. Increasing/decreasing taxes.

2. Increasing/decreasing government expenditures.

3. Selling securities (deficit spending).

Monetary and Fiscal Policy

60. c

Commercial banks establish the prime rate. The executive branch or Congress initiates any price control legislation.

Monetary and Fiscal Policy

61. a

Reducing the required reserve ratio and/or the discount rate. Reducing the required reserve ratio and the discount rate increases the ability of banks to make loans. Those loans create new money, which increases the money supply.

Monetary and Fiscal Policy

62. b

Sell US Treasury bonds to the general public. US Treasury bonds are issued by the US Treasury and not by the Federal Reserve. They are issued to finance operations of the federal government.

Monetary and Fiscal Policy

63. b

The primary function of the Federal Reserve is to carry out monetary policy. The Federal Reserve controls the supply of money enabling it to significantly impact interest rates. The Fed will follow a loose, or easy, monetary policy when it wants to increase the money supply to expand the level of income and employment. In times of inflation and when it wants to constrict the supply of money, the Fed will follow a tight monetary policy. The US Treasury issues bonds to the general public to finance the budget deficits of the federal government.

Monetary and Fiscal Policy

64. a

Increase the reserve requirements. The reserve requirement for a member bank of the Federal Reserve Bank is the percent of deposit liabilities that must be held in reserve. As this requirement is increased, less money is available to be loaned to customers, resulting in a restriction of the money supply.

Monetary and Fiscal Policy

65. c

The government cuts the Federal Funds Rate. The Federal Reserve sets the discount rate, which the Federal Funds Rate is based on. The Fed will lower the discount rate when it wants to increase the money supply. Options (a) and (b) represent expansionary fiscal policy. Option (d) represents restrictive fiscal policy.

Monetary and Fiscal Policy

66. c

M-1 is the measure of the most liquid components of the money supply. M-1 specifically includes currency, checking accounts, NOW accounts, travelers checks and checking money market accounts.

M-2 includes all items of M-1 plus savings accounts, certain money market mutual funds, Overnight Eurodollars and Overnight Repurchase Agreements.

M-3 includes all of M-2 plus certificates of deposit.

Option (a) is incorrect because NOW accounts are included in M-1. Option (b) is incorrect because savings accounts are M-2 and CD's are M-3. Option (d) is incorrect because checking accounts and NOW accounts are included in M-1. Option (e) is incorrect because only three of the five items are included in M-1.

Economics

67. c

Only increasing the discount rate will reduce the money supply. Purchasing Treasury securities and decreasing the reserve requirements for banks will increase the money supply.

Economics

68. d

All of the options have the potential to increase the money supply; however, the Federal Reserve does not control the expenditures of the federal government. Thus, increasing expenditures of the federal government would be fiscal policy, not monetary policy.

Monetary Policy

69. b

Lowering discount rate stimulates the money supply. Selling Treasury securities and increasing the reserve requirement decreases the money supply.

Monetary Policy

70. e

Control of the Federal Reserve Discount Rate, open-market operations, and fiscal policy are all methods of controlling the supply of money in the US economy.

Monetary Policy

71. b

Buying securities on the open market causes a direct increase in the money supply. Whereas selling securities causes a direct decrease in the money supply. Lowering the discount rate and increasing the margin requirement affects the money supply only insofar as to the degree that banks react to these changes.

Monetary Policy (CFP® Certification Examination, released 8/2004)

72. d

The federal funds rate and discount rate are both short-term interest rates. The discount rate is the rate the Federal Reserve charges its member banks for the overnight lending of reserves. The federal funds target rate is also set by the Federal Reserve and is the rate banks charge one another for the overnight lending of reserves. If most banks have reserve deficiencies (they need money), and only a few have excess reserves (high supply of money), market conditions (supply and demand) will cause the federal funds rate to rise. There is a low supply of money and a large demand for money.

A is incorrect. The Federal Reserve is putting cash into the market, increasing the supply of money. Market conditions would cause a decline in the federal funds rate.

B is incorrect. The federal funds rate is an open market rate that fluctuates based on market conditions. It is highly correlated with the discount rate. Therefore, if the Federal Reserve lowers the discount rate, the federal funds rate will likely move lower as well.

C is incorrect. If only a few banks have reserve deficiencies (they need money), and the rest have excess reserves (high supply of money), market conditions (supply and demand) will cause the federal funds rate to decline.

BUSINESS CYCLE THEORIES

Business Cycle

73. c

A typical business cycle can be measured from trough to trough or from peak to peak with expansion and recession in between. A recession follows a peak, and expansion follows a trough, which means the correct answer is (c).

Business Cycle

74. d

An expansion is where employment and output are rising. When employment and output are no longer rising, the phase is the peak. If employment and output begins to decrease, this indicates a recession. Finally, when employment and output are no longer decreasing, the cycle has reached a trough. The intensity indicates the highest and lowest points of the peak or the trough.

FINANCIAL INSTITUTIONS

Safety of Financial Institutions

75. e

Statement 1 is incorrect because the FDIC guarantees amounts up to $100,000 in nonretirement accounts. The excess over $100,000 is at risk. Statement 2 is incorrect because deposits up to $100,000 are guaranteed. Statement 3 is incorrect because funds invested in a mutual fund are subject to market risk and are not guaranteed by the FDIC at all. Statement 4 is incorrect because the FDIC guarantees amounts by depositor and not by accounts.

FDIC

76. d

The FDIC insures separate legal categories of accounts of a legal institution. As a result, the IRA will be insured up to $250,000. The individual accounts owned by John are aggregated and are insured up to $100,000 in total. The joint account will be insured for $70,000.

TIME VALUE OF MONEY

TVM—Future Value/Annual Compounding

77. c

PV	=	($50,000)
i	=	12
n	=	5
PMT	=	$0
FV	=	$88,117.08

TVM—Future Value/Monthly Compounding

78. d

PV	=	($10,000)
i	=	0.91666 (11 ÷ 12)
n	=	84 (7 × 12)
PMT	=	$0
FV	=	$21,522.04

TVM—Future Value/Annual Compounding

79. a

PV	=	($60,000)
i	=	7.5
n	=	8
PMT	=	$0
FV	=	$107,008.67

TVM—Present Value/Annual Compounding

80. b

FV	=	$25,000
i	=	8
n	=	8
PMT	=	$0
PV	=	($13,506.72)

TVM—Present Value/Semiannual Compounding

81. c

FV	=	$75,000
i	=	4.5 (9 ÷ 2)
n	=	12 (6 × 2)
PMT	=	$0
PV	=	($44,224.79)

TVM—Present Value/Monthly Compounding

82. **a**

FV	=	$75,000
i	=	0.8333 (10 ÷ 12)
n	=	60 (5 × 12)
PMT	=	$0
PV	=	($45,584.14)

TVM—Present Value/Quarterly Compounding

83. **b**

FV	=	$57,000
i	=	2.625 (10.5 ÷ 4)
n	=	34 (8.5 × 4)
PMT	=	$0
PV	=	($23,619.30)

TVM—Interest Rate

84. **d**

PV	=	($900)
FV	=	$4,500
n	=	7
PMT	=	$0
i	=	25.8499

TVM—Interest Rate

85. **b**

PV	=	($800)
FV	=	$1,200
n	=	5
PMT	=	$0
i	=	8.4472

TVM—Interest Rate

86. **d**

PV	=	($525)
FV	=	$1,000
n	=	13 (6.5 × 2)
PMT	=	$0
i	=	5.0815

Annual rate of return = 5.0815 × 2 = 10.163

TVM—Compounding Periods

87. b

PV	=	($8,000)
FV	=	$15,000
i	=	12
PMT	=	$0
n	=	5.5468

Note 1: Anytime you calculate for N (term) using a HP 12C you may need to find the answer by trial and error. The HP 12C calculator rounds to the nearest integer when calculating n, and therefore, your answer is not always precise when calculating the term. You must then take what you have and find the exact answer by trial and error methods. The HP 12C will give you 6.0000.

Note 2: If you are using an HP 12C and use correct n of 5.5468 the FV will be $15,023.84, which, of course, looks incorrect. The error is in the way the HP works. If you are using a HP 10B, HP 17BII, Sharp EL-733A, or TI BA II Plus you will get 5.5468 (the correct n). You can mathematically prove this answer by taking 1.12 raised to the 5.5468 power and then multiply by $8,000 to get $15,000.04.

TVM—Compounding Periods

88. a

PV	=	($1)
FV	=	$2
i	=	0.75 (9 ÷ 12)
PMT	=	$0
n	=	7.75 (93 ÷ 12) HP 12C
		7.73 (92.77 ÷ 12) other calculators

TVM—Future Value of an Ordinary Annuity Compounded Annually

89. c

PV	=	$0
PMT_{OA}	=	($1,000)
i	=	10.5
n	=	15
FV_{OA}	=	$33,060.04

TVM—Future Value of an Ordinary Annuity Compounded Quarterly

90. c

PV	=	$0
PMT_{OA}	=	($2,000)
i	=	2.75 (11 ÷ 4)
n	=	28 (7 × 4)
FV_{OA}	=	$82,721.95

TVM—Future Value of an Ordinary Annuity Due Compounded Annually
91. b

PV	=	$0
PMT_{AD}	=	($3,000)
i	=	8
n	=	15
FV_{AD}	=	$87,972.85

TVM—Future Value of an Annuity Due Compounded Quarterly
92. d

PV	=	$0
PMT_{AD}	=	($2,000)
i	=	2.75 (11 ÷ 4)
n	=	28 (7 × 4)
FV_{AD}	=	$84,996.80

TVM—Present Value of an Ordinary Annuity Compounded Annually
93. a

PMT_{OA}	=	$5,000
i	=	14
n	=	4
FV	=	$0
PV_{OA}	=	($14,568.56)

TVM—Present Value of an Ordinary Annuity Compounded Semiannually
94. c

PMT_{OA}	=	$1,500
i	=	5.5 (11 ÷ 2)
n	=	12 (6 × 2)
FV	=	$0
PV_{OA}	=	($12,927.78)

TVM—Present Value of an Annuity Due Compounded Annually
95. d

PMT_{AD}	=	($4,000)
i	=	10.5
n	=	7
FV	=	$0
PV_{AD}	=	$21,168.72

TVM—Present Value of an Annuity Due Compounded Monthly
96. b

PMT_{AD}	=	($1,200)
i	=	0.8333 (10 ÷ 12)
n	=	60 (5 × 12)
FV	=	$0
PV_{AD}	=	$56,949.10

TVM—Present Value of an Annuity Due Compounded Monthly
97. a

PV	=	$200,000
i	=	1.00 (12 ÷ 12)
n	=	60 (5 × 12)
FV	=	$0
PMT_{AD}	=	($4,404.84)

TVM—Payment Calculation for Annuity Due with Quarterly Compounding
98. b

FV	=	$60,000
i	=	2.625 (10.5 ÷ 4)
n	=	20 (5 × 4)
PV	=	$0
PMT_{AD}	=	($2,260.09)

TVM—Payment Calculation for an Ordinary Annuity Using Semiannual Compounding
99. c

FV	=	$150,000
i	=	6 (12 ÷ 2)
n	=	12 (6 × 2)
PV	=	$0
PMT_{OA}	=	($8,891.55)

TVM—Payment Calculation for an Ordinary Annuity Using Monthly Compounding
100. b

PV	=	$19,500
i	=	0.91666 (11 ÷ 12)
n	=	36 (3 × 12)
FV	=	$0
PMT_{OA}	=	($638.40)

TVM—Present Value Analysis of Alternatives

101. a

The best investment opportunity would be the receipt of the 45,000 today.

Option A:	PV	=	$45,000

Option B:	FV	=	$120,000
	i	=	10.5
	n	=	10
	PMT	=	$0
	PV	=	($44,213.86)

Option C:	PMT_{AD}	=	$5,500
	i	=	10.5
	n	=	15
	FV	=	$0
	PV_{AD}	=	($44,935.97)

Option D:	PMT_{OA}	=	$5,500
	i	=	10.5
	n	=	19
	FV	=	$0
	PV_{OA}	=	($44,523.35)

Option E:	PMT_{OA}	=	$5,750
	i	=	10.5
	n	=	17
	FV	=	$0
	PV_{OA}	=	($44,731.47)

TVM—Present Value Analysis of Alternatives

102. c

Option A:	PV	=	$100,000

Option B:	FV	=	$310,000
	i	=	9
	n	=	15
	PMT	=	$0
	PV	=	($85,106.79)

Option C:	PMT	=	$1,200
	i	=	0.75 (9 ÷ 12)
	n	=	132 (11 × 12)
	FV	=	$0
	PV_{OA}	=	($100,327.70)

Option D:

FV	=	$65,000		FV	=	$125,000
i	=	9		i	=	9
n	=	5		n	=	10
PMT	=	$0		PMT	=	$0
PV	=	($42,245.54)		PV	=	($52,801.35)

$42,245.54 + 52,801.35 = $95,046.89

Option E:	n	=	15
	i	=	9
	FV	=	$200,000
	PMT	=	$0
	PV	=	($54,907.61)

$54,907.61 + 42,245.54 = $97,153.15

TVM—Present Value Analysis of Alternatives
103. d

Option A: PV   = $50,000

Option B: FV   = $250,000
            i =   12
            n =   14
            PMT = $0
            PV   =   ($51,154.95)

Option C: FV   = $40,000   FV   = $120,000
            i =   12 i =   12
            n =   4 n =   12
            PMT = $0   PMT = $0
            PV   =   ($25,420.72)   PV   =   ($30,801.01)

$25,420.72 + 30,801.01 = $56,221.73

Option D: PMT = $5,000
            i =   6 (12 ÷ 2)
            n =   18 (9 × 2)
            FV   = $0
            PV_{AD} =   ($57,386.30)

Option E: FV   = $60,000
            i =   12
            n =   3
            PMT = $0
            PV   =   ($42,706.81)

TVM—Present Value on an Annuity Due Adjusted for Inflation Compounded Annually
104. d

PMT = $25,000

i =   3.84615 $\left(\dfrac{1.08}{1.04} - 1.00\right) \times 100$

n =   20
FV   = $0
PV_{AD} =   ($357,681.56)

TVM—Present Value on an Annuity Due Adjusted for Inflation Compounded Annually

105. a

PMT	=	$50,000
i	=	$4.3062 \left(\dfrac{1.09}{1.045} - 1.00 \right) \times 100$
n	=	12
FV	=	$0
PV_{AD}	=	($480,878.04)

TVM—Serial Payments Adjusted for Inflation

106. c

FV	=	$300,000
i	=	$(0.95238)^* \left(\dfrac{1.04}{1.05} - 1.00 \right) \times 100$
n	=	9
PV	=	$0
PMT_{OA}	=	($34,623.42) × 1.05 = $36,354.60 (change sign)

* The interest rate is negative because the inflation exceeds the return.

TVM—Serial Payments Adjusted for Inflation

107. b

$36,354.60* × 1.05 = $38,172.33

*See previous question.

TVM—Serial Payments Adjusted for Inflation

108. b

FV	=	$200,000
i	=	$4.8077 \left(\dfrac{1.09}{1.04} - 1.00 \right) \times 100$
n	=	6
PV	=	$0
PMT_{OA}	=	($29,546.11) × 1.04 = $30,727.95 (change sign)

TVM—Serial Payments Adjusted for Inflation

109. d

$30,727.95* × 1.04 = $31,957.07

*See previous question.

TVM—Future Value of an Annuity Due with Annual Compounding

110. b

The question specifies that the deposits are made at the beginning of each year; therefore, the student is required to calculate the future value of an annuity due. Option (a) is the future value of deposits made at the end of the year. Option (c) is incorrect because the calculation is based on the future value of the deposits made at the end of the year at 10% for 11.5 years, a reversal of the term and the interest rate. Option (d) is similar to (c) except the calculation is based on an annuity due. Option (e) is the present value of an annuity due instead of the future value of an annuity due. The keystrokes used with a financial calculator are:

PMT_{AD}	=	($6,100)
i	=	11.5
n	=	10
PV	=	$0
FV_{AD}	=	$116,510

TVM—Future Value of an Annuity Due with Quarterly Compounding

111. c

<u>Step 1:</u>

PV	=	($1)
n	=	4
i	=	2.875 (11.5 ÷ 4)
PMT	=	$0
FV	=	1.120055
Therefore i =		12.0055

<u>Step 2:</u>

PV	=	$0
PMT_{AD}	=	($6,100)
i	=	12.0055
n	=	10
FV	=	$119,931

Option (a) calculates the future value of a $6,100 deposit made at the end of each quarter for 40 quarters using i = 2.875 (11.5 ÷ 4). This is incorrect because the question specifies an annual deposit and not a quarterly deposit. Option (e) calculates the future value of an annuity due of a $6,100 deposit made at the beginning of each quarter for 40 quarters using i = 2.875 (11.5 ÷ 4). Finally, Option (b) calculates the future value of an annuity due of a $6,100 deposit made annually for 10 years at i = 11.5.

TVM—Present Value of an Annuity Due with Lag Period

112. b

There are two steps in solving this question.

Step 1: Calculate the present value of an annuity of $650 per month for 60 months at a discount rate of 9%. Financial calculations: PMT = $650, i = 0.75 (9 ÷ 12), n = 60 (5 × 12) and solve for PV_{AD} = $31,548. This provides the present value of an annuity one year from now.

Step 2: This amount is further discounted to the present, one year. Financial calculations: FV = $31,548, PMT = 0, i=9, n=1 and solve for PV = $28,943.

Option (a) is the present value of an annuity due of $7,800 ($650 × 12) received for five years at a discount rate of 9%. Option (c) is the present value of Option (a) discounted for one year at 9%. Option (d) is the first part of the correct calculation. Finally, Option (e) is the present value of an ordinary annuity instead of an annuity due.

TVM—Capital Budgeting

113. b

The question presented is the definition of Internal Rate of Return.

TVM—Capital Budgeting

114. a

A positive net present value of a series of discounted cash flows means that the discounted cash flows exceed the investment outlay. Statements 2 and 3 cannot be correct because the question does not provide appropriate information. Statement 4 is not correct because if the internal rate of return were the rate used, the net present value amount would be equal to zero.

TVM—Capital Budgeting

115. b

Statements 1 and 4 are correct. A net present value of a series of discounted cash flows equal to zero means the discounted cash flows are equal to the investment outlay.

TVM—Capital Budgeting

116. a

A negative net present value of a series of discounted cash flows means the investment outlay exceeds the discounted cash flows.

Net present value is the difference between the initial cash outflows and the present value of future cash inflows. If the NPV is negative, the PV of future cash flows is less than the initial investment. IRR is also less than the required rate of return.

An investment with a negative NPV is generally and undesirable investment.

TVM—Ordinary Annuity Payment Calculation Assuming Beginning Balance
117. c

There are two steps to solving this question.

The first step is to compute the future value of the beginning savings balance. PV = $2,500, i = 0.9167 (11 ÷ 12), n = 120 (10 × 12) and solve for FV = $7,472.87. This amount is subtracted from the required balance of $150,000 to arrive at the amount that needs to be funded of $142,527.13.

The second step is to solve for this amount as follows: FV = $142,527.13, i = 0.9167 (11 ÷ 12), n = 120 (10 × 12) and solve for PMT_{OA} = ($656.81).

Shortcut: PV = ($2,500), i = 0.9167 (11 ÷ 12), n = 120 (10 × 12), FV = 150,000, PMT = ($656.81). Option (d) has the correct inputs except the answer is the calculation of an annuity due. Option (a) calculates the annuity due assuming no beginning savings balance. Option (b) calculates the payment required assuming no beginning savings balance. Option (e) calculates the annual payment required assuming a beginning balance and divides that number by 12.

TVM—Capital Budgeting with Annuity Due and Beginning Balance
118. b

The amount to be funded is $147,500, the required amount of $150,000 less the face amount of the bond of $2,500. FV = $147,500, i = .9167 (11 ÷ 12), n = 120 (10 × 12) and solve for PMT_{AD} = $673.56. Option (a) is incorrect because the payment is calculated as if the present value of the bond is projected at 11%, the assumed rate of return. It is unnecessary to project the present amount since the face value at the end is known. Option (c) is the same as Option (a) except the payment is solved as an annuity due. Option (d) calculates the future value correctly ($147,500) except as a regular payment and not an annuity due. Option (e) calculates the annuity due of $147,500 except at an interest rate of 8%, which is the implicit rate of the bond.

TVM—Case Study
119. b

Option (a) is an incorrect statement because the marginal tax rate is the appropriate tax rate to use and not the average tax rate. Option (c) is incorrect because an annuity due payment will be less than a regular payment. Option (d) is incorrect because the rates of return should be greater than the education rate of inflation and not the general rate of inflation. Finally, Option (e) does not compare the after-tax rate of return and may not be appropriate advice.

Mortgage Payment Calculation
120. b

n	=	180
i	=	0.8333 (10 ÷ 12)
PV	=	$148,000 ($185,000 × 0.80)
PMT_{OA}	=	($1,590.42)

Mortgage Interest

121. b

PV	=	$96,000 (120,000 × 0.80)
i	=	0.625 (7.5 ÷ 12)
n	=	180 (15 years × 12)
PMT_{OA}	=	($889.93)

Total payments	$160,187.40
Less principal	(96,000.00)
Total interest	$64,187.40

Rounded to $64.187.

TVM—PV

122. d

Solution:				Alternate Method:		
n	=	120 (10 × 12)		n	=	360 (30 × 12)
i	=	0.6667 (8 ÷ 12)		i	=	0.6667 (8 ÷ 12)
PMT_{OA}	=	$953.89		PMT_{OA}	=	$953.89
FV	=	$114,042		FV	=	$0
PV	=	($130,000)		PV	=	($130,000)

TVM—Mortgage Payment Calculation

123. e

PV	=	$117,463.26 = ($114,042 × 1.03)
n	=	204 (17 × 12) (**Note:** Brian wants to pay off by his retirement.)
i	=	0.5833 (7 ÷ 12)
PMT_{OA}	=	($986.29)

TVM

124. a

PV	=	$120,000
n	=	180
i	=	0.5833 (7 ÷ 12)
PMT_{OA}	=	($1,078.59) × 180 = $194,146.90 – 120,000 = $74,146.90

Note: When calculating this problem, you will need to change the sign of $194,146.90 to positive before subtracting $120,000.

TVM (Released Question—CFP® Certification Examination 8/2004)

125. a

They will accumulate $10,368 more than needed. First, the actual cash need must be determined in future dollars:

PV	=	($300,000)
i	=	4%
n	=	18
FV	=	$607,745

Second, the amount saved must be determined:

PMT	=	($20,000)
i	=	6%
n	=	18
FV	=	$618,113

Finally, the surplus/shortfall must be determined:

Amount saved	$618,113
Less: amount needed	(607,745)
Surplus	$10,368

EDUCATIONAL FUNDING

TVM—Education

126. d

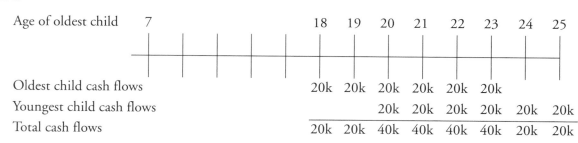

Age of oldest child	7				18	19	20	21	22	23	24	25
Oldest child cash flows					20k	20k	20k	20k	20k	20k		
Youngest child cash flows							20k	20k	20k	20k	20k	20k
Total cash flows					20k	20k	40k	40k	40k	40k	20k	20k

Method: Uneven Cash Flows

Step 1:

Cash Flows

$$CF_{7-17} = (0) \quad (11 \text{ periods})$$

$$CF_{18-19} = 20k \quad (2 \text{ periods})$$

$$CF_{20-23} = 40k \quad (4 \text{ periods})$$

$$CF_{24-25} = 20k \quad (2 \text{ periods})$$

$$i = [(1.12 \div 1.06) - 1] \times 100$$

$$NPV = \$108,663$$

Step 2:

Yearly Payment

$$PV = (\$108,663)$$

$$n = 18 \ (23 - 5)$$

$$i = 12$$

$$FV = 0$$

$$PMT_{OA} = \$14,989$$

TVM—Education

127. a

Method: Account Balance Method

Step 1: Calculate future value of first tuition payment.

PV	=	$12,000
i	=	5
n	=	4
FV$_{@18}$	=	($14,586.08)

Step 2: Calculate present value of 4 tuition payments.

PMT$_{AD}$	=	$14,586.08
i	=	3.81 [[(1.09 ÷ 1.05) − 1] × 100]
n	=	4
PV$_{AD}$	=	($55,210.56)

Step 3: Calculate monthly payment.

$55,210.56 ÷ 3 = $18,403.52 (Sharon's share at age 18)

FV	=	$18,403.52
n	=	48 (4 × 12)
i	=	0.75 (9 ÷ 12)
PMT$_{AD}$	=	($317.56) (Sharon's monthly payment made at the beginning of each month)

Note: There are numerous methods to calculate educational funding needs analysis. This question was solved using the method generally applied to capital needs analysis. If you used the traditional three-step approach illustrated in question 119 or the uneven cash flow method, your answer should be $322 instead of $317.56 (which would change the answer to this question). The reason for this difference is that this problem has been calculated by switching from annual compounding to monthly compounding. Monthly compounding was necessary as indicated by the question. Generally, you should not encounter this problem, most questions will ask for annual payments instead of monthly payments.

TVM—Education

128. d

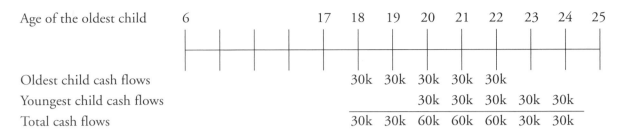

| Age of the oldest child | 6 | | | 17 | 18 | 19 | 20 | 21 | 22 | 23 | 24 | 25 |

Oldest child cash flows					30k	30k	30k	30k	30k			
Youngest child cash flows						30k	30k	30k	30k	30k		
Total cash flows					30k	30k	60k	60k	60k	30k	30k	

<u>Method: Uneven Cash Flows</u>

Step 1:

Cash Flows

CF_{6-17} = 0

CF_{18-19} = 30,000

CF_{20-22} = 60,000

CF_{23-24} = 30,000

i = $[(1.12 \div 1.07) -1] \times 100$

NPV = ($151,693)

Step 2:

Yearly Payment

PV = $151,693

n = 14 (20 − 6)

i = 12

FV = 0

PMT = ($22,886)

Qualified Tuition Plans (QTPs)

129. d

All the statements are correct.

Qualified Tuition Plans (QTPs)

130. b

The contributor/owner can change the beneficiary.

Educational Funding Needs Analysis

131. d

The Roth IRA for Kenneth is the best choice because it keeps an asset out of the son's name (for financial aid purposes). Also, the Roth IRA allows contributions up to $4,000 with an additional catch-up amount of $1,000 for individuals at least 50 years old (for 2007). When Kenneth begins college, John will have attained age 59½, and therefore, he can withdraw funds from his Roth IRA completely income tax free. The Coverdell ESA will not work because contributions are limited to $2,000 per year. Note: Liz will not have attained age 59½, and therefore, earnings withdrawn from her Roth IRA for education costs will be taxable.

Coverdell Education Savings Accounts

132. c

Qualified educational expenses for purposes of Coverdell Education Savings Accounts include elementary, secondary, undergraduate, and graduate level courses.

Federal Education Assistance Programs

133. d

Federal Pell Grants and Supplemental Educational Opportunity Grants issue gifts to students from the government based on financial need. Federal Subsidized and Unsubsidized Stafford Loans require repayment with the interest on the Unsubsidized Stafford Loan being due almost immediately after disbursement. Other government loans include the Federal Perkins Loan and Federal PLUS programs. Although the Federal College Work-Study Program is sponsored by the government, it is administered through colleges. Students work ten to fifteen hours per week at a job that is typically on campus in order to earn a portion of their financial aid package. The Rhodes Scholarship Program is a privately sponsored higher educational program.

Hope Scholarship Credit and Lifetime Learning Credit

134. c

The HOPE scholarship credit can be used for qualified educational expenses for the first two years of college for each student, while the lifetime learning credit is allowed once per year per family. Mike is a senior, and Mary is a junior, and therefore, both are ineligible for the HOPE scholarship credit.

EE Savings Bonds

135. d

Option (a) is incorrect because EE bonds are purchased at one-half of their face value. Option (b) is incorrect because EE bonds have varying interest rates, but face value must be reached in 17 years, for those bonds issued from May 1, 1997 through May 1, 2003. EE bonds issued June 1, 2003 or later reach an original maturity at 20 years. A bond can earn interest for up to 30 years. If you hold your bond long enough, its redemption value will and can exceed its face value. Option (c) is incorrect because to attain tax-free status, EE bonds must be purchased in the name of one or both parents of the student/child.

Educational Funding Needs Analysis

136. c

Option (a) is not the best answer because an UTMA account is not tax efficient. Since Paul is 9, kiddie tax will apply. Option (b) is not the best answer because a Coverdell Education Savings Account has a contribution limit of $2,000. Option (d) is not the best answer because Traditional IRAs do not allow loans. Option (c) is correct. The 529 Plan allows higher contributions and provides tax-free distributions for qualified education expenses distributed after 2001 (for state-sponsored plans) or 2003 (for other eligible educational institutions).

Educational Funding Needs Analysis

137. d

Because of their AGI, Tom and Samantha do not qualify to take the HOPE scholarship credit or lifetime learning credit for 2007. Therefore, Options (a) and (b) are incorrect. Option (c) is incorrect because the Pell Grant is awarded on a financial need basis, for which the family would not qualify.

529 Plans

138. b

Funds used for nonqualified expenses are included in the gross income of the distributee to the extent of the earnings portion of the distributions. Distributions are prorated between earnings and contributions. Thus, only the earnings portion of the $2,000 excess distribution will be included in gross income. Since Statement 1 said $2,000, we know Statement 1 cannot be correct because part of the $2,000 must be a return of capital and the amount included in gross income would have to be less than $2,000. A 10 percent additional tax will be applied to any distribution that is includible in gross income.

Education Funding (CFP® Certification Examination, released 8/2004)

139. c

A parent who claims a child as a dependent is entitled to take the HOPE credit for the educational expenses of the child.

A is incorrect. The Lifetime Learning Credit is equal to 20% of qualified educational expenses up to a certain limit.

B is incorrect. The HOPE credit is available for the first 2 years of postsecondary education

D is incorrect. The contribution limit for Coverdell Education Savings Accounts is applied per year per student (not donor).

CONTRACTS

Suretyship

140. c

The surety may assert a defense, personal to the surety, to limit his/her liability to a creditor. The surety may use the defense of incapacity of the surety to avoid liability to the principal debtor's creditor.

Suretyship

141. a

Release of a co surety by a creditor without the consent or reservation of rights against the other co surety releases the remaining surety to the extent that he/she cannot obtain contribution from the released surety. Thus, Lanning remains liable for 50% of the loan balance.

Contracts

142. e

There are four essential elements of a contract:

1. Agreement.
2. Consideration.
3. Legal capacity.
4. Legal objective.

A writing is not required. Therefore, Statements 2, 3, and 4 are correct.

Contracts

143. a

The promise of one party to perform is consideration for the promise of the other in a bilateral contract (two promises). On the other hand, in a unilateral contract, one party makes a promise in exchange for the other party's act (one promise).

Contracts

144. d

The manner of communications is irrelevant as long as it is communicated as intended by the offeror. Therefore, Statements 2 and 3 are correct, and Statements 1 and 4 are incorrect.

AGENCY

Agency
145. d

(a) is incorrect. A minor can serve as an agent, as long as the minor is capable of carrying out the required duties. (b) is incorrect. A principal, not the agent, must have contractual capacity. (c) is incorrect. The agent is not a party to the contract.

Agency
146. b

An agent has a "duty of loyalty" to the principal. (a) is incorrect. An agency relationship is consensual, not contractual. Consideration need not be given by the principal. (c) is incorrect. The principal is responsible for an agents acts when the agent is acting within his or her authority. (d) is incorrect. Implied authority is a type of actual authority that is necessary for the conduct of the ordinary business of the partnership.

NEGOTIABLE INSTRUMENTS

Negotiable Instruments

147. e

All are correct. In order for an instrument to be negotiable, it must:

- Be written.
- Be signed by the maker/drawer.
- Contain an unconditional promise or order to pay.
- State a fixed amount in money.
- Be payable to order/bearer.
- Be payable on demand or at a definite time.

Negotiable Instruments

148. e

All are correct. In order for an instrument to be negotiable, it must:

- Be written.
- Be signed by the maker/drawer.
- Contain an unconditional promise or order to pay.
- State a fixed amount in money.
- Be payable to order/bearer.
- Be payable on demand or at a definite time.

PROPERTY

Legal Environment

149. c

The characteristics of community property include:

1. Joint interest held by husband and wife.
2. Community property gets a step up to FMV for taxable basis both halves at the death of the first spouses.
3. Transfer requires the consent of both parties.
4. There is no right of survivorship.

Property

150. b

The main characteristic of tenancy by the entirety (joint tenancy between spouses) is that if one of the spouses dies, interest in the property automatically passes to the other spouse by operation of law.

Legal Environment

151. d

The characteristics of tenancy by the entirety are:

1. Joint interest held by husband and wife.
2. Tenancy by the entirety is presumed when the names of both spouses are on the title.
3. Transfer requires the consent of both parties.
4. Each tenant has a right of survivorship.
5. Divorce creates a property ownership as tenants in common.

Property

152. c

Community property and tenancy by the entirety can only be entered into by spouses. Joint tenancy (JTWROS) is often used by spouses to avoid probate but is not limited to spouses.

Uniform Transfers to Minors Act (UTMA)

153. a

All income earned greater than $1,700 (for 2007) in an UTMA by a child who is under the age of 18 is taxed at the rate of the parents.

Uniform Transfers to Minors Act (UTMA)

154. b

If a child is 18 years or older, the income earned by the assets in an UTMA is taxed at the child's income tax rate. Kiddie tax no longer applies once a child attains age 18.

Property

155. b

When property is owned as JTWROS between non-spouses, the gross estate inclusion is based on relative contributions. Since Della paid 1/3 of the purchase price, she will include 1/3 of the date of death value in her gross estate.

Gross estate inclusion = [($60,000/$180,000) × $240,000] = $80,000

CONSUMER PROTECTION

Consumer Legislation (CFP® Certification Examination, released 11/94)

156. b

Each credit card carries a $50 potential liability, which is mitigated with notice prior to any fraudulent use.

Discover Card	$50
Master Card	$50
VISA	$50
Sears	$25
Marshall Fields	$50
Total	$225

Age Discrimination

157. a

The ADEA is intended to prevent arbitrary discrimination based on age. Furthermore, compulsory retirement of most classes of employees before the age of 70 is prohibited.

BANKRUPTCY AND REORGANIZATION

Bankruptcy

158. b

At the end of Chapter 11 proceedings, a corporate creditor had negotiated with creditors for most of the debts of the business. Exceptions to negotiated debts include debts that are provided for in the plan of reorganization (approved by the creditors and the court) and certain nondischargeable debts.

Bankruptcy

159. d

A single creditor may file an involuntary petition for relief under Chapter 11 if he/she has at least $5,000 of unsecured claims and if the debtor has fewer than 12 creditors.

Bankruptcy

160. a

Debts arising from alimony, maintenance, and child support may not be discharged in bankruptcy. This does not include lump-sum property settlement awards.

Bankruptcy

161. c

The bankruptcy estate consists of all the debtor's legal and equitable interests in property, including gifts, insurance proceeds, property settlements, and inheritances received within 180 days of the commencement of bankruptcy proceedings.

Chapter 7 Bankruptcy

162. c

Child support is not dischargeable nor are federal taxes within the last three years. Nonintentional tort claims and consumer debt may be discharged.

Bankruptcy

163. d

Credit card debt will be discharged but not alimony or self-employment tax.

Bankruptcy

164. e

None is dischargeable.

TORTS

Tort Law
165. c

Courts try to provide a remedy for injury when a freedom of action is outweighed by the harm caused by interference with the personal or property rights of another.

Tort Law
166. c

Intent exists when the defendant makes a false representation with knowledge of its falsity or with a reckless disregard for the truth.

Tort Law
167. b

A battery is an intentional unprivileged bodily contact that would be harmful or offensive to a reasonable person.

Tort Law
168. d

Negligence is "conduct that falls below the standards established by law for the protection of others against unreasonable risk of harm." Stan, who knowingly drove his car after taking medicine he knows makes him drowsy, behaved negligently.

PROFESSIONAL LIABILITY—FINANCIAL PLANNERS

Contract

169. a

Under common law, an accountant's liability for negligence is most often restricted to those parties in privity of contract or who are primary beneficiaries of the engagement. This liability may also extend to foreseen third parties.

Note: For additional questions in this area, refer to the Ethics section of Fundamentals.

Liability

170. d

Once the client assumes the advice is fact, the certificant is responsible, even if compensation or a contractual obligation has not occurred.

REGULATORY REQUIREMENTS

Regulatory Requirements

171. a

Liability under Rule 10b-5 requires that the plaintiff (stock purchaser) prove that a CFP® practitioner had the intent (scienter) to deceive investors, the existence of a misstatement or omission of a material fact, its connection with the securities transaction, and reliance on the misstatement (reliance is assumed in omission cases.)

Regulatory Requirements

172. b

In order to be subject to the reporting requirements, a company must have shares listed on a national security exchange or have at least 500 shareholders and total gross assets of at least $5,000,000.

Regulatory Requirements

173. d

The reports include the annual report (Form 10-K), the quarterly reports (10-Q), and a proxy statement. In addition, the current report (8-K) must be filed to disclose material events within 15 days of occurrence.

Regulatory Requirements

174. e

Statements 2 and 3 are correct.

Regulatory Requirements

175. d

The 1933 Act exempts certain types of securities from registration statements. These include securities issued by not-for-profit organizations, domestic governments, banks, savings and loan associations, companies in reorganization, parties regulated by the ICE, receivers or trustees in bankruptcy, and companies in exchange for existing securities if no commission is paid.

Regulatory Requirements

176. b

The 1933 Act states that prospective investors must be provided with a prospectus disclosing pertinent financial and other types of information. The principal purposes for which the offering's proceeds will be used must also be disclosed. Options (a), (c), and (d) are not relevant to an informed decision regarding the purchase of a security.

Regulatory Requirements (CFP® Certification Examination, released 11/94)

177. a

Nothing assures the investor safety while investing and trading in securities (Statement 4). Statements 1, 2, and 3 are correct.

Regulatory Requirements

178. e

If an individual has fewer than 15 clients, registration is not necessary. Therefore, Options (b) and (d) are incorrect. A CFP® practitioner does not necessarily have to register by virtue of the designation; therefore, Options (a) and (c) are incorrect.

INVESTMENT ADVISER REGULATION AND REGISTRATION

Regulatory Environment

179. c

NASD registration is required when products are offered for sale.

Licenses

180. d

Series 6 license qualifies you to sell mutual funds, variable life insurance, variable annuities, and unit investment trusts.

CFP BOARD'S STANDARDS OF PROFESSIONAL CONDUCT

Code of Ethics—Preamble and Applicability

181. a

Statement 2 is incorrect. The *Code of Ethics* applies to individuals who have been certified in the past and retain the right to reinstate their CFP® certification without passing the current CFP® Certification Examination.

Code of Ethics—Composition and Scope

182. c

Both Statements 1 and 2 are correct.

Code of Ethics—Part II—Rules—Integrity

183. b

Option (b) is not correct. Neither a candidate for CFP® certification nor a CFP® certificant can offer personal views as those of CFP Board.

Code of Ethics—Part II—Rules—Competence

184. b

Statement 1 is incorrect. In areas where the CFP Board designee is not professionally competent, the CFP Board designee shall seek the counsel of qualified individuals and/or refer clients to such parties.

Code of Ethics—Part II—Rules—Objectivity and Fairness

185. d

Option (d) is a Rule in the *Code of Ethics* that relates to the Principle of Objectivity, not Fairness.

Code of Ethics—Part II—Rules—Fairness

186. c

Rule 401 relating to the Principle of Fairness explicitly requires that the designee disclose material information relevant to the professional relationship including the designee's address, telephone number, credentials, qualifications, licenses, and compensation structure.

Code of Ethics—Part II—Rules—Confidentiality

187. c

Both Statements 1 and 2 are correct. See Rules 501 and 502 that relate to the Principle of Confidentiality.

Code of Ethics—Part II—Rules—Confidentiality

188. b

For purposes of this Rule, the proscribed use of client information is improper whether or not it actually causes harm to the client.

Code of Ethics—Part II—Rules—Professionalism

189. a

Under Rule 605 relating to the Principle of Professionalism, an individual who only suspects illegal conduct within their firm should notify their direct supervisor, a partner, or co-owner of the firm. The designee should notify the CFP Board once the designee is convinced of illegal conduct in which the firm has not taken appropriate measures to correct.

Code of Ethics—Part II—Rules—Professionalism

190. a

A CFP Board designee who has knowledge (no substantial doubt), which is not required under the *Code of Ethics* to be kept confidential, and which raises a substantial question of unprofessional, fraudulent or illegal conduct by a CFP Board designee or other financial professional, shall promptly inform the appropriate regulatory and/or professional disciplinary body.

Code of Ethics—Part II—Rules—Diligence

191. d

Rule 702 relates to the Principle of Diligence.

Disciplinary Rules and Procedures—Article 1: Introduction

192. c

Both 1 and 2 are correct.

Code of Ethics—Part II—Rules—Confidentiality

193. b

Under Principle 5, a CFP® practitioner may disclose any confidential client information with the specific consent of the client.

Code of Ethics

194. c

The CFP® marks should never have periods between the letters. Therefore, Options (a), (b), and (e) are incorrect. The mark should not be used as part of or incorporated in the name of a firm. Therefore, Option (d) is incorrect. It is appropriate to either capitalize all the letters as shown in Statement 3 or to use large initial capitals with the first letter of each word as shown in Statement 4.

Code of Ethics

195. d

30 hours of continuing education is required every 2 years. The 30 hours must be in at least three areas (e.g., tax, investments, and estates). Two hours of ethics must also be completed.

Code of Ethics—Part I—Principles

196. b

Integrity, Objectivity, and Competence are Principles of the *Code of Ethics and Professional Responsibility.* Disclosure is not.

Code of Ethics—Part I—Principles

197. a

Fairness, Confidentiality, and Professionalism are Principles of the *Code of Ethics and Professional Responsibility.* Proper training is not.

Code of Ethics—Part I—Principles

198. c

Objectivity and Competence are Principles of the *Code of Ethics and Professional Responsibility.* Independence and disclosure are not.

Code of Ethics—Part I—Principles

199. a

Diligence, Confidentiality, and Fairness are Principles of the *Code of Ethics and Professional Responsibility.* Independence is not one of these principles.

Code of Ethics—Part I—Principles

200. c

Never take a sleazy client. Integrity.

Code of Ethics—Part I—Principles

201. d

Marion has violated all of the listed principles.

Disciplinary Rules and Procedures—Article 4: Forms of Discipline

202. c

Suspension is only allowed up to 5 years.

Disciplinary Rules and Procedures—Article 11: Appeals

203. e

If an order of the Board is not appealed within 30 <u>calendar</u> days after notice of the order is sent to the CFP Board designee, such order shall become final.

Disciplinary Rules and Procedures—Article 13: Settlement Procedure

204. a

Statement 2 is incorrect. Submission of an Offer of Settlement does suspend all proceedings conducted pursuant to the *Disciplinary Rules and Procedures.*

Disciplinary Rules and Procedures—Article 15: Reinstatement After Discipline

205. c

Revocation is permanent, and there shall be no opportunity for reinstatement.

Financial Planning Practice Standards—Description of Practice Standards

206. c

The *Practice Standards* were not designed to be a basis for legal liability. Conduct inconsistent with a *Practice Standard* in and of itself is not intended to give rise to a cause of action nor to create any presumption that a legal duty has been breached.

Financial Planning Practice Standards—Practice Standards 100 Series

207. a

Practice Standard 100-1—Defining the Scope of the Engagement.

Financial Planning Practice Standards—Practice Standards 200 Series

208. b

Practice Standard 200-1—Determining a Client's Personal and Financial Goals, Needs and Priorities.

Financial Planning Practice Standards—Practice Standards 200 Series

209. b

Practice Standard 200-1—Determining a Client's Personal and Financial Goals, Needs and Priorities. When appropriate, the practitioner shall try to assist clients in recognizing the unrealistic goals and objectives.

Financial Planning Practice Standards—Practice Standards 200 Series

210. a

Practice Standard 200-2—Obtaining Quantitative Information and Documents.

Financial Planning Practice Standards—Practice Standards 200 Series

211. b

Practice Standard 300-1—Analyzing and Evaluating the Client's Information.

Financial Planning Practice Standards—Practice Standards 400 Series

212. c

Practice Standard 400-1—Identifying and Evaluating Financial Planning Alternative(s).

Financial Planning Practice Standards—Practice Standards 400 Series

213. c

Practice Standard 400-2—Developing the Financial Planning Recommendation(s).

Financial Planning Practice Standards—Practice Standards 400 Series

214. d

Practice Standard 400-3—Presenting the Financial Planning Recommendation(s).

Financial Planning Practice Standards—Practice Standards 500 Series

215. d

Practice Standard 500-1—Agreeing on Implementation Responsibilities.

Financial Planning Practice Standards—Practice Standards 500 Series

216. d

Practice Standard 500-2—Selecting Products and Services for Implementation.

Financial Planning Practice Standards—Practice Standards 600 Series

217. e

Practice Standard 600-1—Defining Monitoring Responsibilities.

A

Absolute liability 79, 94
Accommodation party 172
Accord 165
Adequacy of consideration 156
Adhesion contract 161
Adjustable rate mortgage (ARM) 26, 27
Adjustment of debt 88, 90
Advertising 174
Advisors Act 104
Agency 75, 76, 168
Agency created by agreement 76
Agency created by estoppel 76
Agency created by ratification 76
Agency relationship 75, 76, 111, 168, 169
Agent 75–77, 94, 168, 169, 172
Annuity due 50–54
Anticipatory breach of contract 164
Anti-fraud provisions 104
ARM 26, 27
Asset allocation 6
Assignment 171

B

Bait and switch advertising 174
Balance sheet 7
Bank Insurance Fund (BIF) 40, 145
Bankruptcy 88, 90, 169
Bankruptcy Court 88, 89
Bankruptcy Reform Act of 1978 88
Banks 40, 105, 145, 172
BIF 40, 145
Bonds 146
Breach of contract 95, 163–169
Breach of duty 91
Budgeting 13
Steps 13
Business cycles 37
Business organization 72

C

Capital formation 38
Capital goods 38
Cash equivalents 7
Cash flow 5, 26
Cash flow capacity 26
Certificate of deposit 79
Chapter 7 liquidation 90

Check 13, 40, 78, 79, 104, 145, 146, 170–173
Client data 3, 107, 117
Client planner relationships 3
Client-specific financial plan 5
Closely held business planning 3
Commercial banks 40
Commercial paper 78
Common-law liability to clients 95
Common-law liability to third persons 96
Community property 84
Compensatory damages 166
Compound interest tables 47
Conditions 163
    Concurrent condition 163
    Condition precedent 163
    Condition subsequent 163
Conflicts of interest 76
Consumer 32, 33, 40, 86, 90, 145, 174, 175
Consumer Credit Protection Act 86
Consumer Price Index (CPI) 33, 34
Consumer protection 86, 174, 175
Contract liability 96
Contraction 37
Contraction phase 37
Contracts
    Agreement 72, 73, 154, 155
    Bilateral contract 72, 74
    Consideration 73, 74, 75, 156, 157, 161
    Contractual capacity 72, 158
    Exclusive dealings contract 157
    Executed contract 154, 158
    Executory contract 154, 158
    Express contract 72
    Form 72, 75, 104, 154
    Formal contract 72, 75, 104, 154
    Genuineness of assent 72
    Implied 72, 93, 159, 163
    Informal contract 154
    Legality 72
    Output contracts 157
    Requirements contracts 156
    Unenforceable contract 72, 154
    Unilateral contract 72, 73
    Valid and enforceable contract 72, 154
    Void contract 72, 154
    Voidable contract 72
Contractual liability 79
Corporation 40
Cost of replacement 26

Counter-advertising 174
Coverdell Education Savings Account 63, 64, 68
CPI 33, 34
Credit protection 86
Credit unions 145
Current liabilities 7

D

Damages 95, 96
Debt 11, 25, 87, 88, 89, 90
Debt collection 87
Debt securities 35, 36, 95–101, 103, 104, 146, 162
Debt-to-income ratio 11
Demand 30, 32
Demand curve shift 30
Demonstrated financial need 151
Depression 38
Determining goals and expectations 3
Determining the client's financial status 3
Detrimental reliance 158
Directors 100, 101
Discharge by breach of contact 164
Discharge of debtor from debts 89
Dividends 10
    Stock dividends 99
Downward sloping demand 30
Durable goods 38
Duress 161
Duty of cooperation 77
Duty of loyalty 76
Duty to notify 76
Duty to perform 76

E

Easy monetary policy 35
Economic environment 30
Education funding 57
Educational IRA 68
Elastic and inelastic demand 32
Employee benefits 4, 5
Employer educational assistance program 59
Endorsements
    Blank endorsement 171
    Qualified endorsement 171
    Restrictive endorsement 171
    Special endorsement 171
Equal Credit Opportunity Act 87

Equitable remedies 166
Estimated family contribution (EFC) 151
Ethics 95, 106–108, 110, 112, 114, 115, 117–124, 126–128, 131
Expansion 37
Expansion phase 37
Extension of credit 78

F

Factual cause 91
FAFSA 66, 151, 152
Fair Credit Billing Act 86
Fair Debt Collection Practices Act 87
FDIC 40, 105
Fed 10, 35
Federal Deposit Insurance Corporation (FDIC) 40, 105
Federal methodology 151
Federal Reserve Bank 35
Federal Reserve Board 86
Federal Reserve discount rate 35
Federal Securities Regulation 98
Federal Trade Commission (FTC) 174
Federal Truth-in-Lending Act (Consumer Credit Protection Act) 86
Fee simple 81, 83
Financial aid 66, 67, 151, 152
Financial calculator 47
Financial institutions 40, 41, 145
Financial need 151
Financial plan 5
Financial planning process 3
Financial position 5
Financial services companies 146
Financial status 3, 119
Financing strategies 24
Fiscal policy 35, 36
Fixed annuity payments 53
Fixed outflows 7, 8
Fixed-to-fixed rates 26
Fixed-to-variable rates 26
Fraud 72, 75, 89, 90, 92, 96–98, 101, 104, 160, 166
    Actual fraud 96
    Constructive fraud 96
Fraudulent misrepresentation 160
Free Application for Federal Student Aid (FAFSA) 66, 151, 152
Freehold estates 83

FTC 174
Future value 46–51, 148
Future value of a single sum deposit 46, 147
Future value of an annuity 50

G

Galloping inflation 33
GDP 37, 38
GNP 33
Good faith 80, 90, 113, 158, 164, 172
Government grants 66, 151
Gross Domestic Product (GDP) 37, 38
Gross National Product (GNP) 33

H

Holder 78–80, 86, 101, 170, 171–174
Holder in due course 78, 171
Home mortgages 26
Housing payment ratio 11

I

Impact of inflation 33
Income effect 30
Income tax 5
Independent activity 45
Independent contractor 75
Index-number problems 34
Inflation 32, 33
Injunction 167
Injury to plaintiff 91
Innocent misrepresentation 161
Insider trading 100
Institutional methodology 151
Intentional tort 91
    Assault 92
    Battery 91
    Conversion 93
    Defamation 92
    False imprisonment (false arrest) 92
    Infliction of mental distress 92
    Misrepresentation (fraud or deceit) 92
    Trespass to land 92
    Trespass to personal property 93
Interest rates 36, 48, 140, 141, 149
Internal analysis 16
Investment Adviser Registration Depository (IARD) 105
Investment Company Act of 1940 101

Investment counsel 104
Investment security 98
Involuntary liquidation 88

J

Joint accounts 42
Joint tenancy with right of survivorship 81, 84

L

Legal benefit 74
Legal detriment 74
Liability of parties 79, 172
License renewal process 115
Lifecycle phases 22
Lifecycle positioning 16, 17
Life estate 83
Liquidated damages 166
Liquidation 88
    Involuntary liquidation 88
    Ordinary or straight bankruptcy 88
    Voluntary liquidation 88
Liquidity ratio 11
Loans 40, 66, 67, 69, 151, 152
Long-term liabilities 7

M

Misleading advertising 110
Mistake 160
Mitigation of damages 166
Moderate inflation 33
Monetary policy 35
Money damages 166
    Compensatory damages 166
    Mitigation of damages 166
    Nominal damages 166
    Punitive or exemplary damages 166
Money market mutual funds 146
Mutual fund 50, 52, 146
Mutual rescission 165
Mutual savings banks 145

N

NASD 101, 105
National Association of Securities Dealers, Inc. (NASD) 101, 105
National Credit Union Share Insurance Fund (NCUSIF) 145

NCUSIF 145
Negligence 93–96
Contributory and comparative negligence 93
Implied or express assumption of the risk 93
Last clear chance 93
Negotiable 78, 79, 170–173
Negotiation 171
Net discretionary cash flow 8
Net present value 56
Nominal damages 166
Nominal interest rate 36
Nondischargeable debts 89
Nonnegotiable 78, 172
Novation 165

O

Open-market operations 35
Order for relief 88, 90
Ordinary annuity 50, 51, 53, 55

P

P&I payments 27
Parol evidence rule 162
Partial performance 162, 163
Peak 37
Peak point 37
Personal financial statements 7
Personal property 81
Intangible personal property 81
Tangible personal property 81
Post-certification requirements 115
Potential statutory liability 96
Power of attorney 75
PPI 33, 34
Present value 46, 48, 49, 52, 147, 148
Present value of an annuity 52, 149
Price elasticity 32
Price elasticity of demand 32
Price index 33
Principal 9, 11, 26, 27, 40, 67, 75, 76, 77, 104, 105, 113, 162, 168, 169, 172
Principal and interest payments 27
Principal's right to indemnification 168
Prioritized action items 6
Producer Price Index (PPI) 33, 34
Professional liability 95
Promisee 73
Promisor 73

Promissory estoppel 155, 158
Promissory note 47, 78, 79
Prospectus 98
Proximate causation 91
Proximate cause 96
Proximate or legal cause 91
Proxy statements 101
Public policy issues 174
Punitive or exemplary damages 166

Q

Qualified tuition program (QTP) 59, 60, 65
Quantitative analysis comparison 26
Quasi contract 167

R

Ratio analysis 11
Debt-to-income ratio 11
Housing payment ratio 11
Liquidity ratio 11
Savings ratio 11
Solvency ratio 11
Total payments ratio 11
Rationing by prices 32
Real interest rate adjustment 33
Real property 83
Recession 37
Registration 96, 101–104
Registration statement 96, 98
Regular calculator 47
Regulation 86, 98, 99, 101, 103
Regulatory requirements 98
Release 157, 165
Remedies at law 166
Reorganization (Chapter 11) 90
Representation of authority 110
Rescission 166
Reserve requirements 35
Respective annuity due 53
Restatement of Torts 96
Restitution 158, 159, 166
Return 100
Return on investments 36
Reversion 84
Risk exposure 3
Risk management 3
Risk tolerance 3
Roth IRA 68

S

SAIF 40
Satisfaction 165
Saving and consumption habits 13
Savings and loan associations 40
Savings Association Insurance Fund (SAIF) 40
Savings bonds 65
Savings ratio 11
Section 529 plan 59, 65
Securities Act of 1933 96–98
Securities and Exchange Commission (SEC) 103
Securities Exchange Act of 1934 97, 98, 100, 104
Serial payment 53–55
Shareholders 101
Single ownership accounts 42
Sole proprietorship 42, 45
Solvency ratio 11
Specific performance 166
Statement of cash flows 7, 10
Statement of consideration 170
Statement of financial position 7, 9
Statute of frauds 84, 161, 162
Statutory liability 96
Stock brokerage firms 146
Strict liability 94
Substitute for money 78
Substituted agreement 165
Substitution effect 30
Supply 31, 32

T

Tax deductions 60
Tax Relief Act of 2001 59
Tenancy by the entirety 81, 84

Tenancy in common 81, 84
Tender of complete performance 163
Tight monetary policy 35
Time value of money (TVM) 28
Tolerance for risk 26
Tort law 91
Tort liability 96
Torts 91, 96
Total payments ratio 11
Trough 37
Trough point 37
TVM 28

U

UGMA 69
Unconscionability 161
Undue influence 161
Uniform Gift to Minor's Act (UGMA) 69
Unilateral contract 72, 73
Unit-elastic demand 32

V

Variable outflows 8
Voluntary liquidation 88
Voting
    Voting agreements 162

W

Warranty liability 79
    Presentment warranties 79
    Transfer warranties 79